M000278668

The Artist-Signed Postcard Price Guide

A Comprehensive Reference

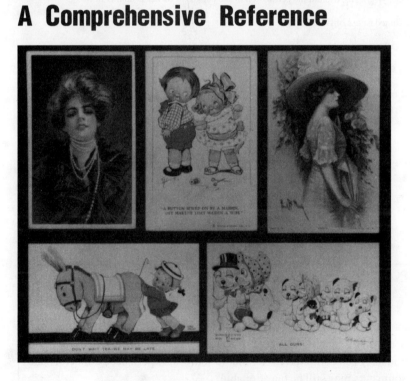

J.L. Mashburn

Thousands of Prices, Representing Millions of Cards

Published by:

WorldComm ®
a division of Creativity, Inc.

Publisher: Ralph Roberts

Editor: Emma Mashburn

Assistant Editor: Kathryn L. Hall

Cover Design: WorldComm®

Interior Design and Electronic Page Assembly: WorldComm®

A Colonial House Production

Printed in the United States of America

First Edition

10 9 8 7 6 5 4 3 2 1

ISBN 1-56664-028-8

Library of Congress Number: 93-060075

The author and publisher have made every effort in the preparation of this book to ensure the accuracy of the information. However, the information in this book is sold without warranty, either express or implied. Neither the author nor WorldComm Press will be liable for any damages caused or alleged to be caused directly, indirectly, incidentally, or consequentially by the information in this book.

The opinions expressed in this book are solely those of the author and are not necessarily those of WorldComm Press.

WorldComm Press—a Division of Creativity, Inc., 65 Macedonia Road, Alexander, North Carolina 28701, (704) 252-9515—is a full service publisher.

AN IMPORTANT NOTICE TO THE READERS OF THIS PRICE GUIDE:

The comprehensive nature of compiling data and prices on the thousands of cards, sets and series in this publication gives many probabilities for error. Although all information has been compiled from reliable sources, experienced collectors and dealers, some data may still be questionable.

The author and publisher will not be held responsible for any losses that might occur in the purchase or sale of cards because of the information contained herein.

The author will be most pleased to receive notice of errors so that they may be corrected in future editions.

Contact: J.L. Mashburn, Colonial House, Box 609, Enka NC 28728 USA.

Contents

DEDICATION

TO THE MEMORY OF

Miss Agnes Patton

Who taught me to appreciate
the great beauty of artist-signed postcards.

ACKNOWLEDGMENTS

Many individuals have made countless and most valuable contributions for making this publication possible. While all cannot be acknowledged, appreciation is extended to the following contributors who have given their time and effort by creating, revising or verifying new artists and checklists or lending cards for scanning.

To **Audrey Buffington**, for her checklist and editing of the works of F. Earl Christy; to **Gordon Gesner** for the works of Philip Boileau; to **Ted Holmes** for contributions on the checklists of Howard Chandler Christy, Clarence Underwood, R. Ford Harper, Coles Phillips, Archie Gunn, Lester Ralph, and others; to **Mrs. C.B. Micklea**, who supplied the checklists and publishers of her wonderful and beautiful Art Deco ladies.

To **Ralph C. Girkins, Jr.,** for the checklists and publisher information from his great collection of the Fidler sisters; **Marilyn Brust** for her Teddy Bears; to **Alyce Thorson, Bob Summerell** and **George Armstrong** for their many fine suggestions and additions to various checklists.

To **Fred Kahn**, fellow North Carolina Dealer-Collector, who allowed the use of many of the cards for scanning purposes and provided his expertise for pricing purposes.

Special thanks also to shop owners **Detlef Hilmer** and his very fine staff, and **Ute Harning** of Munich; and to **Hans Lugmair** of **INFORMATIO** in Vienna. During our twice-yearly visits to Europe since 1984, they have been very helpful in my quest to acquire cards, and to build many of the checklists and information contained in this publication.

And finally, to all collectors and dealers whose combined efforts have made this hobby so wonderful and so fantastically interesting.

*A beautiful lady by Henry Hutt, published
by the German firm of H & S Art*

1

INTRODUCTION

Many acquaintances have asked, "Why in the world do you spend all your time collecting old postcards?" and continue knowingly, "They look like junk to me." These people, of course, have never seen a water color of a beautiful lady signed by Clarence Underwood or Haskell Coffin, a colorful mermaid by E. Schulz, a tantalizing pastel nude by Edward Adrian Dussek, or the playful and majestic children of Bessie Pease Gutmann or Margaret G. Hays.

The beautiful cards of these artists, and hundreds of others in all categories, have made for me a delightful pastime over the past twenty-nine years. One of the most pleasurable moments for me, as a collector, is to finally find the elusive sixth card to complete a set or series and place them all side by side and relish their beauty... or to find a beautiful card by a new artist whose work is unfamiliar...to find a foreign card of one of my favorite artists that has not been documented...and, of course, to find a super rare card that is in great demand! These are some of the great thrills that can only be realized by an avid collector.

Through the many years of collecting beautiful artist-signed postcards, I have felt there was a terrible void in the hobby. I have many times wished that there was a good, comprehensive postcard reference that listed all the different cards produced by an artist, and one that would give the up-to-date value of each card. With the publishing of this first edition of **"The Artist-Signed Postcard Price Guide"** I feel the void has been filled and that my wish is becoming a reality.

Slowly, but surely, near-complete works of most of the leading artists have been compiled. The production of beautiful ladies—both U.S. and foreign—of Harrison Fisher, Philip Boileau, Clarence Underwood, F. Earl Christy, Howard Chandler Christy, James Montgomery Flagg, Henry Hutt, Frank Desch, Archie Gunn, Haskell Coffin, Alfred Dewey, Charles Dana Gibson, Coles Phillips, Lester Ralph, P. Stanlaws, and the three Fidler sisters are all nearly complete in this First Edition.

Other artists' works, both major and minor, which are high in collector esteem (especially of beautiful children, fantasy, animals, blacks, Art Deco, etc.), have tremendous listings and are well represented. Prominent foreign artists, because of their great popularity to collectors, all have listings ... and there will be more in future editions.

As a postcard dealer and collector, I have had many "learning experiences" as a result of not knowing the values of many cards. To sell a card at $10 only to find out later that it was a rare card and worth $100 or more is very frustrating. This is true not only for dealers, but for the collector who may be inexperienced and also uninformed. For instance, there are over 240 cards listed in the reference for Philip Boileau. Values range from $10-15 to $200-250 per card. For those not knowing the difference, **"The Artist-Signed Postcard Price Guide"** can be the tool needed to "check it out."

This reference has been a tremendous undertaking and would have been impossible without the great effort and contributions of many collectors, dealers and postcard historians. We hope that this publication will fill the void for everyone in the hobby, and that your "learning experiences" will be minimized.

Happy Hunting!   *J L Mashburn*   March, 1993.

HOW TO USE THIS PRICE GUIDE

This price guide has been uniquely designed to serve the needs of both the beginning and advanced collector, as well as the established postcard dealer. Our attempt to provide a very comprehensive price guide and reference to artist-signed postcards, both U.S. and foreign, and dating from 1900 through the 1940's makes it possible for even the novice collector to consult it with confidence and ease in finding each particular listing. The following important explanations summarize the general practices that will help the reader benefit from its use.

CATEGORICAL ARRANGEMENT

All cards are arranged by category, and each category is listed in the Table of Contents. The artists are listed under a particular type or motif. If an artist painted both ladies and children, he/she is listed under both "Beautiful Ladies" for their lady cards and "Beautiful Children" for their works of children. Artists are always listed alphabetically in each section.

The most prominent cards, if known, and the value of each are listed for each artist. Otherwise, the values listed are for the generalized cards, or particular topic or theme, by the artist.

LISTINGS

Listings may be identified as follows:

1. **SECTION**   (Beautiful Ladies, Fantasy, etc.)
2. **ARTIST**   (Listed in Bold Capital Letter)
3. **PUBLISHER**   (Listed in Bold Lower Case Letters)
4. **NAME OF SERIES; OR SERIES NUMBER**
5. **TOTAL NUMBER OF CARDS IN SET OR SERIES** (Enclosed in Parentheses when Available in Bold)
6. **CAPTION OR TITLE OF CARD** (Enclosed in Quotation Marks)
   — If no caption, image is identified without quotations.
7. **PRICE OF 1 CARD IN VERY GOOD CONDITION**
8. **PRICE OF SAME CARD IN EXCELLENT CONDITION**

Example of above.

1. **BEAUTIFUL LADIES**
2. **PHILIP BOILEAU**
3. **Reinthal & Newman**
4. **Series 94**
5. **(6)**
6. "At the Opera"
7. $10 - 15
8. $15 - 20

CONDITION AND GRADING OF POSTCARDS

As with old coins, stamps, books, etc., the condition of a postcard is an extremely important factor in determining the price for the collector, the dealer, and for those having found cards and wishing to sell them. Damaged, worn, creased, or dirty cards—cards in less than Very Good condition—are almost uncollectible unless they are to be used as a space filler until a better one is found. Collectors should never buy a damaged card if they expect to sell it.

Grading standards should be used and are very necessary so that the buyer and seller may come to an informed agreement on the value of a card. In **"THE ARTIST-SIGNED POSTCARD PRICE GUIDE,"** two different collectible conditions, **Very Good** and **Excellent,** are used. There are, of course, higher and lower grades, but these two will be most normally seen and will be most normally quoted for postcards sold throughout the hobby.

The leading postcard hobby publications, *Barr's Postcard News* and *Postcard Collector,* have both selected a standard grading system which has been adapted by most dealers. This system is listed below with their permission:

M—MINT. A perfect card just as it comes from the printing press. No marks, bends, or creases. No writing or postmarks. A clean and fresh card. Seldom seen.

NM—NEAR MINT. Like Mint but very light aging or very slight discoloration from being in an album for many years. Not as sharp or crisp.
EX—EXCELLENT. Like mint in appearance with no bends

or creases, or rounded or blunt corners. May be postally used or unused and with writing and postmark only on the address side. A clean, fresh card on the picture side.

VG—VERY GOOD. Corners may be just a bit blunt or rounded. Almost undetectable crease or bend that does not detract from overall appearance of the picture side. May have writing or may be postally used on the address side. A very collectible card.

G—GOOD. Corners may be noticeably blunt or rounded with slightly noticeable bends or creases. May be postally used or have writing on the address side. Less than VG.

FR—FAIR. Card is intact. Excess soil, stains, creases, writing, or cancellation may affect picture. Could be a scarce card that is difficult to find in any condition.

Collectors should keep this in mind if they have cards to sell. **Postcard dealers will always want better condition cards that have no defects.** Therefore, anyone building a collection should also maintain a standard for condition and stick to it. Even if the asking price is a little higher when a card is purchased, it will be worth the extra cost when it is resold.

PRICE GUIDE VALUATIONS

The postcard values quoted in this publication represent an average price in the current retail market. They were compiled from dealer pricing at shows, personal dealer communications, from the author's personal purchasing (both in the U.S. and throughout Europe), from his approval sales, from more than 100 mail auctions, and from his active day-to-day involvement in the hobby.

Values were also compiled from observations of listings in auctions, auction catalogs (U.S., Europe, and Great Britain), prices realized, and fixed price sales in the fine hobby publications, *Barr's Post Card News* and *Postcard Collector,* and other related publications listed in the **Periodicals** section. **In all instances, listings of high and low values were taken for each observation, and these were averaged to obtain the "VG" and "Excellent" prices quoted.**

It must be stressed that this price guide and reference work is intended to serve only as an aid in evaluating postcards. It should not be used otherwise. As everyone is well aware, actual market conditions change constantly, and prices may fluctuate. The trend for postcards, however, seems to always be to the upside.

Publication of this price guide is not intended to be a solicitation to buy or sell any of the cards listed.

Price ranges for cards in both **Very Good** and **Excellent** conditions are found at the end of each listing. Prices for cards in less than **Very Good** condition would be much lower, while those grading above **Excellent** might command relatively higher prices.

Without exception, prices quoted are for **one** card, whether it be a single entity or one card in a complete set or series. Note that after many entries a number is enclosed in parentheses; e.g. (6). This number indicates the total number of cards that are believed to be in a set or a series. The price listed is for one card in the set and is multiplied by this number to determine the value of the complete set.

WHY PRICE RANGES ARE QUOTED

Price ranges are quoted for cards graded both **Very Good** and **Excellent** for four major reasons. Any of the following can determine the difference in the high or low values in each of the listing ranges.

1. Prices tend to vary in different geographical areas across the United States. At the present time they are somewhat higher on the Pacific Coast and other western states, possibly because of shorter supply of dealers resulting also in lesser supply of cards. They tend to be somewhat lower in the East, because of the larger concentration of dealers, and somewhere in-between in the central and midwestern states. For instance, a card with a price range of $6.00-8.00 might sell for $6.00 in the East, $7.00 in the Mid-West and $8.00 in the Far West.

2. Dealer price valuations also vary. Those who continu-

ally set up and sell at postcard shows seem to have a better feel for up-to-date pricing structures, know which cards are selling well, and adjust their prices accordingly. Dealers who sell only by mail, or by mail auction, tend to price their cards(or list estimated values in their auctions) just a bit higher. This is because of the high cost of advertising and mailing. They usually are able to realize these prices because of a wider collector base obtained by the large number of subscribers served by nationally distributed post-card auction publications. These publications also reach some international collectors and those unable to attend shows.

3. "Hot" cards, or those of topics in great demand, also have wider price ranges; as collector interests rise there is a greater disparity in values because of supply and demand. If a dealer has only a small stock of big demand cards he will almost automatically elevate his prices. Those having a large supply will probably not go as high.

4. Card quality, appearance, and the subject matter in a set or series can also cause a variance in price range. Printing quality, more beautiful and varied colors, and sharpness of the image may make a particular card much more desirable and, therefore, it will command a higher price.

Cards that have a wide price range usually are those that are presently the "most wanted" and, subsequently, the best sellers at the time. Most often, dealers will only offer a small discount (or none at all) when selling these because they know there is a good market for them. Cards listed with a narrow price range, on the other hand, are usually those that have been "hot" but have settled down and have established a more competitive trading range. Dealer discounting on these slow-movers tend to be much more prevalent than those in the wide price ranges.

GUIDELINES FOR BUYING AND SELLING CARDS

As noted above, the prices listed in this price guide are **retail** prices—prices that a collector can expect to pay when buying a card from a postcard dealer. It is up to the collector to bargain for any available discount from the dealer.

The **wholesale** price is the price which a collector may expect from a dealer. This price will be significantly lower than the retail price. Most dealers try to operate on a 100% mark-up, and will normally pay around 50% of a card's low retail value. On some high-demand, or "hot" cards, he might be willing to pay up to 60% or 75% if he wants them badly enough. This is especially true with artist-signed cards.

Dealers are always interested in purchasing collections and accumulations of cards. They are primarily interested in those issued before 1915-20, but may be induced to take those issued afterwards if they are clean and in good condition.

Collections: Normally, collections are a specialized group or groups of cards that a person has built over the years. They will be in nice condition, without any damage, and may contain some rarities or high-demand cards, especially if they contain many that are artist-signed.

If the collection is a group of views from the collector's home town or state it would be to his advantage, pricewise, to sell them to a collector or dealer nearby. An ad, placed in the daily newspaper, usually creates a lot of interest and may result in a good sale. Cards should be priced on the high side, or at retail prices, when selling to individuals. The price can always be lowered.

If the collection contains nice artist-signed, topicals, complete sets, as well as views, etc., the seller should contact a postcard dealer to dispose of them. However, as noted above, be prepared to sell to the dealer at around 50% of the value of the collection. The dealer will make an offer, but sometimes the price can be negotiated.
Collectors that know of no dealers in their area may write to the **International Federation of Postcard Dealers (I.F.P.D.)** to the attention of John McClintock, Executive Secretary, P.O. Box 1765, Manassas, VA 22110, and

enclose a double-stamped, self-addressed #10 envelope for a list of members. The list will include dealers that are very interested in purchasing cards and collections. They also sell cards.

Collectors also may dispose of their collections by writing to dealers who advertise in *Barr's Post Card News,* 70 South 6th Street, Lansing, IA 52151 or *Postcard Collector,* P.O. Box 37, Iola, WI 54945. Also, *Collectors News,* P.O. Box 156, Grundy Center, IA 50638-0156, *Paper Collectors' Marketplace,* P.O. Box 128, Scandinavia, WI 54977, and *The Antique Trader,* P.O. Box 1050, Dubuque, IA 52004 all have strong sections on postcards. Write and ask for information on subscriptions or sample copies.

Accumulations: Accumulations are usually groups of many different kinds, many different eras and many different topics, and usually with the good mixed with the undesirable. These can usually be sold to dealers at 20% to 30% of value. Many low-demand cards are worthless to a dealer, but he may take them if there are some good cards in the group. It will be to the seller's advantage to keep the entire accumulation intact. It is possible that just a small number of cards sold separately will make the remaining cards practically worthless.

Buying: The best way to buy postcards, without doubt, is to attend a show where there is a large group of dealers (show dates are normally listed in the postcard periodicals listed above). It is worthwhile to compare prices among dealers before purchasing the cards you desire. A collector has the best of worlds. Dealers at these shows have good cards to offer and a competitive price can usually be negotiated. The collector and dealer can become acquainted and good relationships can be formed.

It is also possible to find cards at Antique Shows, Flea Markets, and Antique Shops. Collectors can, however, waste considerable time and never find suitable cards, as the cards found are usually damaged and of poor quality. For better selection and quality it is best to go directly to the source, and that would be to a postcard dealer, a postcard Approvals dealer, or one who holds postcard auctions.

IDENTIFYING THE AGE OF POSTCARDS

The dating of postcards for year and/or eras of issue can be accurately determined if the card is studied for certain identity points. Research has already been carried out by earlier historians and guidelines have been put in place for this purpose.

There have been seven different eras for the postcard industry. The following helps determine the era of the card in question:

PIONEER ERA (1893-1898)

The Pioneer Era began when picture postcards were placed on sale by vendors and exhibitors at the Columbian Exposition in Chicago in May, 1893. These were very popular and proved to be a great success. The profitability and future of the postcard were greatly enhanced.

Pioneer cards are relatively scarce and hard to find. They can be identified by combinations of the following:

• All have undivided backs.

• None show the "Authorized by Act of Congress" byline.

• Postal cards will have the Grant or Jefferson head stamp.

• Most, but not all, will be multiple view cards.

• The words, "Souvenir of..." or "Greetings from..." wil appear on many examples.

• Postage rate, if listed, is 2 cents.

• The most common titles are "Souvenir Card" or "Mail Card."

• Appeared mostly in the big Eastern cities.

PRIVATE MAILING CARD ERA (1898-1901)

On May 19, 1898, the government gave private printers permission to print and sell postcards. The cards were all issued with the inscription "Private Mailing Card," and today they are referred to as PMC's. It is very easy to identify these because of the inscription. It may be noted that many of the early Pioneer views were reprinted as Private Mailing Cards.

UNDIVIDED BACK ERA (1901-1907)

On December 24, 1901, permission was given for use of the wording "Post Card" to be imprinted on the backs of privately printed cards. All cards during this era had undivided backs and only the address was to appear on the back. The message, therefore, had to be written on the picture side of the card. For this reason many cards have writing on the face of the card. This fault is becoming more acceptable on cards of this era.

DIVIDED BACK ERA (1907-1915)

This era came into being on March 1, 1907. The divided back made it possible for both the address and the message to be on the back of the card. This eliminated writing on the face of the card and proved to be a great boon for collectors. Normally the view colors or images filled the entire card, and there was no white border.

WHITE BORDER ERA (1915-1930)

The White Border Era brought an end to the so-called Golden Era of Postcards. It ended as imports from Germany ceased and publishers in the U.S. began printing postcards to try to fill the void. The cards were of very poor quality and many were reprints of earlier Divided Back Era cards. These are easily distinguished by the white border around the pictured area.

It should be noted that the Europeans and Great Britain continued publishing cards during this era, but because of high tariff rates they were no longer exported in great quantities to the U.S. This is one reason that many of the very collective Art Deco issues and other great cards from those countries did not begin arriving in the U.S. until they were "discovered" in the 70's and early 80's.

LINEN ERA (1930-1945)

Improvements in American printing technology brought

much improved card quality. Publishers began using a linen-like paper containing a high rag content, but used very cheap inks in most of their processes. Until recently, these cards were considered very cheap, drab, and uninteresting. Now they have become very popular with collectors of Roadside America, Blacks, Comics, and Advertising. Views are also becoming more popular as collectors realize that this era too is a great part of our history and heritage, and these cards help to illustrate the changes in our mode of life and the geographic structure of America.

PHOTOCHROME ERA (1939 to present day)

"Modern Chromes," as they are now called by the postcard fraternity, were first introduced in 1939. Publishers such as Mike Roberts, Dexter Press, Curt Teich, and Plastichrome began producing cards that had very beautiful chrome colors and were very appealing to collectors. The growth of this group has been spectacular in recent years, so much so that there are now many postcard dealers who specialize only in chromes.

REAL PHOTO POSTCARDS (1900 to present day)

Real Photo postcards were in use as early as 1900. It is sometimes very difficult to date a card unless it has been postally used or dated by the photographer. The stamp box will usually show the process by which it was printed— AZO, EKC, KODAK, VELOX, and KRUXO are some of the major ones. Careful study of photo cards is essential to make sure they have not been reproduced.

THE ARTIST-SIGNED POSTCARD

The growing popularity of the postcard in the 1890-1905 era was further influenced by use of the works of illustrators, posterists, and commercial artists as designs on the new mailing mediums. Publishers quickly capital-ized on this popularity, and the artist-signed postcard became the rage of the era. Through the years, it has remained the most relished and highly collected type of postcards.

The beautiful renditions of artists such as Mucha,

Koloman Moser, Egon Schiele, etc., became miniature works of art in a new medium that could be handled very easily...and one that could be sent through the mail for advertising or other purposes.

An important feature of these miniature gems was the artist's signature, either name or initials. These became the artist-signed postcards as we know them today. It has been estimated that there were 20,000 worldwide artists who contributed to the production of postcards. The sheer magnitude of this number makes it impossible to list all, even if they were known.

Many artists refused to sign their works because they thought so little of the budding postcard industry, and believed it lowered their standards to participate. Therefore, since very few records were kept, the artists of some of the most beautiful cards, sets, and series can only be listed today as "anonymous."

Frances Brundage, the famous artist of beautiful children, was commissioned to do postcards in Germany and Austria starting as early as 1900. She painted hundreds of very beautiful, classic cards for various publishers but signed only a small number of them. Later, possibly because of the growth in popularity of the postcard industry, many of these originals were released by other publishers using her signature. Therefore, it is possible that the thoughts of lowered standards were forgotten.

American publishers and artists, taking note of the growing popularity and salability of imported European postcards, began searching for and producing images that they felt would be competitive. Some of the first artist-signed cards produced were those by The Detroit Publishing Co. of illustrations from *Life* Magazine's fictional stories. Actual illustrations by Harrison Fisher, Charles Dana Gibson, James Montgomery Flagg, and others were used and adapted as postcards.

These very influential artists, plus many others that followed, began producing countless numbers of beautiful images just for the postcard industry. Paintings and pastels that had been hanging in galleries, originals of magazine covers, prints already selling through magazine advertisements, and renderings meant for advertising were quickly adapted for postcard use, and were sent to Germany to be printed into the tiny, colorful works of art.

Postcard production and sales were booming. Americans, as with people of other countries, became enthralled with the beauty and diverse motifs of the postcard. They also became collectors, placed their choice cards in huge albums, and sent new selections back home to friends when visiting another city or country.

These were the Golden Years of the postcard and collectors hoped they would last forever. However, World War 1 and a high tariff brought an end to importing cards from Germany, and collectors began storing their albums away in attics and cellars as the thrill of collecting waned. Today, those same postcards are again prized and pursued by many, and the hobby is steadily growing. To many of us ... these are still the Golden Years!

E. Chandler, Asher & Co.

SHE: "THE FACE IS VERY GOOD BUT I OBJECT TO THE POSE."
HE: "THEY ARE NOT MADAM THEY ARE FLOWER POTS."

(Author's note: This was probably an early but unsuccessful artist.)

BEAUTIFUL LADIES

	VG	EX
ABIELE, JACK (France)		
Lady/Flower Series	$35 - 40	$40 - 45
ANICHINI, E. (Italy) See Art Deco		
ARMSTRONG, ROLF (U.S.A.)		
K. Co., New York		
Water Color Series 101-112	12 - 15	15 - 20
ASTI, ANGELO (Italy)		
R. Tuck		
Connoisseur Series 2731		
"Beatrice"	8 - 12	12 - 16
"Gladys"	8 - 12	12 - 16
"Irene"	8 - 12	12 - 16
"Juliet"	8 - 12	12 - 16
"Marguerite"	8 - 12	12 - 16
"Rosalind"	8 - 12	12 - 16
Connoisseur Series 2743		
"Helena"	8 - 12	12 - 16
"Madeline"	8 - 12	12 - 16
"Muriel"	8 - 12	12 - 16
"Phyllis"	8 - 12	12 - 16
"Portia"	8 - 12	12 - 16
"Sylvia"	8 - 12	12 - 16
Rotograph Co., NY		
Series T.5268		
"Beatrice"	7 - 10	10 - 12
"Gladys"	7 - 10	10 - 12
"Irene"	7 - 10	10 - 12
"Juliet"	7 - 10	10 - 12
"Marguerite"	7 - 10	10 - 12

"Rosalind"	7 - 10	10 - 12
T.S.N. (Theo Stroefer, Nuremberg)		
Series 508 (8)		
No Captions	6 - 8	8 - 10
Semi-Nude Real Photo Series		
"Epanouissment"	15 - 18	18 - 22
"Fantasie"	15 - 18	18 - 22
"Solitude"	15 - 18	18 - 22
"Une Favorite"	15 - 18	18 - 22
"Volupte"	15 - 18	18 - 22
Others	15 - 18	18 - 22
AVELINE, F.		
Lindberg'in Kirjap. Oy, Helsinki Series	8 - 10	10 - 12
AXENTOWICZ (Poland)		
Heads and full-length	8 - 10	10 - 15
Fantasy	12 - 15	15 - 18
Nudes	12 - 15	15 - 18
AZZONI, N. (Italy) See Art Deco		
BACHRICH, M. (See Art Deco)		
BAILEY, S.C.		
Carlton Pub. Co.		
Series 674	6 - 8	8 - 10
Series 689	8 - 10	10 - 12
BAKST, LEON	20 - 25	25 - 30
BALL, H. LaPRIAK (U.S.A)	3 - 4	4 - 5

F. Aveline, Lindberg, Helsinki
No Caption

C.W. Barber, B.K.W.I. 861/3
"Why Not?"

Court Barber, JW & Co. 415
No Caption

Court Barber, SWSB 1409
"Cherry Ripe"

BALOTINI (Italy)   See Art Deco
BARBER, COURT (U.S.A.)

B.K.W.I.		
Series 861 (12)	6 - 8	8 - 10
Series 686 (6)	8 - 10	10 - 12
Series 1200	6 - 8	8 - 10
Others	6 - 8	8 - 10
Minerva Series 683 Head Studies	8 - 10	10 - 12
R.B.H. Series 688 Head Studies	8 - 10	10 - 12
J.W. & Co. Series	6 - 8	8 - 10
S.W.S.B. Series	10 - 12	12 - 14
Others	6 - 8	8 - 10

BARBER, C.W. (U.S.A.)

B.K.W.I.		
Series 861 (12)	8 - 10	10 - 14
Series 2128 (8)	8 - 10	10 - 14
Carleton Publishing Co.		
Series 676, 678	8 - 9	9 - 12
Series 709, 716	8 - 9	9 - 12
Series 735, 861	8 - 10	10 - 14

BARRIBAL, L. (GB)

B.K.W.I.		
Series XIX Fashion	8 - 10	10 - 12
Series 860 Fashion	8 - 10	10 - 12

"Sweet Simplicity."

L. Barribal, Henderson 2648 *"Sweet Simplicity"*	*L. Barribal, Novitas 15642* *No Caption*	
Carlton Pub. Co.	6 - 8	8 - 10
Henderson	6 - 8	8 - 10
International Art. Pub. Co.		
"Artisque Series"	8 - 10	10 - 12
M. & H.		
Series 15644 Heads	10 - 12	12 - 14
M. Munk, Vienna Heads	8 - 10	10 - 12
Novitas, Germany	8 - 10	10 - 12
Valentine Co.		
"Flags of Nations" Series	6 - 8	8 - 10
"Great Britain"		
"Japan"		
"Scotland"		
"Ireland"		
"Germany"		
"Russia"		
Lindberg's Tryokeria Series (8)	10 - 12	12 - 14
Lindberg'in Kirjap. Oy, Helsinki (6)	10 - 12	12 - 14
BASCH, ARPAD (Hungary) See Art Nouveau		
BENDA, WLADYSLAW T. (W.T.)		
"Rosamond"	8 - 10	10 - 12
"Reverie"	8 - 10	10 - 12
BENTIVOGLIO See Art Deco		
BERTIGLIA, A. (Italy) See Art Deco		

BETRINELLI, MARIA (Italy) See Art Deco		
BIANCHI (Italy) See Art Deco		
BIELETTO, T.	5 - 6	6 - 8
BIRI, S. (Italy) See Art Deco		
BLUMENTHAL, M.L.	4 - 5	5 - 6
BODAREVSKY, N.K.	5 - 6	6 - 8
BOILEAU, PHILIP (Canada-U.S.A.)		

Philip Boileau, born in Canada but finally settling in New York, was one of the great painters and illustrators of beautiful women. His works are collected world-wide and are in great demand by all who love the facial beauty of the selected fair.

Most of his images on postcards were published in the U.S.A. by the New York firm of Reinthal & Newman during the "postcard craze" years of 1905-1918. Other principal publishers were Osborne Calendar Co., with printings of the rare Boileau calendar cards; National Art Co. and advertising cards; and The Taylor, Platt Co. and their scarce, flower-decorated cards and valentine heads issues.

Minor issues of advertising cards were done by Flood & Conklin, Soapine Mfg. Co., S.E. Perlberg Tailors, and others. These various issues, as well as his other advertising card issues, are extremely difficult to find and are very high priced when they surface.

British, European, and Finnish publishers issued Boileau cards which are very elusive and also command very high prices. The R. Tuck Connoisseur Series 2819 and the German K N G Shöne Frauen, along with the KOY Finnish Series, are among those most sought after by collectors worldwide.

Due to the destruction of the infamous Berlin Wall, cards of Russian origin are beginning to surface, and will be a high priority for Boileau collectors. As with other foreign issues, these will command very high prices.

PHILIP BOILEAU

I. AMERICAN PUBLISHERS

  Reinthal & Newman

Series 94 *		
"At the Opera"	10 - 15	15 - 20

"Peggy"	10 - 15	15 - 20
"Schooldays"	10 - 15	15 - 20
"Sweethearts"	10 - 15	15 - 20
"Thinking of You"	10 - 15	15 - 20
"Twins"	10 - 15	15 - 20

* Cards with Series No. on back, add $5.

Series 95 *

"A Mischiefmaker"	10 - 15	15 - 20
"Anticipation"	10 - 15	15 - 20
"Forever"	10 - 15	15 - 20
"Little Lady Demure"	10 - 15	15 - 20
"My Chauffeur"	10 - 15	15 - 20
"Nocturne"	10 - 15	15 - 20
"Passing Shadow"	15 - 18	18 - 22
"Spring Song" **	15 - 18	18 - 22
"Today"	10 - 15	15 - 18
"Tomorrow"	10 - 15	15 - 18
"Winter Whispers"	15 - 18	18 - 22
"Yesterday"	10 - 15	15 - 20

* Cards with Series No. on back, add $5.
** Cards distr. by Chas. H. Hauff, add $5.

Series 109 *

"Evening and You"	20 - 25	25 - 30
"Girl in Black"	20 - 25	25 - 30

Philip Boileau, R&N, No Number
Charles Hauff, "The Twins"

Philip Boileau, R&N 822
"Every Breeze..."

"Her Soul With Purity Possessed"	22 - 27	27 - 32
"In Maiden Meditation"	22 - 27	27 - 32
"June, Blessed June"	20 - 25	25 - 30
"My Moonbeam"	20 - 25	25 - 30
"My One Rose"	20 - 25	25 - 30
"Ready for Mischief"	20 - 25	25 - 30
"The Secret of the Flowers"	22 - 27	27 - 32
"True as the Blue Above"	22 - 27	27 - 32
"Twixt Doubt and Hope"	20 - 25	25 - 30
"Waiting for You"	20 - 25	25 - 30
"With Care for None"	20 - 25	25 - 30

* Cards with Series No. on back, add $5.

200 Series

204 "Rings on Her Fingers"	10 - 15	15 - 20
205 "Question"	10 - 15	15 - 20
205 "Chrysanthemums"	15 - 20	20 - 25
206 "The Enchantress"	10 - 15	15 - 20
207 "A Hundred Years Ago"	10 - 15	15 - 20
208 "Miss America"	12 - 16	16 - 22
209 "Youth"	10 - 15	15 - 20
210 "Joyful Calm"	10 - 15	15 - 20
211 "Chums"	10 - 15	15 - 20
212 "Sweet Lips of Coral Hue"	10 - 15	15 - 20
213 "His First Love"	10 - 15	15 - 20
214 "For Him"	10 - 15	15 - 20
215 "I Wonder"	10 - 15	15 - 20
282 "Ready for the Meeting"	12 - 16	16 - 22
283 "Miss Pat"	12 - 16	16 - 22
284 "Old Home Farewell"	10 - 15	15 - 20
285 "A Serious Thought"	10 - 15	15 - 20
286 "I Don't Care"	12 - 16	16 - 22
287 "The Eyes Say No, The Lips Say Yes"	12 - 16	16 - 22
294 "Blue Ribbons"	15 - 20	20 - 25
295 "A Little Devil"	15 - 20	20 - 25
296 "Once Upon a Time"	10 - 15	15 - 20
297 "My Big Brother"	10 - 15	15 - 20
298 "My Boy"	10 - 15	15 - 20
299 "Baby Mine"	15 - 20	20 - 25

Water Color Series 369-380 *

369 "Vanity"	15 - 22	30 - 40
370 "Haughtiness"	20 - 25	30 - 40
371 "Purity"	15 - 22	30 - 40
372 "Loneliness"	20 - 25	40 - 45
373 "Happiness"	20 - 25	30 - 40
374 "Queenliness"	20 - 25	30 - 40
375 "Whisperings of Love" (Annunciation)	20 - 25	30 - 40
376 "Fairy Tales" (Girlhood)	20 - 25	30 - 40
377 "Parting of the Ways" (Maidenhood)	20 - 25	30 - 40
378 "Here Comes Daddy"	15 - 20	30 - 40
379 "Lullabye" (Motherhood)	20 - 25	30 - 40
380 "Don't Wake the Baby"	15 - 20	30 - 40

Philip Boileau, R&N 827
"Sister's First Love"

Philip Boileau,
Fried. O. Wolter 1058, "Studie"

* Cards without Subtitle, add $5.

445 Series *

1 "Spring Song"	18 - 22	25 - 30
2 "Today"	18 - 22	25 - 30
3 "Tomorrow"	18 - 22	25 - 30
4 "Forever"	18 - 22	25 - 30
5 "My Chauffeur"	18 - 22	25 - 30
6 "Nocturne"	18 - 22	25 - 30

* With German caption, add $5.

474 Series *

1 "Spring Song"	20 - 25	30 - 35
2 "A Passing Shadow"	20 - 25	30 - 35
3 "A Mischiefmaker"	20 - 25	30 - 35
4 "Anticipating"	20 - 25	30 - 35
5 "Yesterday"	20 - 25	30 - 35
6 "Little Lady Demure"	20 - 25	30 - 35

* With German caption, add $5.

700 Series *

750 "Be Prepared"	12 - 15	15 - 20
751 "Absence Cannot Hearts Divide"	12 - 15	15 - 20
752 "A Neutral"	12 - 15	15 - 20
753 "The Chrysalis"	12 - 15	15 - 20
754 "Pensive"	12 - 15	15 - 20
755 "The Girl of the Golden West"	12 - 15	15 - 20

756 "Pebbles on the Beach"	15 - 18	18 - 25
757 "Snowbirds"	15 - 18	18 - 25
758 "One Kind Act a Day"	12 - 15	15 - 20
759 "The Flirt"	12 - 15	15 - 20
760 "In Confidence"	12 - 15	15 - 18
761 "The Coming Storm"	15 - 18	18 - 26

* With German caption, add $5.

800 Series

820 "Devotion"	25 - 30	35 - 40
821 "Golden Dreams"	20 - 25	35 - 40
822 "Every Breeze Carries My Thoughts..."	18 - 22	22 - 26
823 "Priscilla"	25 - 30	35 - 45
824 "Fruit of the Vine"	18 - 22	22 - 25
825 "Butterfly"	25 - 30	35 - 45
826 "When Dreams Come True" *	12 - 15	15 - 20
827 "Sister's First Love" *	12 - 15	15 - 20
828 "The Little Neighbors" *	12 - 15	15 - 20
829 "Peach Blossoms" *	15 - 20	20 - 25
830 "When His Ship Comes In" *	12 - 15	15 - 20
831 "Need a Lassie Cry" *	12 - 15	15 - 20

* With German caption, add $5.

Water Color Series 936-941

936 "A Bit of Heaven"	18 - 22	35 - 40
937 "Chic"	18 - 22	35 - 40
938 "Have a Care"		

Philip Boileau, R&N Watercolor 939
"Just a Wearying for You"

Philip Boileau,
R&N Watercolor 369, "Vanity"

also "Hav a Care"	20 - 25	35 - 40
939 "Just a Wearying for You"	20 - 25	35 - 40
940 "Sunshine"	25 - 30	35 - 40
941 "Sincerely Yours"	20 - 25	35 - 40
2000 Series		
2052 "Thinking of You"	20 - 25	25 - 30
2063 "Chums"	20 - 25	25 - 30
2064 "His First Love"	20 - 25	25 - 30
2065 "Question"	20 - 25	25 - 30
2066 "From Him"	20 - 25	25 - 30
2067 "The Enchantress"	20 - 25	25 - 30
2068 "Joyful Calm"	20 - 25	25 - 30
Others in Series	20 - 25	25 - 30
Unnumbered Series		
"The Dreamy Hour"	15 - 20	25 - 35
"Out for Fun"	15 - 20	25 - 35
Reinthal & Newman Copyright		
Distributed by **Novitas.** No Numbers.		
"A Mischiefmaker"	18 - 22	22 - 25
"A Passing Shadow"	18 - 22	22 - 25
"Anticipating"	18 - 22	22 - 25
"Forever"	18 - 22	22 - 25
"Little Lady Demure"	18 - 22	22 - 25
"My Chauffeur"	18 - 22	22 - 25
"Nocturne"	18 - 22	22 - 25
"Spring Song"	18 - 22	22 - 25
"Today"	18 - 22	22 - 25
"Tomorrow"	18 - 22	22 - 25
"Winter Whispers"	18 - 22	22 - 25
"Yesterday"	18 - 22	22 - 25
Reinthal & Newman Copyright		
Distributed by **J. Beagles & Co., London**		
No No. "Little Lady Demure"	18 - 22	22 - 25
No No. "Nocturne"	18 - 22	22 - 25
No No. "Winter Whispers"	18 - 22	22 - 25
Osborne Calendar Co. *		
459 "Winifred"	75 - 100	100 - 150
940 "A Fair Debutante"	75 - 100	100 - 150
941 "The Blonde"	75 - 100	100 - 150
942 "Phyllis"	75 - 100	100 - 150
943 "Pansies"	75 - 100	100 - 150
944 "True Blue"	75 - 100	100 - 150
945 "Army Girl"	75 - 100	100 - 150
946 "Day Dreams"	75 - 100	100 - 150
947 "Passing Shadow"	75 - 100	100 - 150
948 "The Girl in Brown"	75 - 100	100 - 150
949 "Goodbye"	75 - 100	100 - 150
950 "Passing Glance"	75 - 100	100 - 150
951 "A Winter Girl"	75 - 100	100 - 150
1459 "Rhododendrons"	100 - 125	125 - 165
1489 "At Play"	125 - 150	150 - 175

1738 "Virginia"	125 - 150	150 - 175
2076 "Suzanne"	125 - 150	150 - 175
3525 "Autumn"	125 - 150	150 - 175
3625 "Chrysanthemums"	125 - 150	150 - 175
Others	125 - 150	150 - 175

* The Osborne Calendar Cards are the rarest U.S. Series. Some dealer prices may be somewhat higher!

National Art Company

17 "Spring"	70 - 80	80 - 90
18 "Summer"	70 - 80	80 - 90
19 "Autumn"	70 - 80	80 - 90
20 "Winter"	70 - 80	80 - 90
150 "The Debutantes"	65 - 70	75 - 90
160 "Summer"	70 - 80	80 - 90
161 "Autumn"	70 - 80	80 - 90
162 "Spring"	70 - 80	80 - 90
163 "Winter"	70 - 80	80 - 90
230 "Spring"	80 - 90	90 - 100
231 "Summer"	80 - 90	90 - 100
232 "Autumn"	80 - 90	90 - 100
233 "Winter"	80 - 90	90 - 100

C.N. Snyder Art

"Spring Song"	65 - 75	75 - 85

S.E. Perlberg Co., Tailors (Ad on back)

"My Moonbeam"	65 - 75	75 - 85
"My One Rose"	65 - 75	75 - 85
"Secret of the Flowers"	65 - 75	75 - 85
"True as the Blue Above"	65 - 75	75 - 85
"Twixt Doubt and Hope"	65 - 75	75 - 85

Flood & Conklin

"Girl in Blue"	75 - 85	85 - 95
"The Girl in Brown"	75 - 85	85 - 95
"His First Love"	75 - 85	85 - 95
Others	75 - 85	85 - 95
Soapine Advertising Card	75 - 85	85 - 95

Sparks Tailoring (Ad on back) by **R&N**

"Tomorrow"	65 - 75	75 - 85
A.P. Co. Advertising Card	65 - 75	75 - 85

Holland Magazine (Ad on back)

"Miss Pat"	65 - 75	75 - 85
"Ready for the Meeting"	65 - 75	75 - 85
Metropolitan Life Advertising Card	35 - 40	50 - 60

Will's Embassy Pipe Tobacco Mixtures

"Nocturne"	65 - 75	75 - 85

Worthmore Tay Tailors, Chicago

"Ready for Mischief"	65 - 75	75 - 85

First Nat. Bank, Cripple Creek, CO

"Virginia"	65 - 75	75 - 85

Taylor, Platt *

"Chrysanthemums"	70 - 80	80 - 100

Philip Boileau, R&N 209
"Youth"

Philip Boileau, R&N 205
"?!"

"Poppies"	70 - 80	80 - 100
"Violets"	70 - 80	80 - 100
"Wild Roses"	70 - 80	80 - 100

* 12 cards were supposedly issued;
  however, only 4 have surfaced.

Unsigned, Unknown Publisher *

"Chrysanthemums" **	30 - 35	35 - 45
(To My Sweetheart)		
"Poppies"	30 - 35	35 - 45
(A Greeting from St. Valentine)		
(A Token of Love) 2 types exist.		
"Violets"	30 - 35	35 - 45
(A Gift of Love)		
"Wild Roses"	30 - 35	35 - 45
(To My Valentine)		

* Others may exist.

** Embossed and un-embossed varieties
   exist, and possibly in all four cards.

Wolfe & Co.

"Fancy Free" (Silk) Very Rare!	150 - 200	200 - 250

II. FOREIGN PUBLISHERS

Apollon Sophia

"My Big Brother" (No. 21)	40 - 50	50 - 65

B.K.W.I., German *
"Ready for Mischief"   75 - 100   100 - 125
"June, Blessed June"   75 - 100   100 - 125
* Die-cuts on headbands, necklaces, foil
inside. Others exist without die-cut holes.
Diefenthal, Amsterdam
"The Enchantress"   50 - 75   75 - 85
"Question"   50 - 75   75 - 85
"A Hundred Years Ago"   50 - 75   75 - 85
"C'est Moi"   50 - 75   75 - 85
H & S, Germany
"Au Revoir"   75 - 100   100 - 125
"At Home" (White border)   75 - 100   100 - 125
"Fancy Free" (White border)   75 - 100   100 - 125
"Paying a Call" (White border)   75 - 100   100 - 125
"Paying a Call" (No bord., rev. image)   75 - 100   100 - 125
"I Am Late" (Uns., blue rev. image)   75 - 100   100 - 125
MEU   (Publisher Logo on back)
Untitled, Woman/Dark Hat, Dated 1905 65 - 75   75 - 85
Albert Schweitzer, Germany   50 - 75   75 - 85
H.S. Speelman (Probably Dutch)
"Eva" (Same as "Peggy")   50 - 75   75 - 85
Raphael Tuck
Connoisseur Ser. 2819
"At Home"   125 - 150   150 - 175

Philip Boileau, R&N 820
"Devotion"

Philip Boileau, KNG 8010
"Schöne Frauen"

Philip Boileau, Taylor, Platt Co.
"Chrysanthemums"

Philip Boileau, A.V.N. Jones & Co.
"Spring"

"Au Revoir"	125 - 150	150 - 175
"Fancy Free"	125 - 150	150 - 175
"I Am Late"	125 - 150	150 - 175
"Paying a Call"	125 - 150	150 - 175
"Summer Breezes"	125 - 150	150 - 175

A.V.N. Jones & Co., London
Distributed by **B.K.W.I.**
Series 500

"Spring"	100 - 125	125 - 150
"Summer"	100 - 125	125 - 150
"Fall"	100 - 125	125 - 150
"Winter"	100 - 125	125 - 150

K.K. Oy, Finland

"Baby Mine"	125 - 150	150 - 175
"Sister's First Love"	125 - 150	150 - 175
"Snowbirds"	125 - 150	150 - 175
"Here Comes Daddy" (Light Pastels)	125 - 150	150 - 175

KNG, Germany
Schöne Frauen Series 8010

"I Am Late" (No border)	75 - 100	100 - 125
"Paying a Call" (No border)	75 - 100	100 - 125
"Summer Breezes" (No border)	75 - 100	100 - 125
"Fancy Free"	100 - 125	125 - 150

"Au Revoir"	100 - 125	125 - 150
"At Home"	100 - 125	125 - 150
Schöne Frauen Series 8011		
"I Am Late" (White border)	75 - 100	100 - 125
"Fancy Free"	100 - 125	125 - 150
"Paying a Call" (White border)	75 - 100	100 - 125
"Summer Breezes" (White border)	75 - 100	100 - 125
Schöne Frauen Series 8012		
"I Am Late" (Rev. image, uns., untit.)	75 - 100	100 - 125
"Fancy Free"	75 - 100	100 - 125
Schöne Frauen Series 8013		
"I Am Late" (Reversed image, uns.)	75 - 100	100 - 125
"Paying a Call" (Reversed image, uns.)	75 - 100	100 - 125
"Summer Breezes" (Blue rev. image)	100 - 125	125 - 150
Weinthal Co., Rotterdam	50 - 75	75 - 85
Friedrich O. Wolter, Berlin		
1058 "Studie"	50 - 75	75 - 85

III. RUSSIAN

AWE - Russian/Polish Back		
Real Photo Series		
"Miss America"	125 - 150	150 - 175
"Phillips"		
104 "Winter"	125 - 150	150 - 175
110 "Violets"	125 - 150	150 - 175
111 "Chrysanthemums"	125 - 150	150 - 175
112	125 - 150	150 - 175
116	125 - 150	150 - 175
Unknown Russian Publisher		
Real Photo Ser., Russian-Polish Back		
"The Enchantress"	125 - 150	150 - 175
Unknown Russian Publisher		
"Autumn"	125 - 150	150 - 175
Unknown Russian Publisher		
5 "Rings on Her Fingers" (Unsigned)	125 - 150	150 - 175
18 "A Brotherly Kiss" (Peb. grain Paper)	125 - 150	150 - 175

IV. UNKNOWN PUBLISHERS

Series 682 (6)		
682-1 "Anticipation"	50 - 60	60 - 75
682-2 "True as the Blue Above"	50 - 60	60 - 75
682-3 "In Maiden Meditation"	50 - 60	60 - 75
682-4 Unknown	175 - 200	200 - 225
682-5 "Twins"	50 - 60	60 - 75
682-6 "The Girl in Black"	50 - 60	60 - 75
Unsigned		
"Miss America"	50 - 75	75 - 95
"Miss America" (Signed, 1910, blue ink)	50 - 75	75 - 95

"Rings on Her Fingers"	50 - 75	75 - 95
Unknown Publisher (Possibly Dutch)		
Series R		
R.236 "Miss America"	50 - 75	75 - 95
R.238 "His First Love"	50 - 75	75 - 95
R.239 "Chums"	50 - 75	75 - 95
BOLETTA	6 - 8	8 - 10
BOMPARD, S. (Italy) See Art Deco		
BONORA (Italy) See Art Deco		
BOTTARO (Italy) See Art Deco		
BOUTET, HENRI	20 - 25	25 - 30
BRAUN, W.H. (German)	6 - 8	8 - 10
BREDT, F.M. (German)	5 - 6	6 - 8
BRILL, G.R. (U.S.A.)		
Sporting Girl Series	6 - 8	8 - 9
BROCK, A. (German)	5 - 6	6 - 8
BROWN, J. FRANCIS (U.S.A.)	4 - 5	5 - 6
BRUNELLESCHI (Italy)		
See F. Glamour & Art Deco		
BRUNING, MAX (Germany)	8 - 10	10 - 14
Erotic	12 - 15	15 - 18
BRYSON (U.S.A.)		
S. S. Porter, Chicago		
143 "Secrets"	5 - 6	6 - 8

W.H. Braun, Caklovic VIII-5
No Caption

A. Butcher, Inter-Art Co.
"For Mercy's Sake"

BUKOVAC, PROF. V. (Poland)	4 - 5	5 - 6
BULAS, J. (Poland)	8 - 10	10 - 12
BUSI, ADOLFO (Italy) See Art Deco		
BUTCHER, ARTHUR (GB)		
United Six Girls Series		
"Belgium"	10 - 12	12 - 15
"Britain"	10 - 12	12 - 15
"France"	10 - 12	12 - 15
"Japan"	10 - 12	12 - 15
"Russia"	12 - 15	15 - 18
"Serbia"	12 - 15	15 - 18
"Artisque" Series 1509 (6)	8 - 10	10 - 12
A.R.i.B. Series 1963 (6)	8 - 10	10 - 12
Inter-Art Co.	10 - 12	12 - 14
CALDONA (Italy) See Art Deco		
CARSON, T. See Art Nouveau		
CAUVY, L. See Art Nouveau		
CASTELLI (Italy) See Art Deco		
CELEBRI (Italy) See Art Deco		
CENNI, E. (Italy) See Art Deco		
CHERUBINI (Italy) See Art Deco		
CHIOSTRI & SOFIA See Art Deco		

CHRISTY, F. EARL (U.S.A.)

F. Earl Christy was one of the leading American artists who depicted the beauty of the prestigious American girl, especially of the college and university varieties. Most of his early works were in this category, as he helped start the tradition of glorifying the beauties of the era.

He painted them as very high class, always beautifully dressed, and seemingly in complete command of the situation. They were the girls who attended football games, played golf and tennis, rode in new automobiles and who were gifted with musical talent. His was the *All-American Girl*.

His first College Girl series was published by the U.S.S. Postcard Co. in 1905. This series revealed an artist with promising talents, and he went on to design many of the great "College Girl" series for numerous publishers. Among his most popular works were the Raphael Tuck College Queens and College Kings series.

After the college/university girl fad had run its course, Christy used his many talents to paint beautiful ladies and man/woman lover types. The Reinthal & Newman Co. of

Earl Christy, Platinachrome Co.
"Yale"

Earl Christy, Raphael Tuck 2625
"Princeton"

New York was his major publisher; however, he did many fine series for the Knapp Co., Edward Gross, and others. His images were also published and distributed in Europe and Scandinavia.

F. EARL CHRISTY

Reinthal & Newman
No Number Series

"Love"	12 - 15	15 - 18
"A Sandwich"	12 - 15	15 - 18
"Be With You in a Minute"	10 - 12	12 - 15
"Always Winning"	15 - 18	18 - 22
"Love Dreams"	10 - 12	12 - 15
"Lovingly Yours"	10 - 12	12 - 15
"Swimming"	12 - 15	15 - 18
"A Sweet Surrender Series"		
168 "A Sweet Surrender"	12 - 15	15 - 18
169 "The Pilot"	12 - 15	15 - 18
170 "My Love is Like a Red, Red Rose"	12 - 15	15 - 18
171 "Come Sit Beside Me"	10 - 12	12 - 15
172 "Come With Me	10 - 12	12 - 15
173 "Love All"	15 - 20	20 - 25

"The Siren" Series

228 "Masks Off"	10 - 12	12 - 15
229 "Lovingly Yours"	10 - 12	12 - 15
230 "Be With You in a Minute"	10 - 12	12 - 15
231 "The Rose Maid"	10 - 12	12 - 15
232 "The Siren"	12 - 15	15 - 18
233 "Roses are Always in Season"	10 - 12	12 - 15

"The Path of Love" Series

276 "The Love Song"	10 - 12	12 - 15
277 "Love Dreams"	10 - 12	12 - 15
278 "The Love Story"	10 - 12	12 - 15
279 "The Love Match"	10 - 12	12 - 15
280 "The Love Waltz"	10 - 12	12 - 15
281 "Love"	10 - 12	12 - 15

Water Color Series 363-368

363 "A Bit of Tea and Gossip"	12 - 15	15 - 18
364 "The Sweetest of All"	12 - 15	15 - 18
365 "For the Wedding Chest"	12 - 15	15 - 18
366 "The Message of Love"	12 - 15	15 - 18
367 "The Day's Work"	15 - 18	18 - 22
368 "A Finishing Touch"	12 - 15	15 - 18

Series 428-433

428 "What Shall I Answer?"	10 - 12	12 - 15
429 "I'm Waiting for You"	10 - 12	12 - 15
430 "Tender Memories"	10 - 12	12 - 15

Earl Christy, Raphael Tuck 2766
"College Kings," "Cornell"

Friedman-Shelby Shoe Co.
©F. Earl Christy

431 "A Message of Love"	10 - 12	12 - 15
432 "On the Bridal Path"	10 - 12	12 - 15
433 "Always Winning"	15 - 18	18 - 22
Series 618-623		
618 "The Girl I Like"	12 - 14	14 - 18
619 "The Girl I Like to Chat With"	12 - 14	14 - 18
620 "The Girl I Like to Walk With"	12 - 14	14 - 18
621 "The Girl I Like to Flirt With"	12 - 14	14 - 18
622 "The Girl I Like to Play With"	15 - 18	18 - 22
623 "The Girl I Like to Sing With"	12 - 14	14 - 18
Series 624-629		
624 "By Appointment"	12 - 15	15 - 18
625 "As Promised"	12 - 15	15 - 18
626 "What Shall I Say?"	10 - 12	12 - 15
627 "A Sandwitch"	12 - 15	15 - 18
628 "With Fond Love"	10 - 12	12 - 15
629 "Nearest Her Heart"	10 - 12	12 - 15
Water Color Series 942-947		
942 "Protected"	12 - 14	14 - 16
943 "Someone is Thinking of You"	12 - 14	14 - 16
944 "Are You There"	12 - 14	14 - 16
945 "Love, Here is My Heart"	12 - 14	14 - 16
946 "Worth Waiting For"	12 - 14	14 - 16
947 "Not Forgotten"	12 - 14	14 - 16
ENGLISH REPRINTS		
2106 "On the Bridal Path"	12 - 15	15 - 18
2107 "Tender Memories"	12 - 15	15 - 18
2109 "Nearest Her Heart"	12 - 15	15 - 18
Others	12 - 15	15 - 18
FAS (F.A. Schneider)		
197 Horseback Riding	15 - 18	18 - 25
198 Skates	15 - 18	18 - 25
199 Tennis	20 - 25	25 - 28
200 Golf	20 - 25	25 - 28
201 In an Auto	15 - 18	18 - 25
202 "What the Waves are Saying"	15 - 18	18 - 25
203 Daisies	15 - 18	18 - 25
Edward Gross		
Series 3		
"Black-Eyed Susan"	10 - 12	12 - 15
"God is not All"	10 - 12	12 - 15
"Her Pilot"	10 - 12	12 - 15
"In Deep Water"	10 - 12	12 - 15
"Oldest Trust Co."	10 - 12	12 - 15
"World Before Them"	10 - 12	12 - 15
Knapp Co., N.Y. W.M. Sanford		
Paul Heckscher Import		
Series 304		
1 "Annie Laurie"	12 - 14	14 - 16
2 "The Lost Chord"	12 - 14	14 - 16
3 "Louisiana Lou"	12 - 14	14 - 16

4 "The Rosary"	12 - 14	14 - 16
5 "The Largo"	12 - 14	14 - 16
6 "Love's Old Sweet Song"	12 - 14	14 - 16
7 "Daughter of the Regiment"	12 - 14	14 - 16
8 "Good Night, Beloved"	12 - 14	14 - 16
9 "The Gypsy Maid"	12 - 14	14 - 16
10 "Maryland, My Maryland"	12 - 14	14 - 16
11 "Home, Sweet Home"	12 - 14	14 - 16
12 "Wish I Was in Dixie"	12 - 14	14 - 16

Paul Heckscher Import   W.M. Sanford
Miniature Image Series 304

371 "Annie Laurie"	10 - 12	12 - 15
381 "The Lost Chord"	10 - 12	12 - 15
391 "Louisiana Lou"	10 - 12	12 - 15
401 "The Rosary"	10 - 12	12 - 15
411 "The Largo"	10 - 12	12 - 15
421 "Love's Old Sweet Song"		10 - 12

12 - 15

431 "Daughters of the Regiment"	10 - 12	12 - 15
441 "Good Night, Beloved"	10 - 12	12 - 15
451 "The Gypsy Maid"	10 - 12	12 - 15
461 "Maryland, My Maryland"	10 - 12	12 - 15
471 "Home, Sweet Home"	10 - 12	12 - 15
481 "Wish I was in Dixie"	10 - 12	12 - 15

Paul Heckscher Import

1025-3 "I'm Ready"	12 - 15	15 - 18
Others	12 - 15	15 - 18

Knapp Co. (Continued)

103 Girl in Sailor Blouse and Hat	12 - 15	15 - 18
105 Girl with Lace Collar	12 - 15	15 - 18
114 Girl in Sailor Blouse	12 - 15	15 - 18
115 Beauty, with Pearl Necklace	12 - 15	15 - 18
116 Sweet Girl with Long Curl	12 - 15	15 - 18
119 Blonde Girl with Black Pearls	12 - 15	15 - 18
124 "Prudence"	10 - 12	12 - 15
169 "Let's Go"	12 - 15	15 - 18
176 "Skipper's Mate"	12 - 15	15 - 18
215 "Beauty"	10 - 12	12 - 15
219 "Anna Belle"	10 - 12	12 - 15

Note: There may be cards missing from
103 through 219.

Knapp Co.
Heckscher Import Series 318

"The Best of Chums"	12 - 15	15 - 18
"Blossoming Affection"	12 - 15	15 - 18
"Goodbye Summer"	12 - 15	15 - 18
"The Springtime of Friendship"	12 - 15	15 - 18

Heckscher Import Series 319

"Embracing the Opportunity"	12 - 15	15 - 18
"In Sweet Accord"	12 - 15	15 - 18
"The Message of the Rose"	12 - 15	15 - 18

"Tempting Fate"	12 - 15	15 - 18
Knapp Co. by **Sanford**		
Calendar card, 1916		
"I Wish I Was in Dixie"	15 - 18	18 - 22
Jules Bien, 1907		
College Series 95		
Girl & Boy on Football		
950 "Yale"	15 - 18	18 - 22
951 "Harvard"	15 - 18	18 - 22
952 "Columbia"	15 - 18	18 - 22
953 "Penn"	15 - 18	18 - 22
954 "Princeton"	15 - 18	18 - 22
955 "Cornell"	15 - 18	18 - 22
Chapman, N.Y., 1910		
1032 "A Brisk Walk"	10 - 12	12 - 14
1034 "Waiting Their Turn"	10 - 12	12 - 14
1039 "At the Horse Show"	10 - 12	12 - 14
William B. Christy (His Father)		
Unnumbered Series		
"Harvard"	12 - 15	15 - 18
"Michigan"	12 - 15	15 - 18
"Penn"	12 - 15	15 - 18
"Princeton"	12 - 15	15 - 18
"Yale"	12 - 15	15 - 18
EAS (E.A. Schwerdfeger)		
Girl on Brick Wall Series		
"Columbia"	10 - 12	12 - 15
"Cornell"	10 - 12	12 - 15
"Harvard"	10 - 12	12 - 15
"Penn"	10 - 12	12 - 15
"Princeton"	10 - 12	12 - 15
"Yale"	10 - 12	12 - 15
H. Henninger Co.		
40 Driving	8 - 10	10 - 12
44 In an Auto (Same as **FAS** 201)	10 - 12	12 - 14
45 Daisies	10 - 12	12 - 14
Illustrated Postal Card & Novelty Co.		
Series 133 *		
1 "Cornell"	10 - 12	12 - 14
2 "Harvard"	10 - 12	12 - 14
3 "Yale"	10 - 12	12 - 14
4 "Penn"	10 - 12	12 - 14
5 "Princeton"	10 - 12	12 - 14
6 "Columbia"	10 - 12	12 - 14
* With Silk Applique Dress, add $10-15.		
Series 150 *		
1 "Cornell"	10 - 12	12 - 15
2 "Harvard"	10 - 12	12 - 15
3 "Yale"	10 - 12	12 - 15
4 "Penn"	10 - 12	12 - 15
5 "Princeton"	10 - 12	12 - 15

6 "Columbia"	10 - 12	12 - 15

* With Silk Applique Dress, add \$10-15.
Note: Nos. are on backs of some cards.

Series 160, 1907

160-1 "A Drama"	10 - 12	12 - 14
160-2 "A Critical Moment"	10 - 12	12 - 14
160-3 "The World was Made..."	10 - 12	12 - 14
160-4 "An Attractive Parasol"	10 - 12	12 - 14
160-5 "Getting Acquainted"	10 - 12	12 - 14
160-6	10 - 12	12 - 14

"Sports" Series

552D Swinging	6 - 8	8 - 10
554 Bowling	6 - 8	8 - 10
557 Rowing	6 - 8	8 - 10
562 Swimming	6 - 8	8 - 10
567 Driving Old Car	6 - 8	8 - 10
569 Four Princeton Girls in Auto	6 - 8	8 - 10
572 Golf	10 - 12	12 - 14
574 Princeton Belles in Old Car	6 - 8	8 - 10
577 Buggy	6 - 8	8 - 10
582 Three Yale Girls in Auto	6 - 8	8 - 10
584 Tennis	10 - 12	12 - 15

Series 5006

1

Earl Christy, R&N Watercolor 946
"Worth Waiting For"

Earl Christy, R&N Watercolor 364
"The Sweetest of All"

2			
3 "Swinging"		6 - 8	8 - 10
4			
5			
6			
7			
8 Horse & Buggy		6 - 8	8 - 10
9 Old Car-Harvard		6 - 8	8 - 10
10 Old Car-Yale		6 - 8	8 - 10
11 Old Car-Princeton		6 - 8	8 - 10
12 Old Car-Penn		6 - 8	8 - 10

Platinachrome, 1907
Girl/Pennant form Letter, College Yell

"Chicago"	15 - 18	18 - 25
"Columbia"	15 - 18	18 - 25
"Cornell"	15 - 18	18 - 25
"Harvard"	15 - 18	18 - 25
"Michigan"	15 - 18	18 - 25
"Penn"	15 - 18	18 - 25
"Princeton"	15 - 18	18 - 25
"Yale"	15 - 18	18 - 25

Platinachrome, © 1905 by F. Earl Christy
No Numbers or Captions

Two Women in a Car	8 - 10	10 - 12
Woman Golfing	12 - 15	15 - 18
Woman Bowling	8 - 10	10 - 12
Woman-Ice Hockey	8 - 10	10 - 12

P. Sander, N.Y., 1907 (Ill. P.C. Co.)
Series 198

1 "Is a Caddie always Necessary"	12 - 15	15 - 18
2 "Is horseback riding..."	10 - 12	12 - 15
3 "Trying to make a hit"	10 - 12	12 - 15
4 "A Good Racquet for Two"	14 - 16	16 - 20
5 "Out for a catch"	10 - 12	12 - 15
6 "Hockey is not the only game"	12 - 15	15 - 18

P. Sander, N.Y., 1908
Series 246 (6) Large Hats *

1 Full Photo	6 - 8	8 - 12
2 1910 Calendar	10 - 12	12 - 15
3 Christmas, Silver	5 - 6	6 - 8
4 Christmas, Gold	5 - 6	6 - 8
5 Woman in Easter Egg	5 - 6	6 - 8
6 Valentine	5 - 6	6 - 8

* Full card is signed. Others cropped & uns.
Note: There are 6 diff. cards of each image!
There are various numbers on the fronts.
Series 304-A (6) Signed, 1908

1 Full Card	8 - 10	10 - 12
2 Birthday, White	6 - 8	8 - 10
3 Birthday, Gold	6 - 8	8 - 10
4 Birthday, Silver	6 - 8	8 - 10

5 Woman in Egg	6 - 8	8 - 10
6 Valentine, Checkered	6 - 8	8 - 10
7 Valentine, Gold	6 - 8	8 - 10
8 Horse Shoe, Birthday, White	6 - 8	8 - 10
9 Horse Shoe, Birthday, Gold	6 - 8	8 - 10
10 Horse Shoe, Birthday, Silver	6 - 8	8 - 10

Note: There are 10 diff. cards of each image!
There are various numbers on the fronts.

W.H. Sanford
  Series 371

"Goodbye Summer"	12 - 15	15 - 18
"Tempting Fate"	12 - 15	15 - 18

Stecher Litho Co., N.Y.
  Series 618, Valentines

A "To My Sweetheart"	8 - 10	10 - 12
B "Valentine Thoughts" (Unsigned)	8 - 10	10 - 12
C "To My Valentine" (Unsigned)	8 - 10	10 - 12
D "A Valentine Greeting"	8 - 10	10 - 12
F "A Valentine Greeting"	8 - 10	10 - 12

Souvenir Postcard Co., © F. Earl Christy
  Girl & Football Player with Banner

1 "Michigan"	10 - 12	12 - 15
2 "Chicago"	10 - 12	12 - 15
3 "Princeton"	10 - 12	12 - 15

Earl Christy, Ill. P. C. Co. 150-1
"Cornell"

Earl Christy, Anonymous 336
No Caption

4 "Penn"	10 - 12	12 - 15
5 "Cornell"	10 - 12	12 - 15
6 "Yale"	10 - 12	12 - 15
7 "Harvard"	10 - 12	12 - 15
8 "Columbia"	10 - 12	12 - 15

Raphael Tuck
University Girl Series 2453

"Oberlin College"	20 - 22	22 - 25
"West Point"	20 - 22	22 - 25
"Syracuse U."	20 - 22	22 - 25
"Georgetown"	20 - 22	22 - 25
"U.S. Naval Academy"	20 - 22	22 - 25
"Tennessee"	20 - 22	22 - 25

Series 2590

"Iowa"	20 - 22	22 - 25
"U. of Arkansas"	20 - 22	22 - 25
"Valparaiso U."	20 - 22	22 - 25
"Ames"	20 - 22	22 - 25
"Kentucky"	20 - 22	22 - 25
"Penn State"	20 - 22	22 - 25

Series 2717

"Mary Baldwin Seminary"	15 - 18	18 - 22

University Girl Series 2625

"Columbia"	15 - 18	18 - 22
"Cornell"	15 - 18	18 - 22
"Harvard"	15 - 18	18 - 22
"Penn"	15 - 18	18 - 22
"Princeton"	15 - 18	18 - 22
"Yale"	15 - 18	18 - 22

Series 2626

"U. of Chicago"	15 - 18	18 - 22
"U. of Illinois"	15 - 18	18 - 22
"Indiana U."	15 - 18	18 - 22
"U. of Michigan"	15 - 18	18 - 22
"U. of Minnesota"	15 - 18	18 - 22
"U. of Wisconsin"	15 - 18	18 - 22

Series 2627

"Brown U."	15 - 18	18 - 22
"Tulane of La."	15 - 18	18 - 22
"Vanderbilt U."	15 - 18	18 - 22
"U. of Virginia"	15 - 18	18 - 22
"Williston Seminary"	20 - 22	22 - 25
"McGill College"	20 - 22	22 - 25

Series 2766 "College Kings"

"Columbia"	60 - 70	70 - 80
"Cornell"	60 - 70	70 - 80
"Chicago"	60 - 70	70 - 80
"Michigan"	60 - 70	70 - 80

Series 2767 "College Queens"

"Yale"	60 - 70	70 - 80

"Penn"	60 - 70	70 - 80
"Harvard"	60 - 70	70 - 80
"Princeton"	60 - 70	70 - 80
"Good Luck" Series 276		
"Not only for today..."	10 - 12	12 - 15
"Good luck attend you..."	10 - 12	12 - 15
"Good wishes greet you..."	10 - 12	12 - 15
"May Fortune spin..."	10 - 12	12 - 15

Ullman Mfg. Co.
College Girls, Series 24, C. 1905 (Uns.)

1498 "Penn"	6 - 8	8 - 10
1499 "Columbia"	6 - 8	8 - 10
1512 "Yale"	6 - 8	8 - 10
1513 "Harvard"	6 - 8	8 - 10
1514 "Leland Stanford"	6 - 8	8 - 10
1515 "Cornell"	6 - 8	8 - 10
1516 "Princeton"	6 - 8	8 - 10
1517 "Chicago"	6 - 8	8 - 10

College Football Players,
Series 24, C. 1905, Unsigned

1464 "Harvard	12 - 15	15 - 18
1465 "Princeton"	12 - 15	15 - 18
1466 "Penn"	12 - 15	15 - 18
1467 "Yale"	12 - 15	15 - 18
1518 "Columbia"	12 - 15	15 - 18
1519 "Leland Stanford"	12 - 15	15 - 18
1520 "Chicago"	12 - 15	15 - 18
1521 "Cornell"	12 - 15	15 - 18

Ullman, 1907
Girl in Big College Letter Series

1990 "Chicago"	10 - 12	12 - 15
1991 "Cornell"	10 - 12	12 - 15
1991 "Michigan"	10 - 12	12 - 15
1992 "Michigan"	10 - 12	12 - 15
1993 "Columbia"	10 - 12	12 - 15
1994 "Penn"	10 - 12	12 - 15
1995 "Yale"	10 - 12	12 - 15
1996 "Princeton"	10 - 12	12 - 15
1997 "Harvard"	10 - 12	12 - 15

Other **Ullman** College Girls

569 "Princeton"	6 - 8	8 - 10
574 "Penn"	6 - 8	8 - 10
575 "Harvard"	6 - 8	8 - 10
582 "Yale"	6 - 8	8 - 10

Ullman Mfg. Co., 1905, N.Y.

501 Golf	10 - 12	12 - 15
506 "A Pleasant Ride"	4 - 6	6 - 8
507 "In Fair Japan"	4 - 6	6 - 8
1583 "The Graduate"	8 - 10	10 - 12
Series 93	8 - 10	10 - 12

Earl Christy, Souvenir P.C. Co.
"Yale"

Earl Christy, Julius Bien 953
"Pennsylvania"

U.S.S.P.C. Co., 1905
  College Seal Series
1 "Penn"   10 - 12   12 - 14
2 "Princeton"   10 - 12   12 - 14

3 "Harvard" (also leather) *	10 - 12	12 - 14
4 "Yale"	10 - 12	12 - 14
5 "Michigan"	10 - 12	12 - 14
6 "Chicago"	10 - 12	12 - 14
7 "Columbia"	10 - 12	12 - 14
8 "Cornell"	10 - 12	12 - 14

* Add $5-10 for leather cards.

Valentine & Sons
  "Artotype" Series, No Numbers

"Columbia"	15 - 18	18 - 22
"Penn"	15 - 18	18 - 22

Friedman-Shelby Shoe Co.
  "Big Hat" Series

Shoe Style 3324	20 - 25	25 - 30
Shoe Style 3332	20 - 25	25 - 30
The Style	20 - 25	25 - 30
Red Goose School Shoes	25 - 30	30 - 35
Shoe Style 3339	20 - 25	25 - 30

Greenfield's Delatour Chocolates, 1911

Girl With Big Hat, Walks Right	25 - 30	30 - 35
Bulls-Eye Overalls	20 - 25	25 - 30

UNKNOWN

©1910 F. Earl Christy
  Bust of woman with nosegay & big hat

tied under her chin.	8 - 10	10 - 12
Blue dress and pink flowers	8 - 10	10 - 12
Blue hat and red flowers	8 - 10	10 - 12
Orange hat and yellow flowers	8 - 10	10 - 12

Water Colors

650-5 "Embracing the Opportunity"	10 - 12	12 - 15
656-5 "In Sweet Accord"	10 - 12	12 - 15
657-5 "Vacation Days"	10 - 12	12 - 15

FINNISH ISSUES

Pain.Karjalan Kirjap. Oy, Viipuri
N:O 12 Unsigned, no caption

Same as R&N 173, "Love All"	35 - 40	40 - 45
N:O 6 Signed, no cap. Girl with Umbrella	35 - 40	40 - 45

No Identification Series
  Uns., no caption. Same as R&N 365,

"For the Wedding Chest"	30 - 35	35 - 40

W.& G. American Series N:o 7001/1-35
  Girl w/long stemmed roses handing

one to man behind the chair.	35 - 40	40 - 45

CHRISTY, HOWARD CHANDLER (U.S.A.)

Howard Chandler Christy, although of no relation to F.

Earl Christy, was one of the more prominent illustrators of the 1900-1920 era. He also did illustrations for many magazines and paintings of "prominent people" portraits, but probably gained most of his fame from his World War I Posters.

Among the paintings he was commissioned to do were those of Presidents Harding and Coolidge, Mussolini, Will Rogers, and Amelia Earhart. His historical painting of "Signing the Constitution" now hangs in the Capitol in Washington, D.C.

For the postcard collectors of today he left many renderings of beautiful ladies. These became known as the "Christy Girls" and were adapted to postcards from his magazine illustrations and posters. His most famous cards were those of "The Army Girl" and "The Navy Girl" published by A & V for the Jamestown Exposition of 1907.

HOWARD CHANDLER CHRISTY

Moffat, Yard, & Co., N.Y., 1905
"The Christy Post Card"

1 "Arbutus" (B&W)	8 - 10	10 - 12
2 "At the Opera"	10 - 12	12 - 14
3 "A City Girl" (B&W)	8 - 10	10 - 12
Also appears in partial color.	10 - 12	12 - 14
4 "The Dance"	10 - 12	12 - 14
5 "The Debutante"	10 - 12	12 - 14
6 "Encore"	10 - 12	12 - 14
7 "Mistletoe" (B&W)	8 - 10	10 - 12
Also appears in partial color.	10 - 12	12 - 14
8 "A Moment of Reflection"	10 - 12	12 - 14
9 "Reverie" (B&W)	8 - 10	10 - 12
10 "A Suburban Girl" (B&W)	8 - 10	10 - 12
11 "The Summer Girl" (B&W)	8 - 10	10 - 12
12 "Violets" (B&W)	8 - 10	10 - 12
Also appears in partial color	10 - 12	12 - 14
13 "Waiting"	10 - 12	12 - 14
14 "Water Lilies" (B&W)	8 - 10	10 - 12
15 "The Winter Girl" (B&W)		8 - 10
10 - 12		

Unnumbered Series, 1908

"The American Queen"	10 - 12	12 - 14
"American Beauties"	10 - 12	12 - 14
"At the Theater"	10 - 12	12 - 14
"Canoe Mates"	8 - 10	10 - 12
"Drifting"	8 - 10	10 - 12

H.C. Christy, Anon. (Pain. Karj.)
N:O 2, No Caption

H. Coffin, PCG Co. 205/7
"June Roses"

"Excess Baggage"	8 - 10	10 - 12
"A Fisherman's Luck"	10 - 12	12 - 14
"The Golf Girl"	14 - 16	16 - 20
"Lilies"	8 - 10	10 - 12
"On the Beach"	10 - 12	12 - 14
"Sailing Close"	8 - 10	10 - 12
"A Summer Girl"	10 - 12	12 - 14
"Teasing"	8 - 10	10 - 12
"A Winning Hand"	10 - 12	12 - 14
Series 3, 1909		
"Black-Eyed Susan"	8 - 10	10 - 12
"Gold is Not All"	8 - 10	10 - 12
"Her Pilot"	8 - 10	10 - 12
"In Deep Water"	10 - 12	12 - 14
"Miss Demure"	10 - 12	12 - 14
"The Oldest Trust Company"	8 - 10	10 - 12
"A Plea for Arbitration"	8 - 10	10 - 12
"The Sweet Girl Graduate"	10 - 12	12 - 14
"The Teasing Girl"	10 - 12	12 - 14
Series 4, 1909		
"Au Revoir"	10 - 12	12 - 14
"Congratulations"	10 - 12	12 - 14
"The Heart of America"	10 - 12	12 - 14
"Her Gift"	10 - 12	12 - 14

"Honeymoon"	10 - 12	12 - 14
"Into the Future"	10 - 12	12 - 14
"Life's Beginning"	10 - 12	12 - 14
"Love Spats"	10 - 12	12 - 14
"Mistletoe"	10 - 12	12 - 14
"Overpowering Beauty"	10 - 12	12 - 14
"A Rose on the Lips"	10 - 12	12 - 14
Edward Gross		
Series of 6	10 - 12	12 - 14
Scribner's		
Series of 8	10 - 12	12 - 14
Armour & Co., Chicago, 1901 Ad Card		
"The Howard Ch. Christy Girl" (B&W)	15 - 20	20 - 25
Same, by German Publisher (B&W)	20 - 25	25 - 30
A & V, Jamestown Expo., 1907		
"The Army Girl"	125 - 150	150 - 200
"The Navy Girl"	100 - 125	125 - 150
H. Choate & Co.		
Djer-Kiss Rouge		
& Face Powder Compacts		
"American Brunette"	20 - 25	25 - 30
Curt Teich & Co.		
"Boy Scout Jamboree" (Linen, 1937)	10 - 12	12 - 15
T.P. & Co.		
Judge Co., N.Y.		
Series 751		
"You Have a Wonderful Future!"	12 - 14	14 - 16
"Going Away" (Unsigned)	12 - 14	14 - 16

FOREIGN

Novitas		
Series 21655		
"City Girl"	12 - 14	14 - 18
"Drifting"	12 - 14	14 - 18
"Reverie"	12 - 14	14 - 18
"A Summer Girl"	14 - 16	16 - 20
"Violets"	12 - 14	14 - 18
"The World Before Them"	12 - 14	14 - 18
Series 21657 (6)	12 - 14	14 - 18
Pain. Karjalan Kirjap. Oy, Viipuri		
N:O 2 3 Bathing Girls	16 - 20	20 - 25
CLAY, JOHN C. (U.S.A.)		
Detroit Publishing Co.		
Black & White Series	6 - 8	8 - 10
Rotograph Co.		
Water Color Series 160	10 - 12	12 - 15
"Garden of Love" Ser. (12) Head in Flowers		
Armour & Co., Adv. Card		
"The John C. Clay Girl" (B&W)	10 - 12	12 - 15
Same, by German Publisher (B&W)	12 - 15	15 - 18

CLIRIO, L. (Italy) See Art Deco
COFFIN, HASKELL (U.S.A.)
  R.C. Co.
    Series 205

"A Modern Eve"	12 - 15	15 - 20
"An American Queen"	12 - 15	15 - 20
"The Glory of Autumn"	12 - 15	15 - 20
"The Lure of the Poppies"	12 - 15	15 - 20
"Miss Jack Frost"	15 - 18	18 - 22
"Motherhood"	12 - 15	15 - 20
"Queen of the Court"	18 - 20	20 - 24
"The Spring Maid"	15 - 18	18 - 22
"Vanity Fair"	15 - 18	18 - 22
"Winter's Charm"	15 - 18	18 - 22

  K. Co.
    Water Color Series

215 "Beauty"	15 - 18	18 - 22
216 "Sally"	15 - 18	18 - 22
217 "Ruth"	15 - 18	18 - 22
218 "Billy"	15 - 18	18 - 22

Photo Color Graph Co.
  Series 205 "Art Studies"

1 "Bohemia"	12 - 13	13 - 16
2 "Miss Knickerbocker"	12 - 13	13 - 16
3 "Her First Love Letter"	12 - 13	13 - 16
4 "The Final Touch"	12 - 13	13 - 16
5 "Sweet Sixteen"	14 - 16	16 - 18
6 "Girl From the Golden West"	12 - 14	14 - 16
8 "Pride of the Orient"	12 - 14	14 - 16
9 "News From the Sunny South"	12 - 14	14 - 16
Others	12 - 14	14 - 16

  "Flower & Figure" Semi-Nude Series 280

1 Iris	10 - 12	12 - 16
2 Violet	10 - 12	12 - 16
3 Poppies	10 - 12	12 - 16
4 Narcissus	10 - 12	12 - 16
5 Goldenrod	10 - 12	12 - 16
6 Daffodils	10 - 12	12 - 16
7 Hollyhock	10 - 12	12 - 16
8 Water Lily	10 - 12	12 - 16
9 Nasturtium	10 - 12	12 - 16
10 Rose	10 - 12	12 - 16
11 Sweet Pea	10 - 12	12 - 16
12 Morning Glory	10 - 12	12 - 16

  Fantasy Women Series, Semi-nude

"Celia"	12 - 14	14 - 18
Others	12 - 14	14 - 18

A.R. & C.i.B. Co.

417 "An American Queen"	12 - 15	15 - 20
"The Glory of Autumn"	12 - 15	15 - 20
"The Joy of the Hunt"	12 - 15	15 - 20

"Miss Jack Frost"	12 - 15	15 - 20
"Ruth"	12 - 15	15 - 18
"Winter's Charm"	12 - 15	15 - 18
"Vanity Fair"	12 - 15	15 - 18

H & S Company
1551 D3 "A New York Belle"   10 - 12
12 - 15

1551 D6 "Thoughtful"	10 - 12	12 - 15
Others, With Captions	10 - 12	12 - 15
Others, No Captions	8 - 10	10 - 12

ESK Co.

02 Girl with big Slouch Hat, Sequined white Blouse, No caption	12 - 14	14 - 18
Blue Bell Brand Candies Ad. Cards (2)	15 - 18	18 - 22
Hires Root Beer Girl	20 - 25	25 - 30

COLOMBO (Italy) See Art Deco

CONNELL, MARY	4 - 6	6 - 7

CORBELLA, T. (Italy) See Art Deco
CRAFFONARA See Art Nouveau
CRANDALL, JOHN BRADSHAW

K. Co. N.Y. Series	7 - 8	8 - 12

CRATTA (Italy) See Art Deco
CREMIEUX, ED. (France) See French Glamour
CYRANICUS (Italy) See Art Deco
DANIELL, EVA (GB) See Art Nouveau

Frank Desch, K. Co. 1027-1
"Katharine"

Frank Desch, K. C. 303-3
"Violet"

DAY, FRANCES (U.S.A.)	4 - 5	5 - 6
DAVIS, STANLEY (U.S.A.)	8 - 9	9 - 10
DEDINA, JAN (Poland)	10 - 12	12 - 15
DENNISON (U.S.A.)	3 - 4	4 - 5
DERNINI (Italy) See Art Deco		
DERRANTI, D. (Italy) See Art Deco		
DESCH, FRANK (U.S.A.)		
Knapp Co.		
Series 303		
"Annette"	12 - 15	15 - 18
"Diana"	12 - 15	15 - 18
"Eloise"	12 - 15	15 - 18
"Flora"	12 - 15	15 - 18
"Florence"	12 - 15	15 - 18
"Grace"	12 - 15	15 - 18
"Ida"	12 - 15	15 - 18
"Isabel"	12 - 15	15 - 18
"Laura"	12 - 15	15 - 18
"Lillian"	12 - 15	15 - 18
"Violet"	12 - 15	15 - 18
"Virginia"	12 - 15	15 - 18
Knapp Co.		
Series 309 (12)	12 - 15	15 - 18
Series 50	10 - 12	12 - 15
Others	12 - 15	15 - 18
Knapp Co. Calendars		
9443 "Grace"	15 - 18	18 - 22
9453 "Rosina"	15 - 18	18 - 22
9503 "Laura"	15 - 18	18 - 22
9513 "Felicia"	15 - 18	18 - 22
H. Import Co.		
Series 300	12 - 15	15 - 18
H. Choate & Co.		
Djer-Kiss Rouge & Face		
Powder Compacts		
"Spanish Type"	18 - 20	20 - 25
DEWEY, ALFRED (U.S.A.)		
Boston Sunday Post		
Romantic Baseball Series 22		
"Caught Stealing"	8 - 10	10 - 12
"A Costly Error"	8 - 10	10 - 12
"A Double Play"	8 - 10	10 - 12
"A Sacrifice"	8 - 10	10 - 12
"A Single"	8 - 10	10 - 12
"A Shut-Out"	8 - 10	10 - 12
Reinthal & Newman		
"Weather Forecast" Series 221 (12)	7 - 8	8 - 10
"Eventful Hours" Series 270-275	8 - 10	10 - 12
"Mother & Child" Series 450-455	7 - 8	8 - 10
"Love Signal" Series 456-461	7 - 8	8 - 10
"Moon" Series 462-467	8 - 10	10 - 12

H.W. Ditzler, Gibson Art Co.
No Caption

A.L. Fidler, E. Gross Co.
"American Girl 24"

"Smoke" Series 807-812	7 - 8	8 - 10
De YONGH (U.S.A.)	5 - 6	6 - 7
DIHLEN, W.I. (U.S.A.)	5 - 6	6 - 7
DITZLER, W.H. (U.S.A.)		
Gibson Art		
Water Color Series	6 - 8	8 - 10
DOBROWOLSKI, A. (Poland)		
MJK		
Seasons Series 282 (4)	10 - 12	12 - 15
DOUBEK		
Ackerman Co.		
"Historic Ladies" Series	10 - 12	12 - 15
DUDOVICH, M. (Italy) See Art Deco		
"Eureka" Series IV (6)	12 - 15	15 - 20
DUNCAN, FREDERICK (U.S.A.)		
Reinthal & Newman		
Water Color Series 930-935	12 - 15	15 - 18
K. Co. Series	12 - 15	15 - 18
ELLETTI (Italy) See Art Deco		
ELLIOTT, KATHRYN (U.S.A.)		
Gartner & Bender Issues	4 - 5	5 - 8
ELLKA		
M. Munk, Vienna		
Head Studies	10 - 12	12 - 18

FABIANO   (France) See Deco, Fr. Glamour
FARINI, MAY L.
  Gartner & Bender

Black & White Issues	5 - 6	6 - 8
W/"Feliz Dia" Caption - Lady/Dog	6- 8	8 - 10
Color Issues	10 - 12	12 - 16
FERRARIS, A.V.	8 - 10	10 - 12

FIDLER SISTERS
  Pearle Eugenia Fidler (PEF)
  Pearle Fidler LeMunyan (PFL)
  Alice Luella Fidler (ALF)
  Alice Fidler Person (AFP)
  Elsie Catherine Fidler (ECF)
  Series
    American Girl Series (AGS)
    American Girl No. (AG#)
    Fidler College Series-4 (FC-4)
    Fidler LeMunyan Series-5 (FLS-5)
    Poster Sets (40-45, 50-55) (Poster)
  Distributors for the Publisher, Edward Gross , N.Y.
    #1 - Alphalsa Publishing Co., London E.C.
    #2 - A.R.& C.I.B.
    #3 - Kunjiverlag-Leo Glainer, Innsbruck
    #4 - B.K.W.I.

A.L. Fidler, E. Gross Co.
"American Girl 40"

E.C. Fidler, E. Gross Co.
"American Girl 47"

P.F. LeMunyan, E. Gross Co.
"American Girl 55"

A.L. Fidler, E. Gross Co.
"American Girl 45"

#5 - Paul Heckscher
#6 - The "Alpha" Publishing Co., London, E.C.
#7 - Alfred Stiebel & Co., London, E.C.
#8 - Lammerse, Hoofdsteeg 41, Rotterdam
#9 - K.K. Oy, Finland, Series N:O 1/20
DPC - Decorative Poster Co., Cincinnati, Ser. H.C.
1-12 (on back) - 1908, by the U.S. Lithograph Co.,
Cincinnati, O. (on front)
All cards were copyrighted by **Edward Gross** unless noted otherwise.
I. AMERICAN GIRL SERIES

Card Number

1 **PFL**	8 - 10	10 - 13
2 **PFL**	8 - 10	10 - 13
3 **ALF**	8 - 10	10 - 13
3 Unsigned	10 - 12	12 - 15
4 **PFL**	10 - 12	12 - 15
5 **PFL**	10 - 12	12 - 15
6 **PFL**	8 - 10	10 - 13
7 **PFL**	8 - 10	10 - 12
8 **PFL**	8 - 10	10 - 12
9 **ALF**	10 - 12	12 - 15
10 **ALF**	10 - 12	12 - 15
11 **ALF** - AG #11 on back	12 - 14	14 - 16
11 **ALF** - FCS-4 on back *	10 - 12	12 - 15

12	**ALF** - FCS-4 on back	12 - 15	15 - 18
13	**ALF** - FCS-4 on back	12 - 15	15 - 18
14	**ALF** - FCS-4 on back	10 - 12	12 - 15
15	**ALF** - FCS-4 on back	10 - 12	12 - 15
16	**ALF** - FCS-4 on back	10 - 12	12 - 15
17	**ALF** - FLS-5 on back **	10 - 12	12 - 15
18	**PFL** - FLS-5 on back	12 - 15	15 - 18
18	**PFL** - AG #18 on back	12 - 15	15 - 18
19	**PFL** - FLS-5 on back	10 - 12	12 - 15
20	**PFL** - FLS-5 on back	10 - 12	12 - 15
20	**PFL** - AG #20 on back	10 - 12	12 - 15
21	**ALF** - FLS-5 on back	10 - 12	12 - 15
22	**ALF** - FLS-5 on back	10 - 12	12 - 15
22	**ALF** - AG #22 on back	10 - 12	12 - 15
* FCS-4 = Fidler College Series - 4			
** FLS-5 = Fidler LeMunyan Series - 5			
23	**ALF** - Signed	12 - 15	15 - 18
23	**ALF** - Name in print	10 - 12	12 - 15
23	**ALF** - Die cut	15 - 18	18 - 22
24	**ALF** - Signed	12 - 15	15 - 18
24	**ALF** - Name in print	10 - 12	12 - 15
24	**ALF** - 2-line verse	10 - 12	12 - 15
	Distributor #1		
24	**ALF** - 4-line verse, sign 10 - 12	12 - 15	
25	**ALF**	12 - 15	15 - 18
25	**ALF** - Die cut	15 - 18	18 - 22
26	**ALF**	12 - 15	15 - 18
26	**ALF** - 4-line verse	12 - 15	15 - 18
27	**PFL**	10 - 12	12 - 15
27	**PFL** - 4-line verse	10 - 12	12 - 15
28	**ALF**	10 - 12	12 - 15
28	**ALF** - 4-line verse	10 - 12	12 - 15
29	**PFL**	10 - 12	12 - 15
29	**PFL** - 4-line verse	10 - 12	12 - 15
30	**ALF**	10 - 12	12 - 15
30	**ALF** - Name in print	10 - 12	12 - 15
31	**PFL**	12 - 14	14 - 16
31	**PFL** - Name in print	12 - 14	14 - 16
31	**PFL** - 4-line verse	12 - 14	14 - 16
32	**PFL** - 4-line verse	12 - 14	14 - 16
33	**PFL**	10 - 12	12 - 15
33	**PFL** - 4-line verse	10 - 12	12 - 15
33	**PFL** - Distributor #2	12 - 15	15 - 18
34	**PFL**	10 - 12	12 - 15
34	**PFL** - Distributor #3	12 - 15	15 - 18
35	**ALF** - Name in print	12 - 15	15 - 18
	Distributor #4		
36	**ALF** - Name in print	12 - 15	15 - 18
37	**ALF** - Name in print	10 - 12	12 - 15
37	**ALF** - Distributor #4	12 - 15	15 - 18
38	**ALF** - Name in print	10 - 12	12 - 15

38	**ALF** - Distributor #4	12 - 15	15 - 18
39	**ALF** - Name in print	10 - 12	12 - 15
39	**ALF** - Distributor #1	12 - 15	15 - 18
39	Uns - Distributor #9	20 - 22	22 - 25
40	**ALF** - Name in print	10 - 12	12 - 15
40	**ALF** - Distributor #4	12 - 15	15 - 18
41	**ALF** - Name in print	10 - 12	12 - 15
42	**ALF** - Name in print	10 - 12	12 - 15
42	**ALF** - Distributor #4	12 - 15	15 - 18
43	**ALF** - Name in print	10 - 12	12 - 15
44	**ALF** - Name in print	10 - 12	12 - 15
44	**ALF** - Distributor #4	12 - 15	15 - 18
45	**ALF** - Distributor #4	12 - 15	15 - 18
46	**ALF** - Name in print	10 - 12	12 - 15
47	**ECF** - Name in print	12 - 15	15 - 18
48	**PFL** - Name in print "Stating His Case"	10 - 12	12 - 15
48	**PFL** - Distributor #4	12 - 15	15 - 18
49	**PFL** - Name in print "Considering the Evidence"	10 - 12	12 - 15
50	**PFL** - Name in print "The Sealed Verdict"	10 - 12	12 - 15
51	**PFL** - Name in print "Sentenced for Life"	12 - 15	15 - 18

P.F. LeMunyan, E. Gross Co.
"American Girl 56"

P.F. LeMunyan, E. Gross Co.
"American Girl 79"

#	Description		
52	**PFL** - Name in print	10 - 12	12 - 15
52	**PFL** - Distributor #4	12 - 15	15 - 18
53	**PFL** - Name in print	10 - 12	12 - 15
54	**PFL** - Name in print	10 - 12	12 - 15
54	**PFL** - Distributor #4	12 - 15	15 - 18
55	**PFL** - Name in print Distributor #4	12 - 15	15 - 18
56	**PFL** - Name in print	10 - 12	12 - 15
56	**PFL** - Distributor #4	12 - 15	15 - 18
56	**PFL** - Distributor #5	12 - 15	15 - 18
57	PF**L** - Name in print	10 - 12	12 - 15
58	**PFL** - Name in print	10 - 12	12 - 15
58	**PFL** - Distributor #4	12 - 15	15 - 18
59	**PFL** - Name in print	10 - 12	12 - 15
59	**PFL** - Distributor #4	12 - 15	15 - 18
60	**ECF** - Name in print	12 - 15	15 - 18
61	**ECF** - Name in print	12 - 15	15 - 18
62	**ECF** - Name in print	12 - 15	15 - 18
63	**ALF** - Name in print Distributor #7	12 - 15	15 - 18
64	**ALF** - Name in print	10 - 12	12 - 15
65	**ALF** - Name in print	10 - 12	12 - 15
65	**ALF** - Distributor #7	12 - 15	15 - 18
66	**ALF** - Name in print	10 - 12	12 - 15
67	**ALF** - Name in print	10 - 12	12 - 15
68	**ALF** - Name in print	10 - 12	12 - 15
69	**ALF** - Name in print	10 - 12	12 - 15
69	**ALF** - Distributor #1	12 - 15	15 - 18
70	**ALF** - Name in print	10 - 12	12 - 15
70	**ALF** - Distributor #1	12 - 15	15 - 18
71	**ALF** - Name in print	10 - 12	12 - 15
71	**ALF** - 5-line verse Distributor #1	12 - 15	15 - 18
72	**ALF** - Name in print	10 - 12	12 - 15
73	**ALF** - Name in print	14 - 16	16 - 20
74	**PFL** - Distributor #1	12 - 15	15 - 18
74	**PFL** - Distributor #7	12 - 15	15 - 18
75	**PFL** - Name in print	10 - 12	12 - 15
76	**PFL** - Name in print	10 - 12	12 - 15
77	**PFL** - Name in print	10 - 12	12 - 15
78	**PFL** - Name in print	10 - 12	12 - 15
78	**PFL** - Distributor #1	12 - 15	15 - 18
79	**PFL** - Name in print	10 - 12	12 - 15
79	**PFL** - Distributor #7	12 - 15	15 - 18
80	**PFL** - Name in print Distributor #7	12 - 15	15 - 18
81	**PFL** - Name in print	10 - 12	12 - 15
82	**PFL** - Name in print	10 - 12	12 - 15
83	**PFL** - Name in print	10 - 12	12 - 15
83	**PFL** - Distributor #1	12 - 15	15 - 18
84	**PFL** - Distributor #6		

A.L. Fidler, K.K.OY 1/20
No Caption

P.F. LeMunyan, E. Gross Co.
"American Girl 83"

	"Early Symptoms"	12 - 15	15 - 18
85	**PFL** - Name in print		
	"A Tonic"	10 - 12	12 - 15
85	**PFL** - Distributor #1		
	"A Tonic"	12 - 14	14 - 16
86	**PFL** - Name in print		
	"The Critical Stage"	12 - 14	14 - 16
87	**PFL** - Name in print		
	"Given"	12 - 14	14 - 16
87	**PFL** - Distributor #6		
	"Given"	15 - 16	16 - 18
88	**ALF** - Name in print		
	"The Oriental Dance"	12 - 14	14 - 16
88	**ALF** - Distributor #6		
	"The Oriental Dance"	15 - 16	16 - 18
89	**ALF** - Name in print		
	"The Classic Dance"	12 - 14	14 - 16
89	**ALF** - Distributor #6		
	"The Classic Dance"	15 - 16	16 - 18
90	**ALF** - Name in print		
	"The Ballet"	12 - 14	14 - 16
91	**ALF** - Name in print		
	"Rag-Time"	12 - 14	14 - 16
91	**ALF** - Distributor #8		

	"Rag-Time"	15 - 16	16 - 18
92	**ALF** - Name in print	12 - 14	14 - 16
92	**ALF** - Distributor #1	15 - 16	16 - 18
93	**ECF** - Name in print	12 - 14	14 - 16
93	**ECF** - Distributor #6	14 - 16	16 - 18
94	**PFL** - Name in print	12 - 14	14 - 16
95	**PFL** - Name in print	12 - 14	14 - 16
95	**PFL** - Greeting overprint		12 - 14
14 - 16			
96	**ALF** - Name in print	12 - 14	14 - 16
96	**ALF** - Distributor #6	14 - 16	16 - 18
97	**PFL** - Name in print	12 - 14	14 - 16
98	**ALF** - Name in print	12 - 14	14 - 16
98	**ALF** - Distributor #6	14 - 16	16 - 18
	Greeting overprint	14 - 16	16 - 18
99	**ALF** - Name in print	12 - 14	14 - 16
99	**ALF** - Distributor #6	14 - 16	16 - 18
100	**ECF** - Name in print	12 - 14	14 - 16
101	**PFL** - Name in print	12 - 14	14 - 16
102	**AFP** - Name in print	12 - 14	14 - 16
103	**AFP** - Name in print	12 - 14	14 - 16
104	**PFL** - Name in print	12 - 14	14 - 16
105	**AFP** - Name in print	12 - 14	14 - 16
106	**AFP** - Name in print	12 - 14	14 - 16
107	**AFP** - Name in print	12 - 14	14 - 16
108	**PFL** - Name in print	12 - 14	14 - 16
108	**PFL** - Distributor #6	14 - 16	16 - 18
109	**AFP** - Name in print	12 - 14	14 - 16
109	**AFP** - Distributor #1	14 - 16	16 - 18
110	**PFL** - Name in print	12 - 14	14 - 16
111	**PFL** - Unsigned	12 - 14	14 - 16
112	**ALF** - Name in print	12 - 14	14 - 16
113	**ALF** - Name in print	12 - 14	14 - 16
114	**PEF** - Name in print	12 - 14	14 - 16
115	**ALF** - Name in print	12 - 14	14 - 16
116	**PFL** - Name in print	12 - 14	14 - 16
	Greeting overprint	12 - 14	14 - 16
117	**PFL** - Name in print	12 - 14	14 - 16
118	**AFL** - Name in print	12 - 14	14 - 16
119	**PFL** - Name in print	12 - 14	14 - 16
120	**PFL** - Name in print	14 - 16	16 - 18
121	**ALF** - Name in print	14 - 16	16 - 18
122	**PFL** - Name in print	12 - 14	14 - 16
123	**PFL** - Name in print	12 - 14	14 - 16
124	**PFL** - Name in print	12 - 14	14 - 16
125	**ALF** - Name in print	12 - 14	14 - 16
126	**ALF** - Name in print	12 - 14	14 - 16
	Greeting overprint	12 - 14	14 - 16
127	**ALF** - Name in print	12 - 14	14 - 16
128	**ALF** - Name in print	12 - 14	14 - 16
129			

Alice F. Person, E. Gross Co.
"American Girl 106"

P.F. LeMunyan, E. Gross Co.
"Sentenced for Life"

130		
131 **AFP** - Name in print		
Distributor #1	14 - 16	16 - 18
132 **AFP** - Name in print	14 - 16	16 - 18
133 **AFP** - Name in print	14 - 16	16 - 18
134 **AFP** - Name in print	14 - 16	16 - 18
135 **AFP** - Name in print	14 - 16	16 - 18
136		
137 **AFP** - Name in print	14 - 16	16 - 18
138 **AFP** - Name in print	14 - 16	16 - 18

II. POSTERS

All cards in the Poster series are signed.
Cards 40-45 are Copyright 1909, by Edward Gross, N.Y.
Cards 50-55 are Copyright 1910, by Edward Gross, N.Y.
Cards appear in different colors with as many as
7 colors having been seen of one card.

40 Series

40 **ALF**	12 - 15	15 - 18
40 **ALF** - With big "H"	14 - 16	16 - 20
41 **PEF** - With big "V"	14 - 16	16 - 20
42 **PEF**	12 - 15	15 - 18
42 **PEF** - With "ACO"	14 - 16	16 - 20
42 **PEF** - With block "C"	14 - 16	16 - 20
42 **PEF** - With "B" on sweater	14 - 16	16 - 20

42 **PEF** - With "New Auburn, WI"	14 - 16	16 - 20
43 **PEF**	12 - 15	15 - 18
43 Also **ALF** - With "F"	14 - 16	16 - 20
44 **PEF**	12 - 15	15 - 18
45 **PEF**	12 - 15	15 - 18
45 **PEF** - With "Y" on pennant	14 - 16	16 - 20
45 **PEF** - With "B" on pennant	14 - 16	16 - 20
50 Series		
50 **ALF**	12 - 15	15 - 18
50 **ALF** - With "S" in corner	14 - 16	16 - 20
51 **ALF**	12 - 15	15 - 18
52 **PEF**	12 - 15	15 - 18
52 **PEF** - With "S" on shirt	14 - 16	16 - 20
52 **PEF** - With "MC"	14 - 16	16 - 20
53 **PEF**	12 - 15	15 - 18
53 **PEF** - With "Greet Cornell"	14 - 16	16 - 20
54 **PEF**	12 - 15	15 - 18
54 **PEF** - With "Queens" at top	14 - 16	16 - 20
55 **ALF**	12 - 15	15 - 18

III. OTHERS
 Paul Heckscher
  Series 1025

5 **ALF** - "Butterfly Neighbors"	12 - 15	15 - 18

 Knapp Co. (K Co.)
  Series 1025

5 **ALF** - "Butterfly Neighbors"	12 - 15	15 - 18

 Ullman Mfg. Co
  Series 134

32 **ALF** - "Lucky Moon" Sepia	6 - 8	8 - 10

 U.S. Lithograph Co., Cincinnati
  Distributor - **Decorative Poster Co.**
  College Ladies & Men

H.C. Series 1-12 S/**ALF & PEF**	8 - 10	10 - 12

 M.T. Myers & Son

ALF - Big "H" on Sweater	15 - 18	18 - 22

 Advertising Card
  Reliable Woolens

PEF	15 - 18	18 - 22
FINNEMORE, J.	5 - 6	6 - 7
FISCHER, C. (U.S.A.)	6 - 8	8 - 10

FISHER, HARRISON (U.S.A.)

Harrison Fisher was one of the most prolific of all American illustrators. His works, mainly of beautiful women of the era, are desired by collectors throughout the world. The values of his postcards tend to rise almost yearly.

The principal publisher of Fisher postcards was the New York firm of Reinthal & Newman. They published many of his cards in various series ranging from the No-Numbered series, the 100 series and on through the final and very rare 900 series. They also did the English reprints in the 1000 and 2000 series.

The Detroit Publishing Company, beginning around 1905, published a small group of Fisher cards from what were originally illustrations in stories in the old *Life* magazine. The cards were numbered in the Detroit 14,000 series and were printed mainly in sepia, with a small number being in black and white. Since these were not in color they have not been as popular as the later full-color renditions. The American book publishers who used Fisher's illustrations in their novels issued postcards to advertise their books.   These advertising postcards usually showed a beautiful Fisher lady on one-half of the double card and an order form on the remaining half. These cards are among the most sought after and the most expensive of his American-published cards.

Foreign publishers also produced several series and singles which are very much in demand. Among the most elusive, and also commanding the highest prices, are the cards that were produced in Finland and Russia.

HARRISON FISHER

Detroit Publishing Co.

14028 "I don't see..."	10 - 12	12 - 14
14036 "An important..."	10 - 12	12 - 14
14037 "So you don't Kiss..."	10 - 12	12 - 14
14038 "Between Themselves..."	10 - 12	12 - 14
14039 "Can you give your Answer?"	10 - 12	12 - 14
14040 "I suppose you lost..."	10 - 12	12 - 14
14041 "It's just horrid..."	10 - 12	12 - 14
14042 "Wasn't there..."	10 - 12	12 - 14
14043 "And shall we never..."	10 - 12	12 - 14
14044 "I fear there is no hope..."	10 - 12	12 - 14

Book Advertising Cards
(G&D, Dodd-Mead, etc.)

Double-folded Cards, entire card	85 - 90	90 - 100
With Reply section missing	60 - 70	75 - 85

"The Bill Tippers"
"Featherbone Girl"
"54-40 or Fight"
"Half A Rogue"
"The Hungry Heart"

"Jane Cable"
"Jewel Weed"
"The Man from Brodney's"
"My Lady of Cleeve"
"Nedra"
"The One Way Out"
"A Taste of Paradise"
"The Title Market"
"To My Valentine"
"The Goose Girl"

Armour & Co., U.S. (B&W), narrow size	50 - 60	60 - 70
Armour & Co., German (B&W), narrow	70 - 75	75 - 80
Reinthal & Newman		
Unnumbered Series		
"After the Dance"	10 - 15	15 - 18
"The Critical Moment"	10 - 15	15 - 18
"The Motor Girl"	12 - 18	18 - 22
"Ready for the Run"	10 - 15	15 - 18
"Ruth"	10 - 15	15 - 18
"A Tennis Champion"	15 - 18	18 - 25
"The Winter Girl"	15 - 18	18 - 22
101 Series (12)		
"American Beauties"	10 - 15	15 - 18
"Anticipation"	10 - 15	15 - 18
"Beauties"	12 - 16	16 - 20

Harrison Fisher, R&N 107
"A Fair Driver"

Harrison Fisher, R&N 182
"Miss Santa Claus"

"Danger"	10 - 12	12 - 15
"A Fair Driver"	15 - 18	18 - 22
"Odd Moments"	12 - 15	15 - 18
"The Old Miniature"	12 - 15	15 - 18
"Over the Tea Cup"	15 - 18	18 - 22
"Reflections"	15 - 18	18 - 22
"The Study Hour"	12 - 15	15 - 18
"A Thoroughbred"	15 - 18	18 - 22
"Those Bewitching Eyes"	12 - 15	15 - 18
102 Series (6)		
"American Girl in England"	10 - 15	15 - 18
"American Girl in France"	10 - 15	15 - 18
"American Girl in Ireland"	10 - 15	15 - 18
"American Girl in Italy"	10 - 15	15 - 18
"American Girl in Japan"	10 - 15	15 - 18
"American Girl in Netherlands"	10 - 15	15 - 18
103 Series (6)		
"At Home with Art"	10 - 12	12 - 15
"The Canoe"	10 - 12	12 - 15
"Engagement Days"	12 - 15	15 - 18
"Fisherman's Luck"	12 - 15	15 - 18
"Fore"	20 - 22	22 - 28
"Wanted, an Answer"	12 - 15	15 - 18
108 Series (12)		
"An Old Song"	12 - 15	15 - 18
"The Ambush"	12 - 15	15 - 18
"The Artist"	12 - 15	15 - 18
"The Bride"	20 - 22	22 - 26
"The Debutante"	15 - 18	18 - 22
"Dumb Luck"	15 - 18	18 - 22
"He's Only Joking"	15 - 18	18 - 22
"His Gift"	15 - 18	18 - 22
"The Kiss"	12 - 15	15 - 18
"Lost?"	15 - 18	18 - 22
"Oh! Promise Me"	15 - 18	18 - 22
"Song of the Soul"	15 - 18	18 - 22
"Two Up"	18 - 22	22 - 25
123 Series (6)		
"Making Hay"	10 - 12	12 - 15
"A Modern Eve"	12 - 15	15 - 18
"Taking Toll"	10 - 12	12 - 15
"You Will Marry a Dark Man"	10 - 12	12 - 15
"The Fudge Party"	12 - 15	15 - 18
"In Clover"	12 - 15	15 - 18
180-191 Series		
180 "Well Protected"	15 - 18	18 - 22
181 "The Rose"	15 - 18	18 - 22
182 "Miss Santa Claus"	22 - 25	25 - 30
183 "Miss Knickerbocker"	15 - 18	18 - 22
184 "Following the Race"	15 - 18	18 - 22
185 "Naughty, Naughty!"	20 - 22	22 - 25

186 "The Proposal"	10 - 12	12 - 15
187 "The Trousseau"	10 - 12	12 - 15
188 "The Wedding"	12 - 15	15 - 18
189 "The Honeymoon"	10 - 12	12 - 15
190 "The First Evening..."	10 - 12	12 - 15
191 "Their New Love"	10 - 12	12 - 15
192-203 Series		
192 "Cherry Ripe"	15 - 18	18 - 22
193 "Undue Haste"	15 - 18	18 - 22
194 "Sweetheart"	15 - 18	18 - 22
195 "Vanity"	15 - 18	18 - 22
196 "Beauties"	15 - 18	18 - 22
197 "Lips for Kisses"	15 - 18	18 - 22
198 "Bewitching Maiden"	15 - 18	18 - 22
199 "Leisure Moments"	15 - 18	18 - 22
200 "And Yet Her Eyes..."	15 - 18	18 - 22
201 "Roses"	15 - 18	18 - 22
202 "In the Toils"	15 - 18	18 - 22
203 "Maid to Worship"	20 - 22	22 - 25
252-263 Series		
252 "Dreaming of You"	15 - 18	18 - 22
253 "Luxury"	15 - 18	18 - 22
254 "Pals"	15 - 18	18 - 22
255 "Homeward Bound"	12 - 15	15 - 18
256 "Preparing to Conquer"	15 - 18	18 - 22

Harrison Fisher, R&N 971
"Cynthia"

Harrison Fisher, Russian 024
"The Kiss"

257 "Love Lyrics"	15 - 18	18 - 22
258 "Tempting Lips"	15 - 18	18 - 22
259 "Good Night"	12 - 15	15 - 18
260 "Bows Attract Beaus"	15 - 18	18 - 22
261 "Girlie"	15 - 18	18 - 22
262 "Beauty and Value"	15 - 18	18 - 22
263 "A Prairie Belle"	15 - 18	18 - 22
300 Series		
300 "Auto Kiss"	15 - 18	18 - 22
301 "Sweethearts Asleep"	22 - 25	25 - 30
302 "Behave"	15 - 18	18 - 22
303 "All Mine!"	12 - 15	15 - 18
304 "Thoroughbreds"	20 - 22	22 - 25
305 "The Laugh is on You"	15 - 18	18 - 22
Water Color Series 381-392		
381 "All's Well"	15 - 18	18 - 25
382 "Two Roses"	15 - 18	18 - 25
383 "Contentment"	15 - 18	18 - 22
384 "Not Yet — But Soon"	12 - 15	15 - 18
385 "Smile Even if it Hurts"	15 - 18	18 - 22
386 "Speak!"	15 - 18	18 - 25
387 "Welcome Home"	12 - 15	15 - 18
388 "A Helping Hand"	15 - 18	18 - 22
389 "Undecided"	15 - 18	18 - 25

Harrison Fisher, R&N 186
"The Proposal"

Harrison Fisher, 30/25
"Merry Christmas"

Harrison Fisher, 30/25
"King of Hearts"

Harrison Fisher, 30/25
"My Hero"

390 "Well Guarded"	15 - 18	18 - 22
391 "My Lady Waits"	15 - 18	18 - 22
392 "Gathering Honey"	15 - 18	18 - 22
400-423 Series		
400 "Looking Backward"	18 - 20	20 - 25
401 "Art and Beauty"	15 - 20	20 - 25
402 "The Chief Interest"	15 - 20	20 - 25
403 "Passing Fancies"	15 - 20	20 - 25
404 "The Pink of Perfection"	15 - 20	20 - 25
405 "He Won't Bite"	18 - 22	22 - 26
406 "Refreshments"	15 - 20	20 - 25
407 "Princess Pat"	18 - 22	22 - 28
408 "Fine Feathers"	15 - 20	20 - 25
409 "Isn't He Sweet?"	18 - 22	22 - 25
410 "Maid at Arms"	18 - 22	22 - 28
411 "He Cometh Not"	15 - 20	20 - 25
412 "Can't You Speak?"	18 - 22	22 - 28
413 "What Will She Say?"	15 - 20	20 - 25
414 "Music Hath Charm"	15 - 20	20 - 25
415 "Do I Intrude"	15 - 20	20 - 25
416 "My Queen"	18 - 22	22 - 28
417 "My Lady Drives"	15 - 18	22 - 25
418 "Ready and Waiting"	15 - 20	20 - 25
419 "The Parasol"	15 - 20	20 - 25

420 "Tempting Lips"	15 - 20	20 - 25
421 "Mary"	18 - 22	22 - 25
422 "Courting Attention"	15 - 20	20 - 25
423 "My Pretty Neighbor"	18 - 22	22 - 28
600-617 Series		
600 "Winter Sport"	20 - 25	25 - 30
601 "Winter Whispers"	20 - 25	25 - 30
602 "A Christmas Him"	20 - 25	25 - 30
603 "A Sprig of Holly"	20 - 25	25 - 30
604 "Snow Birds"	20 - 25	25 - 30
605 "A Christmas Belle"	20 - 25	25 - 30
606 "The Serenade"	20 - 25	25 - 30
607 "The Secret"	20 - 25	25 - 30
608 "Good Morning, Mama"	20 - 25	25 - 30
609 "A Passing Glance"	20 - 25	25 - 30
610 "A Fair Exhibitor"	20 - 25	25 - 30
611 "Paddling Their Own Canoe"	18 - 20	20 - 25
612 "Tea Time"	20 - 25	25 - 30
613 "The Favorite Pillow"	20 - 25	25 - 30
614 "Don't Worry"	20 - 25	25 - 30
615 "June"	20 - 25	25 - 30
616 "Sketching"	20 - 25	25 - 30
617 "Chocolate"	20 - 25	25 - 30
700-705 Water Color Series		
"The Senses"		
700 "The First Meeting" Sight	20 - 25	25 - 30
701 "Falling in Love" Smell	20 - 25	25 - 30
702 "Making Progress" Taste	20 - 25	25 - 30
703 "Anxious Moments" Hearing	20 - 25	25 - 30
704 "To Love and Cherish" Touch	20 - 25	25 - 30
705 "The Greatest Joy" Common Sense	20 - 25	25 - 30
762-773 Series		
762 "Alone at Last"	12 - 15	15 - 18
763 "Alert"	15 - 18	18 - 22
764 "Close to Shore"	15 - 18	18 - 22
765 "Looks Good to Me"	12 - 15	15 - 18
766 "Passers By"	12 - 15	15 - 18
767 "At the Toilet"	15 - 18	18 - 22
768 "Drifting" *	12 - 15	15 - 18
769 "Her Favorite Him" *	12 - 15	15 - 18
770 "The Third Party" *	12 - 15	15 - 18
771 "Inspiration" *	15 - 18	18 - 22
772 "Dangers of the Deep" *	12 - 15	15 - 18
773 "Farewell" *	12 - 15	15 - 18

* Add $5 to prices if German caption.
  Cards are usually slightly oversized
  and have "Universal" copyright.
  800 Series

819 "Here's Happiness"	15 - 18	18 - 22

Cosmopolitan/Star
  800 Series

Harrison Fisher, R&N 271
"Reflections"

Harrison Fisher, R&N 2049
"Beauty & Value"

832 "Wireless"	20 - 25	25 - 30
833 "Neptune's Daughter"	20 - 25	25 - 30
834 "Her Game"	20 - 25	25 - 30
835 "All Mine"	18 - 20	20 - 25
836 "On Summer Seas"	20 - 25	25 - 30
837 "Autumn Beauty"	20 - 25	25 - 30
838 "The Only Pebble"	20 - 25	25 - 30
839 "A Love Score"	25 - 30	30 - 35
840 "Spring Business"	20 - 25	25 - 30
841 "The King of Hearts"	20 - 25	25 - 30
842 "Fair and Warmer"	20 - 25	25 - 30
843 "Baby Mine"	20 - 25	25 - 30
844 "Compensation"	20 - 25	25 - 30
845 "Sparring for Time"	20 - 25	25 - 30
846 "Confidences"	20 - 25	25 - 30
847 "Her Future"	20 - 25	25 - 30
848 "Day Dreams"	20 - 25	25 - 30
849 "Muriel"	20 - 25	25 - 30
856 "Song of the Soul"	15 - 20	20 - 25
860 "By Right of Conquest" *	18 - 22	22 - 25
861 "The Evening Hour" *	18 - 22	22 - 25
862 "Caught Napping" *	20 - 25	25 - 30

863	"A Novice" *	20 - 25	25 - 30
864	"Winners" *	20 - 25	25 - 30
865	"A Midsummer Reverie" *	25 - 30	30 - 35
866	"When the Leaves Turn" *	20 - 25	25 - 30
867	"Over the Teacup" *	20 - 25	25 - 30
868	"A Ripening Bud" *	20 - 25	25 - 30
869	"I'm Ready" *	20 - 25	25 - 30
870	"Reflections" *	20 - 25	25 - 30
871	"Peggy" *	20 - 25	25 - 30
872	"Penseroso" *	20 - 25	25 - 30
873	"The Girl He Left Behind" *	20 - 25	25 - 30
874	"A Spring Blossom" *	20 - 25	25 - 30
875	"A Study in Contentment" *	20 - 25	25 - 30
876	"A Lucky Beggar" *	20 - 25	25 - 30
877	"Roses" *	20 - 25	25 - 30

* With **Cosmopolitan Print Dept.** byline add $5 to prices.

900-979 Series

970	"Chums"	50 - 75	75 - 100
971	"Cynthia"	50 - 75	75 - 100
972	"A Forest Flower"	50 - 75	75 - 100
973	"The Dancing Girl"	50 - 75	75 - 100
974	"Each Stitch a Prayer"	50 - 100	100 - 125
975	"The Sailor Maid"	75 - 100	100 - 125
976	"My Man"	75 - 100	100 - 125
977	"My Hero"	75 - 100	100 - 125
978	"Her Heart's in the Service"	75 - 100	100 - 125
979	"Somewhere in France"	100 - 125	125 - 150

1001-1005 Series English Reprints

1001	"Cherry Ripe"	20 - 25	25 - 30
1002	"Beauties"	20 - 25	25 - 30
1003	"Vanity"	20 - 25	25 - 30
1004	"Maid to Worship"	20 - 25	25 - 30
1005	"And Yet Her Eyes Can Look Wise"	20 - 25	25 - 30

2000 Series English Reprints

2040	"Love Lyrics"	15 - 20	20 - 25
2041	"A Fair Exhibitor"	18 - 22	22 - 28
2042	"Can't You Speak"	15 - 20	20 - 25
2043	"Serenade"	15 - 20	20 - 25
2044	"Undecided"	15 - 20	20 - 25
2045	"Behave!"	15 - 20	20 - 25
2046	"Princess Pat"	20 - 25	25 - 30
2047	"Good Little Indian"	15 - 20	20 - 25
2048	"Chocolate"	15 - 20	20 - 25
2049	"Beauty and Value"	15 - 20	20 - 25
2050	"Contentment"	15 - 20	20 - 25
2051	"Preparing to Conquer"	15 - 20	20 - 25
2053	"The Kiss"	15 - 20	20 - 25
2054	"What to See in America"	15 - 20	20 - 25
2069	"Paddling Their Own Canoe"	15 - 20	20 - 25
2076	"Good Morning, Mama"	15 - 20	20 - 25

2086 "The Pink of Perfection"	15 - 20	20 - 25
2087 "He Won't Bite"	18 - 22	22 - 28
2088 "Following the Race"	15 - 20	20 - 25
2089 "The Rose"	15 - 20	20 - 25
2090 "Well Protected"	15 - 20	20 - 25
2091 "Sketching"	15 - 20	20 - 25
2092 "Ready and Waiting"	15 - 20	20 - 25
2093 "The Parasol"	15 - 20	20 - 25
2094 "Courting Attention"	15 - 20	20 - 25
2095 "Mary"	15 - 20	20 - 25
2096 "Refreshments"	15 - 20	20 - 25
2097 "Isn't He Sweet?"	18 - 22	22 - 28
2098 "The Old Miniature"	15 - 20	20 - 25
2100 "Odd Moments"	15 - 20	20 - 25
2101 "Tea Time"	15 - 20	20 - 25
2102 "Good Night!"	15 - 20	20 - 25
2103 "A Prairie Belle"	15 - 20	20 - 25
Others	15 - 20	20 - 25

FOREIGN ISSUES

FINNISH

Harrison Fisher, R&N 2088
"Following the Race"

Harrison Fisher,
Publisher at Polyphot, No Caption

All Finnish cards are very rare and extremely elusive. None have the R&N Copyright and all are untitled. The cards are titled using names from similar R&N images. However, several have not appeared as postcards before and are named only if the title is known. Three have been entitled by the author until the true name or caption surfaces.

30/25 Series

"Snowbird" *	150 - 175	175 - 225
"Merry Christmas" titled by Author *	150 - 175	175 - 225
"Welcome Home," variety *	150 - 175	175 - 225
"A Midsummer Reverie"	140 - 165	165 - 220
"Close to Shore"	140 - 165	165 - 220
"Winners"	140 - 165	165 - 220
"My Hero"	140 - 165	165 - 220
"Winifred" *	140 - 165	165 - 220
"When the Leaves Turn"	125 - 150	150 - 175
"My Man"	125 - 150	150 - 175
"King of Hearts"	125 - 150	150 - 175
"Not Yet, But Soon"	125 - 150	150 - 175
"Autumn's Beauty"	125 - 150	150 - 175
"On Summer Seas"	125 - 150	150 - 175
"Baby Mine"	125 - 150	150 - 175
"Muriel"	120 - 140	140 - 165
"Caught Napping"	120 - 140	140 - 165
"Beauty and Value"	120 - 140	140 - 165
"Day Dreams"	120 - 140	140 - 165
"Stringing Them" * **	120 - 140	140 - 165
"All Mine"	120 - 140	140 - 165
"Two Roses"	120 - 140	140 - 165
"Reflections"	120 - 140	140 - 165
"Love Lyrics"	120 - 140	140 - 165
"An Idle Hour"	120 - 140	140 - 165

Note: Unsigned cards add $20-25 each.
* Image never before seen on
an R&N postcard.
** Name from Bowers-Budd-Budd
Book, "Harrison Fisher"

The N:O Numbered Series

N:O 5 "Playing the Game", Unsigned	175 - 200	200 - 250
N:O 10 "Midsummer Reverie" Untitled	175 - 200	200 - 250
N:O 4 "Close to Shore" (764)		165 - 190
190 - 240		
N:O 7 "A Novice" (863)	165 - 190	190 - 225
N:O 11 "At the Toilet" (767)		165 - 190
190 - 225		
N:O 13 "Welcome Home" (387)	165 - 190	190 - 225

W. & G. American Series
   No. 7001/1-35

Unsigned, no numbers, no captions
"Following the Race" (184)	165 - 190	190 - 250
"American Beauties" (101)		165 - 190

190 - 250
"Alert" (763)	165 - 190	190 - 250
"Yet Some Prefer Mountains" (571)	165 - 190	190 - 250
"At the Toilet" (767)	165 - 195	190 - 250

**W. & G. American Series
No. 7001/36-50**

Unsigned, no numbers, no captions
"A Sprig of Holly" (603)	165 - 190	190 - 250
"The Favorite Pillow" (613)	165 - 190	190 - 250
"Girlie" (261)	165 - 190	190 - 250

**W. & G. American Series
No. 7031/1-7**

Unsigned, no numbers, no captions
"Eavesdropping" * **	200 - 225	225 - 250

* Image never before seen on
an R&N postcard.
** Titled by Author.

**Pain. Karjalan Kirjap. Oy,
Viipuri Series**

Numbered, unsigned, no captions
N:O 5 "Playing the Game" *	175 - 200	200 - 250
N:O 10 "A Midsummer Reverie" (865)	175 - 200	200 - 250

*Harrison Fisher, R&N 976
"My Man"*

*No Identification Series, N:05
"Playing the Game"*

N:O 4 "Close to Shore" (764)	160 - 190	190 - 235
N:O 7 "A Novice" (863)	160 - 190	190 - 235
* Image never before seen on an R&N postcard.		

K.K. Oy N:O 1-20 Series
Signed, no numbers, no captions

"Mistletoe" * **	200 - 225	225 - 275
"Thoroughbreds" (304)	160 - 190	190 - 235
* Image never before seen on an R&N postcard.		
** Titled by Author.		

The Publisher at Polyphot Series
Unsigned, no numbers, no captions

"Eavesdropping" * **	200 - 225	225 - 275
"A Sprig of Holly" (603)	150 - 175	175 - 225
"Alert" (763)	150 - 175	175 - 225
"Don't Worry" (614)	150 - 175	175 - 225
"Following the Race" (184)	150 - 175	175 - 225
* Image never before seen on an R&N postcard.		
** Titled by the Author.		

The "No Identification" Series
Unsigned, no numbers, no captions

"Autumn's Beauty" (837)	175 - 200	200 - 250
"Following the Race" (184)	175 - 200	200 - 250
"Contentment" (383)	175 - 200	200 - 250
"The Only Pebble" (838)	175 - 200	200 - 250

The S & K Kouvola
Reversed Image Series
Unsigned, no numbers, no captions

"Snowbird" *	225 - 250	250 - 300
"Winners" (864)	225 - 250	250 - 300
"Study in Contentment" (875)	225 - 250	250 - 300
* Image never before seen on an R&N postcard.		

The Real Photo Card Series
Signed, no numbers, no captions

"American Beauties" (Ser. 101)	75 - 85	85 - 100
"Daydreams" (848)	75 - 85	85 - 100
"Drifting" (768)	75 - 85	85 - 100
"A Novice" (863)	75 - 85	85 - 100
"Alone at Last" (762) has caption	75 - 85	85 - 100

The Otto Andersin, Pori Series
Unsigned, no numbers, no captions

"Close to Shore" (765)	225 - 250	250 - 300
"Drifting" (768)	225 - 250	250 - 300

A 72-PAGE BOOK, **"THE SUPER RARE POSTCARDS OF HARRISON FISHER,"** PUBLISHED IN MARCH, 1992, ILLUSTRATES WITH ALL PHOTOS ALL THE FINNISH POSTCARDS LISTED ABOVE. THE BOOK

Harrison Fisher, S&K, Kouvola
"Winners"

Harrison Fisher, S&K, Kouvola
"Snowbird"

These three Finnish-published reversed image S&K, Kouvola postcards (publisher byline shown above) may be the rarest Harrison Fisher cards in existence. They are images of "Snowbird," "Winners," and "Study in Contentment," which range in price from $200 - $300.

Harrison Fisher, S&K, Kouvola
"Study in Contentment"

Harrison Fisher, Phillips 828, "Teacup Time"

IS AVAILABLE FROM: COLONIAL HOUSE, P.O. BOX 609, ENKA, NC 28728. PRICE IS $11.95, PLUS $2 POSTAGE IN THE U.S. AND $4 IN CANADA AND OVERSEAS. THE BOOK WAS WRITTEN BY J.L. MASHBURN AND IS A MUST FOR ALL FISHER COLLECTORS.

RUSSIAN

Richard Phillips Backs

No. 117 "Hexenaugen"	75 - 100	100 - 150
No. 83 "A Taste of Paradise"	75 - 100	100 - 150
No. 834 "Vanity"	75 - 100	100 - 150
Others	75 - 100	100 - 150

Russian-Polish Real Photo Types
AWE With Russian/Polish Back

"Miss Knickerbocker" (183)	75 - 100	100 - 150
"Miss Santa Claus" (182)	75 - 100	100 - 150
Others	75 - 100	100 - 150

Russian-English Backs

No. 24 "Sport" (Following the Race)	75 - 100	100 - 150
Others	75 - 100	100 - 150

Apollon Sophia

No. 21 "La Musique" (The Artist)	75 - 90	90 - 125
Others	75 - 90	90 - 125
Other Russian	75 - 100	100 - 125

GERMAN-AUSTRIAN

MEU

"In the Country" (131)	70 - 75	75 - 80

MEU/Alfred Schweiser

Either, or both, no captions	75 - 100	100 - 125
"Vienne" Series 806	60 - 75	75 - 80
JTK "Kron-Trier" Series	60 - 75	75 - 80

M.J.S.

"The Kiss" (no caption) (108 Series)	40 - 50	50 - 60

Uitg de Muinck & Co, Amsterdam

"The Honeymoon" (189)	50 - 60	60 - 75
186 R "The Kiss" (108 Series)	50 - 60	60 - 75

Friedrich O. Wolter

"Peggy" (871)	40 - 50	50 - 60

FLAGG, JAMES MONTGOMERY (U.S.A.)

James Montgomery Flagg is better known for his World War 1 and World War 11 Posters than for his earlier postcard works. His poster, depicting a new, more stern and business-like, and younger-appearing Uncle Sam (pointing the recruiting finger to the men of America and entitled "I Want You For U.S. Army") was the most famous

James Montgomery Flagg
World War I Poster Card

Archie Gunn, B. Bergman
No Caption

poster from both wars. Others of note were his renditions of Lady Liberty in "Wake Up, America," and the controversial "Tell That to the Marines."

Flagg's early postcard works were published by the Detroit Publishing Co. These were black and white and were not as popular as some of the later issues of Reinthal & Newman and the T.P. & Co. His "Miss Behaving" Series, by Reinthal & Newman, was his best and most colorful and seems to be the choice of most collectors.

JAMES MONTGOMERY FLAGG

Detroit Publishing Co.
 B&W 14000 Series

14011 "The Sweet Magic of Smoke"	8 - 10	10 - 15
14149 "Sir Charles"	8 - 10	10 - 15
14150 "It Certainly Wasn't"	8 - 10	10 - 15
14151 "For Heavens Sake"	8 - 10	10 - 15
14152 "So Sensible"	8 - 10	10 - 15
14153 "Not Bad to Take"	8 - 10	10 - 15
14154 "Beyond More Conjecture"	8 - 10	10 - 15

14155 "A Cold Proposition"	8 - 10	10 - 15
14156 "If You Get Gay"	8 - 10	10 - 15
14157 "If You're a Perfect Gent"	8 - 10	10 - 15
14158 "Make it Pleasant for Him"	8 - 10	10 - 15
Henderson Litho		
501 "Engaged - His Attitude"	6 - 8	8 - 10
2503 "Something on Account"	6 - 8	8 - 10
Reinthal & Newman		
"Miss Behaving" Series		
288 "A Club Sandwich"	10 - 12	12 - 15
289 "Putting Out the Flames"	10 - 12	12 - 15
290 "Miss Behaving!"	10 - 12	12 - 15
291 "The Most Exciting Moment"	10 - 12	12 - 15
292 "The Real Love Game"	10 - 12	12 - 15
293 "Dry Goods"	12 - 15	15 - 18
TP & Co., N.Y.		
Series 738 (Sepia)		
"Trouble Somewhere"	6 - 8	8 - 10
Series 751		
"The Hypnotist"	10 - 12	12 - 14
"The Only Way to Eat an Orange"	10 - 12	12 - 14
"Say When"	10 - 12	12 - 14
Series 818-8		
"Holding Hands"	10 - 12	12 - 14
Series 818-10		

F.T., M. Munk, Vienna 479
No Caption

F.T., M. Munk, Vienna 479
No Caption

C.D. Gibson, Pictorial Comedy
Head 6

C.D. Gibson, Detroit 14065
"The Gibson Girl"

"In the Hands of the Receiver"	10 - 12	12 - 14
FONTAN, LEO (France) See French Glamour		
FOSTER, F.D. (U.S.A.)	4 - 5	5 - 6
FRANZONI (Italy) See Art Deco		
FREIXAS, J. (U.S.A.)		
Winsch, Copyright	20 - 25	30 - 40
F.T.		
M. Munk, Vienna		
Series 479	12 - 15	15 - 18
GAIGHER, H. (Austria)	4 - 5	5 - 6
GALLAIS, P. (France) See French Glamour		
GAYAC (France) See French Glamour		
GERBAULT (France) See French Glamour		
GIBSON, CHARLES DANA (U.S.A.)		
Detroit Publishing Co.		
B&W 14000 Series		
14000 "Has She a Heart?"	8 - 10	10 - 12
14003 "Their Presence of Mind"	8 - 10	10 - 12
14004 "Melting"	8 - 10	10 - 12
14005 "When Hunting..."	8 - 10	10 - 12
14006 "Last Days of Summer"	8 - 10	10 - 12
14008 "The Dog"	8 - 10	10 - 12
14009 "Who Cares"	8 - 10	10 - 12
14017 "Good Game for Two"		10 - 12

G. Herve, Lapina 5064
"The Smoker"

Maude Humphrey, Gray Litho
P.C. 38, No Caption

12 - 15
14019	"Here it is Christmas"	8 - 10	10 - 12
14029	"The Half Orphan"	8 - 10	10 - 12
14046	"Bathing Suits"	10 - 12	12 - 14
14048	"The Half Orphan"	8 - 10	10 - 12
14050	"America Picturesque"	8 - 10	10 - 12
14051	"The Stout Gentleman"	8 - 10	10 - 12
14052	"No Wonder the Sea Serpent..."	8 - 10	10 - 12
14054	"Stepped On"	8 - 10	10 - 12
14055	"Mr. A Merger Hogg..."	8 - 10	10 - 12
14057	"Ill Blows the Wind..."	8 - 10	10 - 12
14059	"Rival Beauties"	8 - 10	10 - 12
14065	"The Gibson Girl"	12 - 15	15 - 18
14066	"Jane"	10 - 12	12 - 15
14067	"Mabel"	10 - 12	12 - 15
14068	"Amy"	10 - 12	12 - 15
14069	"Eleanor"	10 - 12	12 - 15
14070	"Margaret"	10 - 12	12 - 15
14071	"Molly"	10 - 12	12 - 15
14072	"Helen"	10 - 12	12 - 15
14074	"The Sporting Girl"	12 - 15	15 - 18
14185	"The Eternal Question"	10 - 12	12 - 15

James Henderson & Sons
  Sepia Heads

"Annie"	8 - 10	10 - 12
"Clorinda"	8 - 10	10 - 12
"Gladys"	8 - 10	10 - 12
"Maude"	8 - 10	10 - 12
"Nina"	8 - 10	10 - 12
"Peggy"	8 - 10	10 - 12
"Beatrice"	8 - 10	10 - 12
"Bertha"	8 - 10	10 - 12
"Eileen"	8 - 10	10 - 12
James Henderson & Sons		
Comic Series (36)	5 - 6	6 - 8
Schweizer & Co.		
Embossed, Sepia Series	10 - 15	15 - 18
Pictorial Comedy Series	10 - 12	12 - 15
GILBERT, C. ALLEN (U.S.A.)	5 - 6	6 - 8
Calendar, 1911	6 - 8	8 - 10
GILSON, T. (U.S.A.) See Blacks	6 - 7	7 - 8
GNISCHAF, RUAB (Germany)	6 - 8	8 - 10
GODELA, D. (Italy)		
Series 272 Head Studies	12 - 15	15 - 18
Series 296 Head Studies	12 - 15	15 - 18
GOBBI, D. (Italy) See Art Deco		
GOTTARO	4 - 6	6 - 8
GRAF, MARTE See Art Deco and Silhouettes		
GRANDE (Italy) See Art Deco		
GREENE, FREDERICK (U.S.A.)	5 - 6	6 - 7
GREFE, WILL (U.S.A.)		
Moffat, Yard Co.		
"Playing Card Queens" (Rounded Corners)		
"Club"	15 - 18	18 - 22
"Diamond"	15 - 18	18 - 22
"Heart"	15 - 18	18 - 22
"Spade"	15 - 18	18 - 22
Series 3	10 - 12	12 - 15
GRILLI, S. (Italy) See Art Deco		
GRIMBALL, M.M. (U.S.A.)		
Gutmann & Gutmann	12 - 15	15 - 18
See Beautiful Children		
GROSS, BELLA	5 - 6	6 - 8
GROSZE, MANNI (Italy) See Art Deco, Silhouettes		
GUARINO, ANTHONY	4 - 5	5 - 6
GUARNERI (Italy) See Art Deco		
GUNN, ARCHIE (GB)		

Archie Gunn was born in England and began painting portraits at an early age. His first works were very impressive, and he was commissioned to do portraits of some of the important Earls and Prime Ministers. Upon graduation from college and from the Art Academy in London, he began designing posters for some of London's principal theaters.

Archie migrated to New Rochelle, New York in 1888 at the age of 25. There he made his home and began illustrating magazines, did some portrait painting and magazine covers, as well as posters for some of the New York play productions. Later, during the postcard era, he painted beautiful ladies that were quickly adapted for postcards. His cards were published by National Art, P. Sander, Novelty Mfg. & Art Co., and Illustrated Postal Card Co.

Archie Gunn was not as well known as Boileau, Fisher, Earl Christy, Howard C. Christy, and Underwood, but today's collectors are finding that his work was very beautiful and they have begun collecting his cards in earnest.

ARCHIE GUNN

J. Bergman		
B&W Series (6)	6 - 7	7 - 8
National Art Co.		
13 "Bowling Girl"	8 - 10	10 - 12
14 "Tennis Girl"	12 - 14	14 - 18
15 "Skating Girl"	8 - 10	10 - 12
16 "Yachting Girl"	7 - 8	8 - 10
"City Belles" Series		
33 "Miss New York"	10 - 12	12 - 14
34 "Miss Philadelphia"	10 - 12	12 - 14
35 "Miss Boston"	10 - 12	12 - 14
36 "Miss Chicago"	10 - 12	12 - 14
37 "Miss Pittsburgh"	10 - 12	12 - 14
39 "Miss Toronto"	10 - 12	12 - 14
40 "Miss Washington"	10 - 12	12 - 14
41 "Miss Seashore"	8 - 10	10 - 12
70 "Miss St. Louis"	10 - 12	12 - 14
71 "Miss Milwaukee"	10 - 12	12 - 14
72 "Miss Detroit"	10 - 12	12 - 14
77 "Miss Cleveland"	10 - 12	12 - 14
87 "Miss San Francisco"	10 - 12	12 - 14
88 "Miss New Orleans"	10 - 12	12 - 14
89 "Miss Troy"	10 - 12	12 - 14
90 "Untitled"	6 - 8	8 - 9
"Clans"	7 - 8	8 - 10
"College Belles"	8 - 10	10 - 12
"National Belles"	8 - 10	10 - 12
214 "Lady & the Bear"	8 - 10	10 - 12
217 "Devotion"	8 - 10	10 - 12
219 "Yuletide"	8 - 10	10 - 12
220 "Sables"	8 - 10	10 - 12

221 "Ermine"	8 - 10	10 - 12
222 "Driving"	8 - 10	10 - 12
223 "Automobiling"	10 - 12	12 - 14
276 "The Fencer"	8 - 10	10 - 12
277 "On Guard"	8 - 10	10 - 12
Full-Length Santa	8 - 10	10 - 12

Illustrated Postal Card & Novelty Co.

WW1 Army Series 1368 (12)	6 - 8	8 - 10

"The American Spirit"
"Army, Navy, and Reserves"
"Don't Worry About Me"
"If Wishes Came True"
"Lest We Forget"
"None but the Brave Deserve..."
"Pals"
"Parting is Such Sweet Sorrow"
"Repairing a Man of War"
"Rosemary! That's for Remembrance"
"Shoulder Arms"
"When the Last Goodbyes are Whispered"

WW1 Army Series 1371 (12)	6 - 8	8 - 10

"A Parting Message"
"Hello! I Haven't Heard from You"
"Don't Worry, We're Alright"
"Guardian Spirits"
"Letters are Always Welcome"
"Liberty and Union Now and Forever"
"Pleasant Memories"

M. Ichnowski, "Wisla," Krakow 116, Polish Caption

M. Ichnowski, "Pocztowki," Krakow 43, "Rusalka"

"The Rose for Remembrance"
"Sentry Moon"
"Warmth in the Camp and..."
"We Won't Come Back Till it's Over..."
"Worthwhile Fighting for..."

Statler Calendar Cards, 1912 (12)	10 - 12	12 - 15
A.C.		
Women, 4-line verse (2)	6 - 7	7 - 8
Anonymous		
B&W No captions		
Girl holding basketball	8 - 10	10 - 12
Girl wading in water	6 - 8	8 - 10
Girl at wheel of sailboat	6 - 8	8 - 10
Girl holding golf club	12 - 14	14 - 18
Girl holding golf club, but in Color	15 - 18	18 - 22
Beautiful Lady, red bow, red dress	6 - 8	8 - 10
Beautiful Lady, pink bow, pink dress	6 - 8	8 - 10
Beautiful Lady, Bust, holding 3 roses	6 - 8	8 - 10
B&W/Sepia, Women, no captions (3)	5 - 6	6 - 7
Lowney's Chocolates		
Golf Girls Series (6)	12 - 14	14 - 18
GUZERONI (Italy) See Art Deco		
HAMMICK, J.W. (GB)		
Photocom		
"Celesque" Series		
531 "The Motor Girl"	10 - 12	12 - 14
532 "The Society Girl"	10 - 12	12 - 14
533 "The Ball Room Girl"	10 - 12	12 - 14

534 "The Sporting Girl"	12 - 15	15 - 18
535 "The Sea Side Girl"	10 - 12	12 - 15
HARDY (GB) See Art Deco		
HARE, J. KNOWLES (U.S.A.)		
P. Heckscher		
Series 1009 (6)		
1 "Eugenie"	8 - 10	10 - 12
2 "Rosamond"	8 - 10	10 - 14
3 "Beryl"	8 - 10	10 - 12
4 "Clarice"	8 - 10	10 - 12
5 "Madeline"	8 - 10	10 - 12
6 "Charmion"	8 - 10	10 - 12
Series 1026 (6)	8 - 10	10 - 14
Statler Advertising Cards, 1912 (13)	12 - 14	14 - 16
HARMONY, H.	5 - 6	6 - 7
HARPER, R. FORD		
Reinthal & Newman		
Water Color Series		
350 "Peg O' My Heart"	10 - 12	12 - 16
351 "My Summer Girl"	10 - 12	12 - 16
352 "Love's Locket"	10 - 12	12 - 16
353 "True Blue"	12 - 14	14 - 18
354 "The Favorite Flower"	12 - 14	14 - 18
355 "Miss Innocence"	10 - 12	12 - 16
Gibson Art Co. Issues	8 - 10	10 - 12
P. Heckscher		
Series 1010	10 - 15	15 - 18
Series 1013	10 - 15	15 - 18
Series 1025	10 - 15	15 - 18
P. Sander		
Lady Santa Claus (4)	25 - 30	35 - 40
HARRISON (U.S.A.)	6 - 7	7 - 8
HARTLEIN, W.	4 - 5	5 - 6
HAYDEN, A.E.	3 - 4	4 - 5
HEINZE, A.	5 - 6	6 - 8
HELLI (ICART) (France) See Fr. Glamour		
Series 153 (6)	60 - 70	70 - 80
HEROUARD (France) See Fr. Glamour		
HERSCHEL, OTTO (Austria)	6 - 8	8 - 10
HERVE, G.		
Lapina		
Series 5064 "Smoker"	6 - 8	8 - 10
HIDLER, G. HOWARD		
Platinachrome		
National Girl Series	6 - 8	8 - 10
HILLSON, D.		
Girl Series in Red & Black (23)	6 - 8	8 - 10
HOFER, A.	6 - 8	8 - 10
HOROWITZ, H.		
Raphael Tuck		
Series 1 "A Dream of Fair Women" (6)	8 - 9	9 - 10

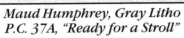

Maud Humphrey, Gray Litho
P.C. 37A, "Ready for a Stroll"

Hamilton King
"The Horse Show Girl"

HORSFALL, MARY (GB)	6 - 8	8 - 10
HOHENSTEIN, A. (Russia) See Art Nouveau		
HUMPHREY, MAUD		
Gray Litho. Co., N.Y. (G in Diamond)		
All her lady postcards are unsigned.		
P.C. 36, P.C. 37, P.C. 37-A, P.C. 38	15 - 18	18 - 22
P.C. 11, P.C. 12, P.C. 13	15 - 18	18 - 22
P.C. 6, P.C. 8, P.C. 10	15 - 18	18 - 22
P.C. 20, P.C. 135, P.C. 141	15 - 18	18 - 22
37A "Ready for a Stroll"	15 - 18	18 - 22
1, 7, 16, 18, 25, 37, 139	15 - 18	18 - 22
Others	15 - 18	18 - 22
Silk-like types	20 - 22	22 - 25
HUNT, ESTHER		
National Art Co.		
9 - 12 Little Chinese Girls	5 - 6	6 - 7
HUNTER, LILLIAN W. (U.S.A.)	6 - 8	8 - 10
HUTT, HENRY (U.S.A.)		
Detroit Publishing Co.		
B&W 14000 Series		
14202 "Sincerity"	8 - 10	10 - 12
14203 "Curiosity"	8 - 10	10 - 12
14204 "Tired of Life"	8 - 10	10 - 12
14205 "Expectancy"	8 - 10	10 - 12

14207 "Frivolity"	8 - 10	10 - 12
14208 "Courageous"	8 - 10	10 - 12
14209 "Shy"	8 - 10	10 - 12
14210 "Disappointment"	8 - 10	10 - 12
14211 "Pleasure"	8 - 10	10 - 12
14212 "Joy"	8 - 10	10 - 12
14213 "Whimsical"	8 - 10	10 - 12
H & S, Germany	10 - 12	12 - 15
ICART, LOUIS (France) See Fr. Glamour		
ICHNOWSKI, M. (Poland)	6 - 8	8 - 10
IRIBE, PAUL	12 - 15	15 - 18
JARACH, A. (France) See Fr. Glamour		
JIRASEK, A.J. (Austria)	4 - 5	5 - 7
JONES, J. (U.S.A.)		
P. Gordon, 1908		
"Opera Girl"	6 - 7	7 - 8
"Vacation Girl" (Unsigned)	4 - 5	5 - 6
College Girl Series	6 - 7	7 - 8
JOZSA, KARL (Austria) See Art Nouveau		
KALOUS, GRET	6 - 8	8 - 10
KAULBACK (German)	5 - 6	6 - 7
KAVAL, M. (France) See Art Deco		
KELLER, A.I.		
Historical Sweethearts Series	4 - 5	5 - 6
"The Introduction"		
"The Wooing of Anne Hathaway"		
"The Proposal"		
"The Wedding"		
Others	4 - 5	5 - 6
KEMPF, TH. (Austria) See Art Nouveau		
KENYON, ZULA	6 - 8	8 - 12
KIEFER, E.H. (GB)		
Bamforth & Co. (16)		
"Could You Be True"	8 - 10	10 - 12
"Dear Heart"	8 - 10	10 - 12
"Good Bye"	8 - 10	10 - 12
"I'm Growing Fond of You"	8 - 10	10 - 12
"I Love a Lassie"	8 - 10	10 - 12
"My Chum"	8 - 10	10 - 12
"There's Nobody Like You"	8 - 10	10 - 12
"You Know You're Not Forgotten"	8 - 10	10 - 12
"Waiting For You"	8 - 10	10 - 12
"When Dreams Come True"	8 - 10	10 - 12
"When You Feel Dreamy"	8 - 10	10 - 12
"When You Feel Naughty..."	8 - 10	10 - 12
"When You're Traveling..."	8 - 10	10 - 12
"When Your Heart Aches..."	8 - 10	10 - 12
"Would You Care"	8 - 10	10 - 12
"Would You Learn to Love Me"	8 - 10	10 - 12
KIMBALL, ALONZO (U.S.A.)		
Reinthal & Newman		

Hamilton King
"Palm Beach Girl"

Hamilton King
"Newport Girl"

Series 122, Lovers	6 - 8	8 - 9
KING, HAMILTON (U.S.A.)		
Coca Cola Girl Advertising Card	350 - 375	375 - 400
Bathing Beauty Series (12)		
"Asbury Park Girl"	10 - 12	12 - 15
"Atlantic City Girl"	10 - 12	12 - 15
"Bar Harbor Girl"	10 - 12	12 - 15
"Cape May Girl"	10 - 12	12 - 15
"Coney Island Girl"	10 - 12	12 - 15
"Long Beach Girl"	10 - 12	12 - 15
"Larchmont Girl"	10 - 12	12 - 15
"Manhattan Beach Girl"	10 - 12	12 - 15
"Narragansett Girl"	10 - 12	12 - 15
"Newport Girl"	10 - 12	12 - 15
"Palm Beach Girl"	10 - 12	12 - 15
"Ocean Grove Girl"	10 - 12	12 - 15
41 "After the Ball" (Basketball)	15 - 17	17 - 20
Other Series	10 - 12	12 - 15
KINNYS, THE (U.S.A.)	6 - 8	8 - 10
KIRCHNER, RAPHAEL (Austria) See Art Nouveau, Art Deco and Fr. Glamour		
KISH, L.	4 - 5	5 - 6
KLAVITCH, RUDOLF See Art Nouveau		
KNOEFEL		

Novitas
  Illumination Series

Series 668 Nudes (4)	15 - 20	20 - 25
Series 20888 Mother/Baby	10 - 12	12 - 15
Series 15662 With Japanese Lantern	15 - 18	18 - 20
Other Illumination Series	12 - 15	15 - 18

M. Munk, Vienna
  Illumination Series

Series 1992 With Japanese Lantern	15 - 18	18 - 22

KOEHLER, MELA (Austria) See Art Deco,
  Art Nouveau

Early Works	40 - 50	50 - 60
After 1915	20 - 25	25 - 30

KOISTER (France) See French Glamour
KOPAL   See Art Nouveau
KOSEL, H.C.   See Nudes
  B.K.W.I.

Series 181	10 - 12	12 - 15
KOTAS, V.	6 - 8	8 - 10

KOVIES, K. See Art Deco

KRAUSZ, J.V. (Austria)	8 - 10	10 - 12
KRENNES, H. (Poland)	8 - 10	10 - 12

KUANI, C. COLAN See Art Deco
KUCHINKA, JAN (Czech.)
  Praha-Podol 150

Erotic Series	25 - 30	30 - 35

KUDERNY
  M. Munk, Vienna

Series 606	10 - 12	12 - 18
Series 634	8 - 10	10 - 15
Series 841, Semi-Nudes	12 - 15	15 - 18
Series 835, Tiny Men	12 - 15	15 - 18

KURT, E. MAISON

Fantasy Deco Series	15 - 20	20 - 25
KUTEW, CHRISTO (Poland)	6 - 8	8 - 10

LARRONI (Italy) See Art Deco
LASKOFF   See Art Nouveau

LAURENS, P.A. (Czech.)	6 - 8	8 - 10
LEARNED	5 - 6	6 - 7
LeDUEI	10 - 12	12 - 14
LEINWEBER, R.	6 - 8	8 - 10

LENOLEM (France) See French Glamour
  Meissner & Buch

Series 219	12 - 15	15 - 20
LHUER, VICTOR	15 - 18	18 - 22

LONGLEY, CHILTON (U.S.A.) See Art Deco

LORENZI, FABIO	15 - 18	18 - 22
M.M.S.	5 - 6	6 - 8

MSM

Meissner & Buch	10 - 12	12 - 15
MALUGANI, G.	15 - 20	20 - 25

Marjorie Mostyn, R. Tuck
W.C. 2397, "A Maiden Fair"

X.P. Nikolaki, R&N 887
"Dullness Reigns"

MANASSE (Austria)	5 - 6	6 - 8
MANNING, FREDERICK S. (U.S.A.)		
Series 117 Portraits	8 - 10	10 - 12
Others	6 - 8	8 - 10
MANNING, REG (U.S.A.)	7 - 8	8 - 9
MANUEL, HENRI (France) See Fr. Glamour		
MANSELL, VIVIAN (GB)		
National Ladies Series	8 - 10	10 - 12
MARCO, M.		
Raphael Tuck		
Series 2763 (Asti-type)	6 - 8	8 - 10
MARTIN-KAVEL		
Head Studies Series 5027-5036	10 - 12	12 - 15
Lapina Nudes	12 - 15	15 - 18
MAUZAN (Italy) See Art Deco		
MAYER, LOU (U.S.A.)		
Reinthal & Newman		
400 Series	7 - 8	8 - 10
500 Series	8 - 10	10 - 12
Fantasy Series 878-883	12 - 15	15 - 18
Ullman Mfg. Co.		
Pretty Girl Series	5 - 8	8 - 10
MAZZA, A See Art Nouveau		
McFALL, J.V. (U.S.A.)	4 - 5	5 - 6

McLELLAN, CHAS. A.	4 - 5	5 - 6
McMEIN, A. (U.S.A.)		
Novitas		
Head Studies Series 15672	10 - 12	12 - 15
Osh Kosh Pennant Girls (6)	10 - 12	12 - 15
MESCHINI G. (Italy) See Art Deco		
METLIKOVITZ, L. (Italy) See Art Deco		
MEUNIER, H. See Art Nouveau		
MEUNIER, SUZANNE See Fr. Glamour		
MIKI (Finland) See Art Deco		
MILLER, MARION	3 - 4	4 - 5
MILLIERE, M. (France) See Fr. Glamour		
MOLINA, ROBERTO		
"Diabolo" Series	10 - 12	12 - 14
MONESTIER, C. (Italy) See Art Deco		
Others	5 - 6	6 - 7
MONIER, MAGGY	15 - 18	18 - 22
MONTEDORO See Art Deco		
MORAN, LEON (U.S.A.)	5 - 6	6 - 7
MOSER, KOLOMAN (Austria)		
See Art Nouveau		
MOSTYN, MARJORIE (GB)		
Raphael Tuck		
Series 108 "Jewel Girls"	10 - 12	12 - 15
Series 11 "Fair of Feature"	10 - 12	12 - 15

A. Pennel, M. Munk 1114
"Eisblume"

G.L. Pew, Anonymous 109/4
No Caption

W. Color Ser. 2397 "A Maiden Fair"	8 - 10	10 - 12
MUHLBERG, S.	8 - 10	10 - 12
MURCH, FRANK	3 - 4	4 - 5
MUSSINO (Italy) See Art Deco		
MUTTICH, C.V. (Czech.)		
Head Studies	5 - 8	8 - 10
Others	5 - 8	8 - 10
MYER (U.S.A.)	4 - 5	5 - 6
NANNI, G. (Italy) See Art Deco,		
Horses/Dogs With Ladies		
NAST, THOMAS, JR.		
Tennis card "Love Game"	15 - 18	18 - 20
Others	6 - 8	8 - 10
NEY (France) See French Glamour		
NICZKY, E.	5 - 6	6 - 8
NIKOLAKI, Z.P.		
Reinthal & Newman		
Ladies Series	6 - 8	8 - 10
NORDSTROM-FEIND, ANNA		
FDB & Co.		
Fisk Hats	6 - 8	8 - 10
NOWICKA, N. (Poland)	10 - 12	12 - 15
NYSTROM, JENNY See F. Tales, Fantasy	10 - 12	12 - 15
O'NEILL, FRANK C. (U.S.A.)	5 - 6	6 - 7
ORLANDI, V. (Italy) See Art Deco		
ORLOFF (Russian)	10 - 12	12 - 14
PAGONI, A. (Italy) See Art Deco		
PALANTI, G. (Italy) See Art Deco		
PAPERITZ, G.	6 - 8	8 - 10
PARKINSON, ETHEL	6 - 8	8 - 9
PATELLA (Italy) See Art Deco		
PAUL, M. (German)	4 - 5	5 - 6
PAUSINGER, C.V.	8 - 10	10 - 12
PELTIER, L. (France) See Fr. Glamour		
PENNELL		
M. Munk, Vienna		
Series 913 Sporting Girls	6 - 8	8 - 10
Series 1114 Sporting Girls	6 - 8	8 - 10
PENOT, A. (France) See Fr. Glamour		
PERAS (France) See French Glamour		
PETER, OTTO (German)	6 - 8	8 - 10
PEW, G.L.		
Aquarelle Series 109	6 - 8	8 - 10
Aquarelle Series 2239	6 - 8	8 - 10
Leubrie & Elkus (L&E)		
Series 2221, 2223 Heads	8 - 10	10 - 12
PETERSON, L. (U.S.A.) See Cowboys/Indians		
H.H. Tammen		
Love & Life Series	5 - 6	6 - 8
PHILLIPS, COLES (U.S.A.)		

The creator of The Fadeaway Girl was born in Springfield, Ohio in 1881. There was very little of the artistic temperament in his early years; rather more of the healthy, fun-loving boy's capacity to fall into deviltry, and it was not until his college days that he realized his natural ability to draw might be of use to him. In an effort to work his way through Kenyon College at Gambier, Ohio, he earned his first money as an artist illustrating and decorating the college monthly magazine.

After graduation, he moved to New York and for some time picked up varied experience in clerking and working at odd jobs. He became a solicitor in one of the city's largest advertising and designing houses. There, he represented his chosen field, and thereby cultivated a keen business head and a practical knowledge of commercial art.

He soon used this knowledge to good advantage by forming a dozen artists into an advertising organization of his own. This new venture, however, caused his painting to suffer from neglect and he finally retired from it altogether and rented a studio. He enhanced his technical training by attending the Chase School in the afternoons and the Free Art School in the evenings.

Phillips worked a month on his first drawing. Life Publishing Co. accepted this rendering as a double-page cartoon and he immediately became a regular contributor. His Fadeaway Girls, glorifying *Life* covers, were an immediate success. So original was the conception that the Fadeaway Girl will always stand for Coles Phillips, and Coles Phillips will always stand for the Fadeaway Girl.

Coles finally settled in New Rochelle, a New York suburb just 45 minutes from Broadway, where his studio overlooked Long Island Sound. His model for most all of his works was his beautiful and slender wife, Tess.

The Coles Phillips Girl typifies the subtle charm of American womanhood. In the drawing room or in the kitchen, breaking hearts or baking pies, or enjoying the

Coles Phillips, Life Publishing Co.
"Which?"

Coles Phillips, Life Publishing Co.
"Summer Fiction"

Coles Phillips, Life Publishing Co.
"The Sandman"

Coles Phillips, Life Publishing Co.
"A Call to Arms"

stillness of the great outdoors, a real woman from the tip of her dainty feet to the soft glory of her head, she stands out from her flat background and answers completely to a young man's fancy at its highest and best.

The values of Coles Phillips cards have accelerated in recent years because of their popularity with signed-artist collectors. Significant too, is their scarcity as collectors have come to realize that there were relatively few of them published.

COLES PHILLIPS
* **Cards listed with an asterisk**
are Fadeaway Girls images.

Life Publishing Co., 1907		
Life Series 1		
"Her Choice"	25 - 28	28 - 32
Life Publishing Co., 1909		
C. Coles Phillips Series		
"Arms and the Man" *	30 - 35	35 - 40
"Between You and Me..." *	30 - 35	35 - 40
"Birches" *	30 - 35	35 - 40

Coles Phillips, Life Publishing Co.
"Birches"

Coles Phillips, Life Publishing Co.
"R.S.V.P."

Coles Phillips, Life Publishing Co., "Her Choice"

"Home Ties" *	30 - 35	35 - 40
"Illusion" *	30 - 35	35 - 40
"Inclined to Meet" Ser. 2 *	35 - 38	38 - 42
"Reflections"	30 - 35	35 - 40
"R.S.V.P."	22 - 25	25 - 30
"The Sand Man"	22 - 25	25 - 30
"The Sand Witch"	22 - 25	25 - 30
"Such Stuff as Dreams are Made Of"	22 - 25	25 - 30
"Summer Fiction"	22 - 25	25 - 30
"What Next?" Ser. 2	25 - 28	28 - 35
"Which?" Ser. 2	25 - 28	28 - 35

Life Publishing Co., 1910

"A Call to Arms" *	30 - 35	35 - 40
"All Wool and Face Value" Ser. 2	25 - 28	28 - 35
"And Out of Mind as..." Ser. 2	25 - 28	28 - 35
"Discarding from Strength" Ser. 2 *	30 - 35	35 - 40
"Hers"	22 - 25	25 - 30

P.F. Volland & Co., Chicago
© by Life Publishing Co.

"Latest in Gowns..."	22 - 25	25 - 30
"Long Distance Makes..." *		30 - 35
35 - 40		
"Memories" *	30 - 35	35 - 40
"My Christmas Thoughts..." *	30 - 35	35 - 40
"The Survival of the Fittest" *	30 - 35	35 - 40

C.P. Co., Inc., N.Y.

Painting of Alice Joyce *	30 - 35	35 - 40

ADVERTISING

*Lyman Powell, Granberg's,
Stockholm, No Caption*

*Lester Ralph, R&N 816
"For All Eternity"*

R. Stafford Collins, N.Y.		
Community Silver Plate		
Ad for Brunner Fl. Jeweler	28 - 30	30 - 35
Community Silver Plate		
"A Case of Love at First Sight"	28 - 30	30 - 35
Book Advertisement		
"The Dim Lantern," by Temple Bailey	30 - 35	35 - 40
Calendar Cards, With Verse	28 - 30	30 - 35
Unsigned - Ten unsigned Fadeaway Girls have been attributed to Coles Phillips.		
Prices of these are:	15 - 18	18 - 22
PILLARD	5 - 6	6 - 7
PINOCHI (Italy) See Art Deco		
PIOTROWSKI, A. (Poland)	5 - 6	6 - 8
POWELL, LYMAN (U.S.A.)		
"Eventful Days" Series		
"Graduation Day"	6 - 8	8 - 10
"Engagement Day"	6 - 8	8 - 10
"Wedding Day"	6 - 8	8 - 10
"Birthday"	6 - 8	8 - 10
Flower Series 783	6 - 8	8 - 10
PUTTKAMER		
Erotic Lovers Series 8027 (6)	15 - 18	18 - 22
QUINNELL, CECIL W.		

B.K.W.I.
"The Jewel Girls" Ser. 251

"Pearl"	8 - 10	10 - 12
"Ruby"	8 - 10	10 - 12
"Emerald"	8 - 10	10 - 12
"Topaz"	8 - 10	10 - 12
"Turquoise"	8 - 10	10 - 12
"Sapphire"	8 - 10	10 - 12
"Glad Eye" Series	8 - 10	10 - 12
RABES, MAX (German)	5 - 6	6 - 8

RALPH, LESTER (U.S.A.)
Reinthal & Newman
"Dancing" Series 801-806

"The La Furlana"	12 - 14	14 - 18
"The Cortez"	12 - 14	14 - 18
"The Half and Half"	12 - 14	14 - 18
"The Tango"	12 - 14	14 - 18
"The One Step"	12 - 14	14 - 18
"The Maxie"	12 - 14	14 - 18
Series 813-818 *		
813 "The Awakening of Love"	10 - 12	12 - 14
814 "The Stage of Life"	10 - 12	12 - 14
815 "Up in the Clouds"	10 - 12	12 - 14
816 "For All Eternity"	12 - 14	14 - 18
817 "In Proud Possession"	10 - 12	12 - 14
818 "The Home Guard"	8 - 10	10 - 12

* With German caption add $2.

The Knapp Co., N.Y.
Paul Heckscher Series 392

1	8 - 10	10 - 12
2 "An Offer of Affection"	8 - 10	10 - 12
3 "Weathering it Together"	8 - 10	10 - 12
4	8 - 10	10 - 12
5 "Four-In-Hand"	8 - 10	10 - 12
6 "Her First Mate"	8 - 10	10 - 12
7 "Two is Company Enough"	8 - 10	10 - 12
8 "Weathering Together"	8 - 10	10 - 12
9 "Fellow Sports"	12 - 14	14 - 16
10 "Diana of the Shore"	10 - 12	12 - 14

H. Import Series 307

1 "Take Me Along"	8 - 10	10 - 12
4 "A Stroll Together"	10 - 12	12 - 14
7 "Two is Company Enough"	8 - 10	10 - 12
Others	8 - 10	10 - 12

H. Import Series 308

1 "Confidential Chatter"	8 - 10	10 - 12
3 "A Social Call"	8 - 10	10 - 12
5 "The Wings of the Wind"	8 - 10	10 - 12
6 "A Surprise Party"	8 - 10	10 - 12
9 "Fellow Sports"	10 - 12	12 - 14
Others	10 - 12	12 - 14

Series 1026

2 "Feathered Friends"	8 - 10	10 - 12
Others	8 - 10	10 - 12

Series 7 *

9523 "Fellow Sports"	10 - 12	12 - 14
9543 "Favored by Fortune"	10 - 12	12 - 14
9563 "Two is Company Enough"	10 - 12	12 - 14
9573 "Her First Date"	10 - 12	12 - 14
9583 "A Challenge from the Sea"	10 - 12	12 - 14
9593 "A Game in the Surf"	10 - 12	12 - 14
9603 "Diana of the Shore"	10 - 12	12 - 14
9613 "Four-In-Hand"	10 - 12	12 - 14
9623 "Fellow Sports"	12 - 14	14 - 16
9633 "An Offer of Affection"	10 - 12	12 - 14
Others	10 - 12	12 - 14

* This series also adapted as Knapp
  Calendars. Add $5 if Knapp Calendars.

C.W. Faulkner

Series 1314B

"Fast Companions"	10 - 12	12 - 14

Series 1315D

"Her Proudest Moment"	10 - 12	12 - 14
Others	10 - 12	12 - 14

RAPPINI (Italy) See Art Deco		
READING	7 - 8	8 - 10
REED, MARION	3 - 4	4 - 6
REYNOLDS (U.S.A.) See Cowboys, Indians		
Cowgirl Series	5 - 6	6 - 7
REYZNER, M.	6 - 8	8 - 10
REZSO, KISS		
Mayar Rotophot Tarsasag, Budapest		
"Studienkopf, Siren Lady" **Series 68-73**	10 - 12	12 - 14
RICCO, LORIS (Italy) See Art Deco		
ROBERTY, L.		
M. Munk, Vienna		
Bather Series 1124	10 - 12	12 - 15
RUMPEL, F.	6 - 8	8 - 10
RUNDALZEFF, M. (Russia)	6 - 8	8 - 10
RUSSELL, MARY LA F.	6 - 7	7 - 8
RYAN, E. (U.S.A.) See Art Nouveau		
Winsch Backs		
Non-Art Nouveau Ladies		
"Blissful Moments, etc."	5 - 6	6 - 7
SLS (SAMUEL L. SCHMUCKER) (U.S.A.)		
Detroit Publishing Co.		
Butterfly Series	100 - 120	120 - 150
Childhood Days Series	150 - 160	160 - 175
Mermaid Series	135 - 150	150 - 165
Fairy Queens Series	150 - 160	160 - 175
Drinks Series	125 - 135	135 - 145
Smokers Series, Unsigned	125 - 135	135 - 145

S.L. Schmucker, Winsch
"Peaceful Thanksgiving"

S.L. Schmucker, Winsch
"Halloween"

S.L. Schmucker, Winsch
"I greet thee Valentine"

S.L. Schmucker, Winsch
"My Valentine think of me"

National Girl Series	125 - 135	135 - 145
Winsch, Copyright		
Halloween		
1911 Series	60 - 75	75 - 85
1912 Series	80 - 100	100 - 125
1913 "Magic" Series	100 - 120	120 - 150
Others	40 - 50	50 - 60
1914 "Magic" Series	60 - 75	75 - 100
Others	40 - 50	50 - 60
1915 W/Small Children	100 -120	120 - 140
1915 No Copyright		
Series 28 Checkerboard	115 - 125	125 - 150
Raphael Tuck		
Series 100 (6)	35 - 45	45 - 60
Unsigned Ladies Valentines &		
Other Holiday types	20 - 25	25 - 30
Silk Inserts	20 - 25	25 - 30
SAGER, XAVIER (France)		
See French Glamour, Fantasy		
ST. JOHN		
National Art		
"National Girls" Series	10 - 12	12 - 14
"Foreign Girls" Series	6 - 8	8 - 10
"The Four Seasons"	10 - 12	12 - 15
"State Girl" Series	6 - 8	8 - 10
Montgomery Co., Chicago		
103 "Shopping"	8 - 10	10 - 12
104 "Promenade"	8 - 10	10 - 12
106 "Beauties"	8 - 10	10 - 12
SALMONI (Italy) See Art Deco		
SANTINO (Italy) See Art Deco		
SCATTINI (Italy) See Art Deco		
SCHILBACH	6 - 8	8 - 10
SCHLOSSER, R. (Germany)	5 - 6	6 - 8
SCHUTZ, ERIC (Austria)		
B.K.W.I. Series 128	8 - 10	10 - 12
SCHMUTZLWER, L. See Color Nudes		
Moderne Kunst Series	6 - 8	8 - 10
SGALLI, S. (Italy) See Art Deco		
SHARPE	6 - 8	8 - 9
SHERIE	5 - 6	6 - 7
SICHEL, N.	5 - 6	6 - 8
SIMM, PROF. FRANZ (Germany)	5 - 6	6 - 8
SIMONETTI (Italy) See Art Deco		
SITSCHKOFF (Russia)	10 - 12	12 - 15
SOLDINGER, A. (Poland)	8 - 10	10 - 12
SOLOMKO, S. (Russia)		
Lapina, Paris		
"Russian Princess" Series		
"Queen Aeviakovna"	15 - 18	18 - 22
"Wassillisa Mikouichuna"	15 - 18	18 - 12

Solomko, Russian
No Caption

P. Stachiewicz, Akropol,
Krakow 152-49, Polish Caption

"Princess Apaaksia"	15 - 18	18 - 22
"Princess Warrior Nastasia"	20 - 22	22 - 25
"Princess Mary, The White Swan"	20 - 22	22 - 25
"Princess Zabava Poutiatichna"	15 - 18	18 - 22
T.S.N. (Theo Stroefer, Nuremberg) *		
15 "Parisiene"	14 - 16	16 - 18
175 ""Phantasy"	16 - 18	18 - 22
"Dream of Icarius"	14 - 15	15 - 18
"Pearl of Creation"	15 - 18	18 - 22
"Vanity" (Semi-nude)	15 - 20	20 - 25
"Circe" (Semi-nude)	15 - 20	20 - 25
"The Tale" (Fantasy)	15 - 16	16 - 18
"The Blue Bird" (Fantasy)	18 - 20	20 - 22
"Magician Circle" (Semi-nude)	15 - 20	20 - 25
154 "Temptations" (Semi-nude)	15 - 20	20 - 25
"Glow Worm" (Fantasy)	15 - 18	18 - 20
Other T.S.N. (Many)	8 - 10	10 - 12
* With Russian backs, add $4-5.		
STACHIEWICZ, P.	8 - 10	10 - 12
STAMM, MAUD	5 - 6	6 - 7
STANLAWS, P. (U.S.A.)		
Edward Gross, N.Y.		
Stanlaws Series 1-12 No Captions	14 - 16	16 - 22
Knapp Co., N.Y.		

Dobrowolski, K.V. 282-3
"Autumn"

An Example of Postcard Beauty

900 Series

"A Midsummer Maid"	14 - 15	15 - 18
"After the Matinee"	14 - 15	15 - 18
"Daisies Won't Tell"	14 - 15	15 - 18
"Fair as the Lily"	15 - 18	18 - 20
"Fresh as the Morn"	15 - 18	18 - 20
"Girl of the Golden West"	14 - 15	15 - 18
"Kissed by the Snow"	15 - 18	18 - 20
"The Pink Lady"	15 - 18	18 - 22
"School Days"	15 - 18	18 - 22

K. Co.
Distributed by A.R.&C.i.B.
900 Series Reprints, Called Series 550

"A Midsummer Maid"	15 - 18	18 - 22
"Daisies Won't Tell"	15 - 18	18 - 22
"Girl of the Golden West"	15 - 18	18 - 22
"The Pink Lady"	15 - 18	18 - 22

Series 551

"After the Matinee"	15 - 18	18 - 22
"Kissed by the Snow"	15 - 18	18 - 22
"School Days"	15 - 18	18 - 22
"Fair as the Lily"	15 - 18	18 - 22

Reinthal & Newman
Military Ladies Series

981 U.S.A.	15 - 18	18 - 22

982 Serbia	12 - 14	14 - 16
983 Belgium	12 - 14	14 - 16
984 France	12 - 14	14 - 16
985 Italy	12 - 14	14 - 16
986 Greece	12 - 14	14 - 16
987 Great Britain	12 - 14	14 - 16
988 Russia	12 - 14	14 - 16

H. Choate & Co.
Djer-Kiss Rouge & Face Powder Compacts

"Silver Blonde"	22 - 25	25 - 28
STRETTI, VICTOR (Czech.)	6 - 8	8 - 10

TAM, JEAN (France) See French Glamour
TERZI, A. (Italy) See Art Deco

TONAILO, A.	6 - 7	7 - 8

TORNROSE, ALEX

Welles Head Series (B&W)	6 - 8	8 - 9
Others	6 - 7	7 - 8

TOULOUSE-LAUTREC (France)

"Cabaret Bruant"	600 - 700	700 - 900
"La Goule au Moulin Rouge"	1500 - 1600	1600 - 1800

Card recently sold for $1800.
TRAVER, C. WARD (U.S.A.)
H & S Art Co.

"The Beauty of the Season"	8 - 10	10 - 12

Clarence Underwood
R.C. Co. 1437, "Diana"

Clarence Underwood
R.C. Co. 1445, "Sylvia"

"Sweet Seventeen"	8 - 10	10 - 12
Others	8 - 10	10 - 12
TUHKA, A. (Finland) See Art Deco		
TWELVETREES, C.	5 - 6	6 - 8
See Beautiful Children		
UNDERWOOD, CLARENCE (U.S.A.)		

Clarence Underwood was another of the more important illustrators of magazine covers and magazine fiction. Those who have seen his beautiful color plates of "Vera," of "Grace Kingsley" and "Dolly Fitzhugh," of "Edna Gray," of "Lynne Halsell" and "Emma Zane" in the fictional story, "Manifest Destiny," in a 1907 edition of *Century Magazine* can realize just what a great illustrator he was.

He also benefitted directly from the great postcard era. This painter of beautiful ladies did work for Reinthal & Newman of New York, but his most beautiful images were published by the R. Chapman Co. (better known as the R.C. Co., N.Y.). They did the 1400 Series Water Colors of his ladies wearing big, beautiful, and colorful hats. These will always be some of the most beautiful work ever done by an American artist.

Marcus Munk, the famous postcard publisher of Vienna, also did many of his images on postcards. These were mainly of loving couples, with colorful backgrounds and many were sports-oriented. Other foreign publishers also produced his works and they were very popular in Europe; however, Underwood was unable to gain the great U.S. popularity attained by his fellow American artists—Fisher, Boileau and Earl Christy.

CLARENCE UNDERWOOD

C.W. Faulkner		
Series 5	10 - 12	12 - 14
Series 1010	10 - 12	12 - 14
1278 "A Symphony of Hearts"	8 - 10	10 - 12
National Art		
"Playing Card" Series		
78 "Hearts" Two men, two ladies	8 - 10	10 - 12
79 "Poker" Five men	8 - 10	10 - 12
80 "Bridge" Four women	8 - 10	10 - 12
81 "Euchre" Five men	8 - 10	10 - 12
Reinthal & Newman		
300 Series Water Colors		

Clarence Underwood
R.C. Co. 1436, "Constance"

Clarence Underwood
R.C. Co., 1441, "Rosabella"

345 "The Flirt"	10 - 12	12 - 15
346 "Pretty Cold"	10 - 12	12 - 15
347 "Her First Vote"	25 - 30	30 - 35
348 "It's Always Fair Weather"	10 - 12	12 - 15
349 "Rain or Shine"	10 - 12	12 - 15
350 "Pleasant Reflections"	10 - 12	12 - 15
R.C. Co., N.Y.		
1400 Water Color Series		
1436 "Constance"	15 - 18	18 - 22
1437 "Diana"	15 - 18	18 - 22
1438 "Vivian"	15 - 18	18 - 22
1439 "Phyllis"	15 - 18	18 - 22
1440 "Celestine"	15 - 18	18 - 22
1441 "Rosabella"	15 - 18	18 - 22
1442 "Juliana"	15 - 18	18 - 22
1443 "Victoria"	22 - 25	25 - 30
1444 "Aurora"	15 - 18	18 - 22
1445 "Sylvia"	15 - 18	18 - 22
1446 "Virginia"	15 - 18	18 - 22
1447 "Doris"	15 - 18	18 - 22
Frederick A. Stokes Co.		
Series 1		
"A Problem of Income"	7 - 8	8 - 10
"Castles in the Smoke"	7 - 8	8 - 10
"For Fear of Sunburn"	8 - 9	9 - 12

"Knight Takes Queen"	7 - 8	8 - 10
Series 2		
"Love Me, Love My Cat"	8 - 9	9 - 12
"Love Me, Love My Dog"	8 - 9	9 - 12
"Love Me, Love My Donkey"	7 - 8	8 - 10
"Love Me, Love My Horse"	8 - 9	9 - 12
Series 3		
"When We're Together Fishing"	8 - 9	9 - 12
"When We're Together at Luncheon"	7 - 8	8 - 10
"When We're Together Shooting"	8 - 9	9 - 12
"When We're Together in a Storm"	7 - 8	8 - 10
Series 4		
"Beauty and the Beast"	8 - 9	9 - 12
"The Best of Friends"	8 - 9	9 - 12
"Expectation"	8 - 9	9 - 12
"The Promenade"	8 - 9	9 - 12
Series 5		
"A Lump of Sugar"	8 - 9	9 - 12
"After the Hunt"	8 - 9	9 - 12
"The Red Haired Girl..."	10 - 12	12 - 14
"Three American Beauties"	10 - 12	12 - 14
Series 6		
"Feeding the Swans"	7 - 8	8 - 10
"A Pet in the Park"	7 - 8	8 - 10
"Posing"	7 - 8	8 - 10
"A Witch"	8 - 10	10 - 12
Series 7		
"An Old Melody"	7 - 8	8 - 10
"Over the Teacups"	7 - 8	8 - 10
"The Opera Girl"	7 - 8	8 - 10
"The Violin Girl"	8 - 10	10 - 12
Series 8		
"At the Races"	8 - 10	10 - 12
"Embroidery for Two"	7 - 8	8 - 10
"Out for a Stroll"	7 - 8	8 - 10
"Two Cooks"	7 - 8	8 - 10
Series 14		
"Their First Wedding Gift"	7 - 8	8 - 10
"Their Love of Old Silver"	7 - 8	8 - 10
"Two and an Old Flirt"	7 - 8	8 - 10
"Vain Regrets"	7 - 8	8 - 10
Series 15		
"A Lesson in Motoring"	8 - 10	10 - 12
"A Skipper and Mate"	7 - 8	8 - 10
Series 19		
"The Only Two at Dinner"	7 - 8	8 - 10
"The Only Two at the Game"	8 - 10	10 - 12
"The Only Two at the House Party"	7 - 8	8 - 10
"The Only Two at the Opera"	7 - 8	8 - 10
Series 22		
"The Greatest Thing in the World"	7 - 8	8 - 10

Clarence Underwood, Novitas
"Wer wird Siegen?"

Clarence Underwood, R&N 347
"Her First Vote"

"The Last Waltz"	7 - 8	8 - 10
"Lost?"	7 - 8	8 - 10
"Love on Six Cylinders"	8 - 10	10 - 12
Taylor, Platt & Co.		
Series 782		
"A Fisherman's Luck"	10 - 12	12 - 15
"A Heart of Diamonds"	10 - 12	12 - 15
"A Modern Siren"	10 - 12	12 - 15
"Daisies Won't Tell"	10 - 12	12 - 15
"The Glories of March"	10 - 12	12 - 15
"His Latest Chauffeur"	10 - 12	12 - 15
"Indicating a Thaw"	10 - 12	12 - 15
"The Magnet"	10 - 12	12 - 15
"Let's Paddle Forever"	10 - 12	12 - 15
"Love Has It's Clouds"	10 - 12	12 - 15
"Stolen Sweets"	10 - 12	12 - 15
"True Love Never Runs Smooth"	10 - 12	12 - 15
Osborne Calendar Co.		
Calendar Cards		
1521 "Fancy Work"	15 - 18	18 - 22
1621 "Music Hath Charm"	15 - 18	18 - 22
A.R. & Co.		
1283 "Des Meeres und der Liebe Wellen"	10 - 12	12 - 14
M. Munk, Vienna		

F. Earl Christy, P. Sander 304-A

Series 303 (8)
Beautiful Ladies with Pets, No captions 8 - 10   10 - 12
Series 377, 385, 387, & 388 10 - 11   11 - 12
Series 742 *
"Love Laughs at Winter" 8 - 10   10 - 12
"Love on Wings" 12 - 15   15 - 18
"Under the Mistletoe" 8 - 10   10 - 12
"The Sender of Orchids" 8 - 10   10 - 12
"The Last Waltz" 8 - 10   10 - 12
"The Greatest Thing" 8 - 10   10 - 12
Others 8 - 10   10 - 12
* Series 742 A,B,C,D,E,F,G & H.
All same as Series 742 but with
German captions, add $3.
Series 832, 834, 837 & 860 *
"A Penny for Thought" 8 - 10   10 - 12
"A Problem of Income" 8 - 10   10 - 12
"Cherry Ripe" 8 - 10   10 - 12
"He Loves Me..." 8 - 10   10 - 12
"How to Know Wildflowers" 12 - 15   15 - 18
"Only a Question of Time" 8 - 10   10 - 12
"The Sweetest Flower that..." 8 - 10   10 - 12
"Skipper and Mate" 10 - 12   12 - 15
"Love and Six Cylinders" 12 - 15   15 - 18
* With German captions, add $3.
Novitas, Germany
400 Series
445 "Gestrand nis" 8 - 10   10 - 12
447 "Einig" 10 - 12   12 - 14
449 "Zutunftplane" 12 - 14   14 - 16
Others 10 - 12   12 - 14
Others, without captions 8 - 10   10 - 12
20,000 Series
20391 No caption 8 - 10   10 - 12
20392 No caption 8 - 10   10 - 12
20451 "Wer Wird Siegen" 8 - 10   10 - 12
20452 "Dem Fluck Entgegen" 8 - 10   10 - 12
20453 No caption (Lovers of Beauty) 8 - 10   10 - 12
20454 "Liebe Auf Eis" 8 - 10   10 - 12
20455 "Abwesend, Aber Nicht Vergessen" 8 - 10   10 - 12
20456 No caption 8 - 10   10 - 12
20457 "Zwei Seelen und ein Genankt" 8 - 10   10 - 12
20458 "Zukunpt Staune" 8 - 10   10 - 12
20459 No caption 8 - 10   10 - 12
20460 "Glucklitch Tagt" 8 - 10   10 - 12
FINLAND
W. & G. (Weilin & Goos)
American Ser. N:O 7001 1-35
6 cards with no captions 20 - 22   22 - 25
RUSSIA
Phillips "The Last Waltz Together" 15 - 20   20 - 25

L. Usabal, S. & G. SiB 733/1
No Caption

L. Usabal, S&G SiB 733/6
No Caption

UNIERZYSKI, J. (Poland)	5 - 6	6 - 8
UPRKA, JOZA (Czech.)	6 - 8	8 - 10
USABAL (Italy) See Art Deco, Ladies with Horses, Ladies with Dogs		
P.F.B. (in Diamond) Series 3796 (6)	12 - 14	14 - 16
E.A.S.B.		
Series 111 Lovers under the Mistletoe	8 - 10	10 - 12
Series 103 Lovers Dancing	8 - 10	10 - 12
Series 114 Lovers Dancing	10 - 12	12 - 14
Erkal		
Series 339 (6) On Toboggan Sled	10 - 12	12 - 14
Series 343 (6) Skiing	10 - 12	12 - 14
Series 336 (6) Tennis	15 - 18	18 - 22
Series 318, 356 (6) Lovers		10 - 12
12 - 15		
Series 301, 308, 367 (6) Hats	8 - 10	10 - 12
Series 1318 (6) Lovers on Couch	10 - 12	12 - 15
Series 347 (6) "Gypsy" Heads	8 - 10	10 - 12
Series 330, 337, 357 (6) Dancing, Kissing	8 - 10	10 - 12
G. Kuais		
Series 1393 Hats	6 - 8	8 - 10
Gurner & Simon		
Series 2027 (6) Lovers at the Bar	6 - 8	8 - 10
S. & G.		

J. Unierzyski, ANCZTC 534
No Caption

J. Unierzyski, ANCZTC 530
No Caption

H. Uziemblo, G. Polska 620
"Aniecka"

H. Uziemblo, G. Artystyezna 18
"Basia"

Series 694 Couples, man in Uniform	5 - 6	6 - 7
S.W.S.B.		
Series 128 Lovers Kissing	8 - 10	10 - 12
Series 1007, 1068 Couples Dancing	8 - 10	10 - 12
Series 1070 Lesbian Dancers	20 - 22	22 - 25
Series 1108 Nude in Fur	12 - 15	15 - 18
Series 1256 Couples Dancing	8 - 10	10 - 12
Series 1295-1300 Dancing/Blacks	18 - 20	20 - 22
Series 1356 Heads/Smoking	10 - 12	12 - 14
Series 303		
"Ladies Smoking"	10 - 12	12 - 14
Series 1356 Smoking	10 - 12	12 - 14
Series 4668, 4669, 4670 (6)		
Women in Uniform	8 - 10	10 - 12
Series 1091, 6380, 6383 (6) Dancing	6 - 8	8 - 10
Anonymous		
Series 20468 Couples Dancing	8 - 10	10 - 12
UZLEMBLO, HENRY (Poland)	6 - 8	8 - 10
VALLET, L. (France) See French Glamour		
VEITH, E.	5 - 6	6 - 8
VERNON, EMILE	3 - 4	4 - 5
VINNOY (France) See Art Deco		
VOGLIO, BENITO (France)	8 - 10	10 - 12
VOIGHT, C.A.	3 - 4	4 - 5
WACHTEL, WILHELM (German)	6 - 8	8 - 10
WAPALLOKA (Russia)	6 - 8	8 - 10
WASILKOWSKI, K. (Poland)	8 - 10	10 - 12
WASKO, EDWIN G.	5 - 6	6 - 8
WEZEL, A. (Austria)	8 - 10	10 - 12

Joza Uprka, Josef Pithrat E-3, No Caption

Fr. Zmurko, ANCZYC 279
Russian Caption

Fr. Zmurko, ANCZYC 438
No Caption

WICHERA, R.R.
  M. Munk, Vienna

Series 112, 322, 411 **(6)**	8 - 10	10 - 12
Series 224, 450, 530, 683 **(6)**	10 - 12	12 - 15
Series 229, 633, 1101 **(6)**	10 - 12	12 - 15
Series 1163 **(6)**	8 - 10	10 - 12
Series 559, 5590 **Big Hats (6)**	12 - 14	14 - 18
Series 684 **Semi-Nudes (6)**	12 - 15	15 - 20

WIEDERSEIM, GRACE (also G. Drayton)
  Armour & Co.

"American Girl" Series		
"The Wiederseim Girl"	30 - 35	35 - 40
"The Wiederseim Girl" (German Pub.)	35 - 40	45 - 50

ZABCZINSKY, W. See Art Deco
ZANDRINO (Italy) See Art Deco

ZELECHOWSKI, K. (Poland)	8 - 10	10 - 12
ZENISER, JOSEF	6 - 8	8 - 10
ZEUMER, BRUNO (German)	5 - 6	6 - 8

ZMURKO, FR. (Poland) See Color Nudes

ANCZYC Series	8 - 10	10 - 12

LADIES & DOGS

BALOTINI (Italy)

Chiostri, Ballerini & Fratini 316
No Caption

Nanni, Uff. Rev. Stampa 300-1
No Caption

Busi, Ballerini & Fratini
No Caption

Series 312	12 - 15	15 - 18
BARBER, COURT (U.S.A.)		
S.W.S.B.		
"Beauties"	8 - 10	10 - 12
1228 "Following the Race"	8 - 10	10 - 12
Anonymous		
Series 2023	8 - 10	10 - 12
Series 2024	8 - 10	10 - 12
BARRIBAL (GB)		
H.N. & N.		
15645 Girl in Furs, W/Dog	6 - 8	8 - 10
BERTIGLIA, A. (Italy)		
Series 163 (6)	12 - 14	14 - 16
BIANCHI, ALBERTO (Italy)		
Series 483 (6)	8 - 10	10 - 12
Series 2020 (6)	10 - 12	12 - 14
BOMPARD, SERGE (Italy)		
Uff. Rev. Stampa &		
Dell Anna & Gasparini		
Series 11, 17 (6)	15 - 18	18 - 20
Series 343 (6)	12 - 14	14 - 16
Series 457 (6)	15 - 18	18 - 20
Series 461 (6)	12 - 14	14 - 16
Series 637 (6) W/puppies	14 - 16	16 - 18
BUSI, ADOLFO (Italy)		

Meschini, Ditta A. Guarneri 2411
No Caption

Meschini, Ditta A. Guarneri 2411
No Caption

Meschini, Ditta A. Guarneri 2411
No Caption

Nanni Uff. Rev. Stampa 300-3
No Caption

C.E.I.C.		
Series 159	14 - 16	16 - 18
Dell, Anna & Gasparini		
Series 170 (6)	14 - 16	16 - 18
Series 533 (6)	15 - 18	18 - 20
CHIOSTRI, SOFIA (Italy)		
Series 316	22 - 25	25 - 30
CHRISTY, EARL (U.S.A.)		
R&N		
942 "Protected"	10 - 12	12 - 15
COLOMBO, C. (Italy)		
Series 330 (6)	12 - 14	14 - 18
Series 530, 894 (6)	15 - 16	16 - 20
Series 1165 (6)	15 - 16	16 - 20
Series 1494 (6)	10 - 12	12 - 16
Series 1763 (6)	15 - 16	16 - 18
CORBELLA, T. (Italy)		
Uff. Rev. Stampa		
Dell, Anna & Gasparini, Degami		
Series 117 (6)	10 - 12	12 - 15
Series 230 (6)	12 - 15	15 - 18
Series 233 (6)	15 - 18	18 - 22
Series 237 (6)	15 - 18	18 - 22
Series 335 (6)	12 - 15	15 - 18
Series 464, 624 (6)	12 - 14	14 - 16

Series 516, 578 (6)	15 - 18	18 - 22
Series 530, 1085 (6)	12 - 15	15 - 18
Degami		
Series 2224, 2258 (6)	22 - 25	25 - 30
Series 4646 (6)	15 - 18	18 - 22
DIETZE		
Series 6026	10 - 12	12 - 14
DUNCAN, FREDERICK (U.S.A.)		
Reinthal & Newman		
931 "A Reserved Seat"	10 - 12	12 - 15
934 "Call of the Country"	10 - 12	12 - 15
FISHER, HARRISON		
Reinthal & Newman		
103 "Wanted, an Answer"	12 - 15	15 - 18
180 "Well Protected"	15 - 18	18 - 22
254 "Pals"	15 - 18	18 - 22
385 "Smile..."	15 - 18	18 - 22
390 "Well Guarded"	15 - 18	18 - 22
405 "He Won't Bite"	18 - 22	22 - 26
409 "Isn't He Sweet"	18 - 22	22 - 25
412 "Can You Speak"	18 - 22	22 - 28
417 "My Lady Drives"	15 - 18	18 - 22
FRANZONI (Italy)		
B.K.W.I.		
Series 369 (6)	10 - 12	12 - 15

Busi, Uff. Rev. Stampa
No Caption

A. Nash, Heckscher 703
"Love Me, Love My Dog"

F. Spotti, Uff. Rev. Stampa 158-2
No Caption

Usabal, PFB 3968-2
No Caption

Series 6309 (6)	12 - 15	15 - 18
P.R.S.		
Series 50 (6) Hi Fashion	12 - 15	15 - 18
GUZERONI (Italy)	10 - 12	12 - 15
GRANDE		
Series 437 (6)	12 - 15	15 - 18
MAUZAN (Italy)		
Uff. Rev. Stampa		
Series 326 (6)	12 - 14	14 - 16
Series 453 (6)	12 - 14	14 - 16
Series 491 (6)	10 - 12	12 - 15
MESCHINI, G. (Italy)		
Citta A. Guarneri, Milan	35 - 40	40 - 50
MONESTIER (Italy)		
Series 36 (6)	12 - 15	15 - 18
NANNI (Italy)		
Series 205 (6)	15 - 18	18 - 22
Series 300 (6)	15 - 18	18 - 22
NASH, A.		
Heckscher		
703 "Love Me, Love My Dog"	10 - 12	12 - 14
PENNELL (U.S.A.)		
M. Munk, Vienna		
"My Companion"	8 - 10	10 - 12

PLANTIKOW	8 - 10	10 - 12
RALPH, LESTER (U.S.A.)		
Knapp Co.		
"Weathering it Together"	10 - 12	12 - 14
"Fellow Sports"	10 - 12	12 - 14
"A Stroll Together"	10 - 12	12 - 14
"Favored by Fortune"	10 - 12	12 - 14
RAPPINI (Italy)	8 - 10	10 - 12
SANTINO, M. (Italy)		
Series 6783 (6)	12 - 14	14 - 16
SCHUBERT (Austria)		
M. Munk, Vienna	6 - 8	8 - 10
SPOTTI, F.		
Uff. Rev. Stampa		
Series 158	8 - 10	10 - 12
TERZI, A. (Italy)		
Series 341, 349, 399 (6)	10 - 12	12 - 14
Series 457, 482, 973 (6)	12 - 13	13 - 16
Series 976, 559, 969 (6)	12 - 14	14 - 18
UNDERWOOD, CLARENCE (U.S.A.)		
M. Munk, Vienna		
"My Companion"	8 - 10	10 - 12
USABAL		
S.W.S.B.		

A. Busi, Degami 687
No Caption

Harrison Fisher, 30/25
"Winners"

Series 4689	8 - 9	9 - 10
Series 1336 (6)	8 - 10	10 - 12
P.F.B.		
Series 3968 (6)	12 - 14	14 - 16

LADIES AND HORSES

BARBER, COURT (U.S.A.)		
"Miss Knickerbocker"	8 - 10	10 - 12
"In Summer Days"	8 - 10	10 - 12
"Thoroughbreds"	10 - 12	12 - 14
2022 "Ready to Ride"	8 - 10	10 - 12
BARRIBAL, L. (GB)		
Artisque Series 2234 (6)	10 - 12	12 - 15
Artisque Series 2236 (6)	10 - 12	12 - 15
BERTIGLIA, AURELIO		
Series 227 (6)	10 - 12	12 - 14
Series 2132 (6)	12 - 14	14 - 16
Series 2151 (6)	10 - 12	12 - 14
BIANCHI (Italy)		
Series 2020 (6)	10 - 12	12 - 14
BORRMEISTER (Germany)	8 - 10	10 - 12
BOMPARD, SERGE (Italy)		
Series 343 (6)	12 - 15	15 - 18
Series 457 (6)	12 - 15	15 - 18
Series 641 (6)	12 - 14	14 - 16
Series 931 (6)	12 - 14	14 - 16
Series 556 (6)	10 - 12	12 - 14
BUSI, ADOLFO (Italy)		
C.E.I.C.		
Series 157 (6)	12 - 15	15 - 18
Degami		
Series 687 (6)	10 - 12	12 - 15
COLOMBO (Italy)		
Series 202 (6)	12 - 15	15 - 18
Series 488, 813 (6)	15 - 18	18 - 22
Series 1676, 1869 (6)	15 - 18	18 - 22
CORBELLA, T. (Italy)		
Series 117, 464 (6)	12 - 15	15 - 18
Series 237, 316, 330 (6)	14 - 17	17 - 20
Series 532 (6)	15 - 18	18 - 22
CYRANICUS (Italy)		
Series 150 (6)	10 - 12	12 - 14
Series 430 (6)	12 - 14	14 - 16
FISHER, HARRISON		
Reinthal & Newman		
108 "Dumb Luck"	15 - 18	18 - 22
304 "Thoroughbreds"	20 - 22	22 - 25
K.K. Oy "Thoroughbreds"	160 - 190	190 - 235
864 "Winners"	20 - 25	25 - 30
30/25 "Winners"	140 - 165	165 - 220

J.N. Loga, ANCZYC 84-2
No Caption

Simonetti, AMAG O34
No Caption

S & K Kouvola "Winners"	225 - 250	250 - 300
GUERZONI (Italy)		
B.K.W.I.		
Series 710 (6)	8 - 10	10 - 12
HORSFALL, MARY (GB)	10 - 12	12 - 14
KASKELINE, F.		
SWSB		
Series 1119	8 - 10	10 - 12
MAUZAN (Italy)		
Series 383 (6)	12 - 15	15 - 18
NANNI (Italy)		
Series 116, 257 (6)	12 - 15	15 - 18
Series 307 (6)	15 - 18	18 - 22
Series 374 (6)	14 - 16	16 - 18
OPLATEK	8 - 10	10 - 12
PENNELL (U.S.A.)	8 - 10	10 - 12
PERINI, T. (Italy)	8 - 10	10 - 12
PLANTIKOW	8 - 10	10 - 12
RAPPINI (Italy)		
Series 1002 (6)	10 - 12	12 - 15
Series 1092, 2019 (6)	9 - 11	11 - 13
SANTINO (Italy)		
Series 68 (6)	8 - 10	10 - 12

Court Barber
"Victress"

Harrison Fisher, R&N Series 108
"Dumb Luck"

SIMONETTI (Italy)		
Series 41 (6)	12 - 15	15 - 18
Series 90 (6)	10 - 12	12 - 15
STOLTE, F.		
Series 25 (6)	8 - 10	10 - 12
TERZI, A. (Italy)		
Uff. Rev. Stampa		
Series 320 (6)	10 - 12	12 - 16
USABAL, L.		
S.W.S.B.		
Series 257, 328, 345 (6)	8 - 10	10 - 12
Series 320 (6)	7 - 8	8 - 10
Series 1201 (6)	7 - 8	8 - 10
Series 4700 (6)	8 - 10	10 - 12
Series 1180, 1181 (6)	6 - 8	8 - 10
Erkal		
Series 307, 320, 335 (6)	10 - 12	12 - 14
WALLACE (U.S.A.)	8 - 10	10 - 12
WFA		
Series 204 (6)	6 - 8	8 - 10

ART DECO

The great new Art Deco movement began around 1910—just as the Art Nouveau era was ebbing—and continued through the "flapper era" and into the early 1930's. It brought the beautiful, strong, deep and vibrant colors of the new art. Due to the great influx of Art Deco postcards to the U.S., there has been a great demand for them in recent years as more and more American collectors discover their scintillating beauty.

Basically, for the postcard collector there are two types of Art Deco. The first, and most sought-after, were the earlier works of Brunelleschi, Chiostri, Montedoro, Bentivoglio, Meschini and Scattini, and a small number of the works of Adolfo Busi, Colombo and T. Corbella. Most of these artists did paintings of beautiful women in their mode of dress of the era, with vibrant and colorful geometrical design and beautiful scenic backgrounds.

The second type was predominantly of ladies in fashionable attire by Italian artists, starting around 1915 and continuing through the 1920's. This was a great era...they bobbed their hair, smoked cigarettes (with a holder), wore tight-fitting little hats and coats and flapper dresses... Wonderful!

The Italian artists were the most prolific painters of Art Deco. The cards were produced predominantly in sets of six depicting a particular theme. Beautiful ladies, smartly dressed and pictured with wild animals, sleek dogs or colorful horses, played a dominant role, while those engaged in tennis and golf and other sports were a close second. Busi, Corbella, Nanni, Mauzan and Colombo seem to generate the most interest for today's collector.

The principal publishers of the Italian artists were **Dell Anna & Gasparini, Milano; Ditta A. Guarneri, Milano; Uff. Rev. Stampa, Milano; Ballerini & Fratini, Florence; Degami, Majestic and "Ultra."**

Unfortunately, very few minor works by American artists, such as Chilton Longley, have become highly collectible. Additionally, many early linen cards were printed in the Art Deco vein. However, most all are unsigned. At the present time, Art Deco cards hold the distinction of being one of the most pursued artist-signed types in the postcard hobby.

ART DECO LADIES

	VG	EX
ANICHINI,EZIO (Italy)		
"Fairies" Series	20 - 25	25 - 30
Dancer Series	22 - 25	25 - 28
Silhouette Series 458	15 - 18	18 - 22
Series 435	15 - 18	18 - 22
Others	15 - 18	18 - 22
ANLURNY		
Series 2590	12 - 15	15 - 18
AZZONI, N. (Italy)		
Series 517 (6)	15 - 20	20 - 25
Others	12 - 15	15 - 18
BACHRICH, M.		
Ladies/Fashion	10 - 12	12 - 15
Ladies/Sports	12 - 15	15 - 18
Dance Series 102	12 - 15	15 - 18
BALLETTI, P. (Italy)		
Ladies/Fashion	12 - 15	15 - 18
BENTIVOGLIO		
Lady & Greyhound	35 - 40	40 - 45
Others	25 - 30	30 - 35
BERTIGLIA, AURELIO (Italy)		
Uff. Rev. Stampa and		

Bentivoglio
No Caption

Brunelleschi, "Femmes" Series
No Caption

Dell, Anna & Gasparini

Ladies/Heads	12 - 15	15 - 18
Ladies/Fashion	12 - 15	15 - 18
Ladies/Animals	15 - 18	18 - 22
Ladies/Tennis-Golf	15 - 18	18 - 22
Harlequins	15 - 18	18 - 22
Ladies/Harlequins	18 - 22	22 - 25
Ethnic/Blacks	8 - 22	22 - 25
Series 163 Big Hats	15 - 18	18 - 20
Series 241 Semi-Nudes	20 - 22	22 - 26
Series 224 Lovers Kissing	10 - 12	12 - 15
Series 2062 Couples	10 - 12	12 - 14

BETTINELLI, MARIO (Italy)

Series 884	10 - 12	12 - 14
Others	8 - 10	10 - 12

BIANCHI, ALBERTO (Italy)
Uff. Rev. Stampa and
P.A.R.

Series 2024, 2041 (6) Walking	10 - 12	12 - 14
Series 2154 (6) Hi Fashion	10 - 12	12 - 15
Ladies/Heads	10 - 12	12 - 15
Ladies/Fashion	10 - 12	12 - 15
Ladies/Animals	12 - 15	15 - 18
Ladies/Tennis-Golf	15 - 18	18 - 22

BIRI, M. (Italy)

S. Bompard, G.D.M. 542
No Caption

S. Bompard, G.D.M. 542
No Caption

Ladies/Harlequins	18 - 22	22 - 25
Others	12 - 15	15 - 18
BOMPARD, S. (Italy)		
Uff. Rev. Stampa &		
Dell, Anna & Gasparini		
Series 208, 431, 508, 931 (6) Fashion	10 - 12	12 - 14
Series 461 (6) Doing Nails, Fashion	10 - 12	12 - 14
Series 464, 467, 439 (6) Heads	10 - 12	12 - 15
Series 474 (6) Semi-Nudes	18 - 20	20 - 25
Series 534, 914, 955 476 (6) Heads	10 - 12	12 - 15
Series 407, 472, 496 (6) Hi Fashion	10 - 12	12 - 15
Series 506, 985 (6) Hi Fashion	10 - 12	12 - 15
Series 401, 449 (6) Hi Fashion	15 - 18	18 - 22
Series 971, 972, 987 (6) Hi Fashion	15 - 18	18 - 22
Series 321, 940, 951 (6) Hi Fashion	15 - 18	18 - 22
Series 907, 950, 956 (6) Fashion	15 - 18	18 - 22
Series 948 (6) Sitting, Fashion	15 - 18	18 - 20
Series 986 (6) With Doll	20 - 22	22 - 25
Series 456, 967, 987 (6) With Hats	15 - 18	18 - 22
Series 994 (6) Woman/child, Snowing	12 - 14	14 - 16
Series 458, 498 (6) Lovers-hugging	10 - 12	12 - 14
Series 498, 609 (6) Lovers, talk-hug	10 - 12	12 - 14
Series 448, 988 (6) Lovers/hug, flowers	12 - 14	14 - 16
Series 433 (6) Small Image-kissing	8 - 10	10 - 12
Series 462 (6) Taking his pulse	12 - 15	15 - 18

Series 960 (6) Fixing his tie	12 - 15	15 - 18
Golf/Tennis	15 - 20	20 - 22
Erotic/Semi-Nude	20 - 22	22 - 25
BONORA (Italy)		
Ladies	15 - 18	18 - 22
Harlequins	20 - 25	25 - 30
BOTTARO, E. (Italy)		
Series 135, Ladies 1900's	20 - 25	25 - 30
Series 123, Bathers 1900's	25 - 30	30 - 35
Others 1920's	12 - 15	15 - 18
BRUNELLESCHI, UMBERTO (Italy)		
"Femmes" Series (6)	150 - 175	175 - 200
Silhouettes	150 - 175	175 - 200
Advertising	50 - 60	60 - 75
BUHNE, BUNTE		
Deco Silhouette Ser. 225-228	12 - 15	15 - 18
BUSI, ADOLFO (Italy)		
Dell, Anna & Gasparini		
Series 112 (6) Diabolo	18 - 22	22 - 25
Series 100 (6) Fantasy	25 - 30	30 - 35
Series 153 (6) Pajamas	15 - 18	18 - 22
Series 126 (6) Girls/Fruit	15 - 18	18 - 22
Series 110, 193, 1020 (6) Fashion	18 - 20	20 - 22
Series 628 (6) Scarfs/Heads	20 - 22	22 - 25
Series 437 (6) "Gypsy" type	15 - 18	18 - 22

A. Busi, Degami
No Caption

A. Busi, Degami
No Caption

Series 558 (6) Couples on sled	15 - 20	20 - 22
Series 575 (6) Lovers in Moonlight	15 - 20	20 - 25
Series 615 (6) Couples/Autos	22 - 25	25 - 28
Series 651 (6) At the Beach	18 - 20	20 - 22
Series 3038, 3540, 3555 (6)	15 - 20	20 - 25
Golf/Tennis	20 - 22	22 - 25
Harlequins	15 - 18	18 - 22
CADORIN, G. (Italy)		
Ladies/Fashion	10 - 12	12 - 15
CASTELLI, V. (Italy)	10 - 12	12 - 15
CESARE (Italy)	10 - 12	12 - 14
CHERUBINI, M. (Italy)		
Uff. Rev Stampa		
Series 790 Deco National Ladies	15 - 18	18 - 22
Series 423, 977 (6) Off-shoulder Fash.	12 - 15	15 - 18
Series 997 (6) With Cupids	12 - 15	15 - 18
Series 408 (6) In Bubbles	10 - 12	12 - 15
Series 959 (6) Beauties	15 - 18	18 - 22
CHIOSTRI, CARLO (Italy) 1900's	12 - 15	15 - 20
CHIOSTRI, SOFIA (Italy)		
Ballerini & Fratini		
Most Series have 4 cards		
Comics, Flowers & Fruits in Deco style	12 - 15	15 - 18
Series 320 Lady/Wild Animal	35 - 45	45 - 55
Series 220 Santas	20 - 25	25 - 35

Cyranicus, Uff. Rev. Stampa
No Caption

Cyranicus, Uff. Rev. Stampa
No Caption

T. Corbella, Uff. Rev. Stampa 332-5
No Caption

T. Corbella, Uff. Rev. Stampa 233-6
No Caption

Black Robe Santa	25 - 30	30 - 40
Series 181 Bathers	25 - 30	30 - 40
Series 243 Witches	25 - 30	30 - 40
Series 316 W/Animals	25 - 28	28 - 32
Series 238 Mermaids	35 - 45	45 - 55
Series 317 Mermaids	35 - 40	40 - 50
Harlequins	25 - 30	30 - 35
Others, Colored Background	25 - 30	30 - 40
Others, Season Greetings	15 - 18	18 - 25
Signed FOFI	10 - 15	15 - 18
CLIRIO, L. (Italy)		
Series 29	15 - 18	18 - 22
COLIN, PAUL	15 - 20	20 - 25
COLOMBO, E. (Italy)		
Del, Anna & Gasparini;		
Uff. Rev. Stampa		
Series 416 (6) Couples, w/umbrella	10 - 12	12 - 15
Series 436, 451, 453 (6) Hats	15 - 18	18 - 22
Series 228, 445, 560 (6) Hi Fashion	20 - 22	22 - 25
Series 443, 522 (6) Hi Fashion	14 - 16	16 - 18
Series 360, 419, 981 Hi Fashion	18 - 22	22 - 25
Series 178, 539, 925 Hi Fashion	18 - 20	20 - 22
Series 948 (6) "Egyptian"	15 - 18	18 - 20
Series 459 (6) Heads	14 - 16	16 - 18

Chiostri, Ballerina & Fratini 320
No Caption

T. Corbella, Uff. Rev. Stampa 516-2
No Caption

Kathryn Elliott, G.O.M. 1986
No Caption

Chiostri, Ballerini & Fratini 209
No Caption

Series 478 (6) Dancers	18 - 20	20 - 22
Series 894, 936 (6)	12 - 15	15 - 18
Golf/Tennis	18 - 20	20 - 22
Harlequins	18 - 20	20 - 22
Colonial-style Deco Ladies, Lovers	12 - 15	15 - 18
CORBELLA, TITO (Italy)		
Dell, Anna & Gasparini;		
Uff. Rev. Stampa;		
Miss Edith Cavell Series	20 - 25	25 - 28
Series 127-M (6) Small Images	8 - 10	10 - 12
Series 162-M (6) Sm. Image, Lovers	6 - 8	8 - 10
Series 162, 355 (6)	14 - 16	16 - 20
Series 160, 203 (6) Hi Fashion	10 - 12	12 - 14
Series 408 (6) Fans	12 - 15	15 - 18
Series (6) Chair and Fans	16 - 18	18 - 22
Series 233, 356, 546, 718 (6) Heads	12 - 14	14 - 16
Series 130, 203, 763 (6) Hi Fashion	10 - 12	12 - 14
Series 282, 316, 317 (6) Fashion	12 - 14	14 - 18
Series 118, 324 (6) Hats	12 - 14	14 - 16
Series 357 (6) T. Bear-Cupids	14 - 16	16 - 20
Series 344, 467 (6) Hi Fashion	16 - 18	18 - 22
Series 236, 516 (6)	12 - 15	15 - 18
Series 162, 234, 269 (6) Lovers-kissing	8 - 10	10 - 12
Series 225, 367, 531 (6) Lovers-kissing	8 - 10	10 - 12
Degami		
Series 319 (6)	16 - 18	18 - 22

S. Bompard
Uff. Rev. Stampa 991-2

S. Bompard
Uff. Rev. Stampa 991-4

M. Dudovich, Ballerini & Fratini
Series 95, No Caption

M. Dudovich, Ballerini & Fratini
Series 95, No Caption

M. Dudovich, Ballerini & Fratini
Series 95, No Caption

M. Dudovich, Ballerini & Fratini
Series 95, No Caption

Chiostri, Dell Anna & Gasperini
No Caption

A. Busi, Degami 628
No Caption

Series 2249 (6) "Gypsy"	10 - 12	12 - 14
Series 2250 (6) In oval	8 - 10	10 - 12
Series 2072 (6) Outside	12 - 14	14 - 16
Series 2214, 2224, 2228 (6)	15 - 18	18 - 22
Series 3016, 3055 (6)	15 - 18	18 - 22
Series 617 (6) Lovers-kissing	8 - 10	10 - 12
Colonial-style Deco Ladies, Lovers	12 - 15	15 - 18
Golf/Tennis	18 - 20	20 - 22
Erotic/Semi-Nudes	18 - 22	22 - 24
COSTANZA, G. (Italy)		
Ladies	12 - 15	15 - 18
Comics/Erotic	12 - 15	15 - 18
CRAMER, RIE	10 - 12	12 - 15
CROTTA		
Uff. Rev. Stampa		
Series 3029 (6) Lovers Kissing	8 - 10	10 - 12
CYRANICUS		
Series 204 (6)	12 - 15	15 - 18
Ladies/Heads	12 - 15	15 - 18
Ladies/Fashion	12 - 15	15 - 18
Ladies/Animals	15 - 18	18 - 22
Ladies Golf/Tennis	15 - 18	18 - 22
DE MARZO	22 - 25	25 - 35
DERNINI, D. (Italy)		
Ladies	15 - 18	18 - 22

DERRANTI, D.
  "Elite" Series 2568   25 - 30   30 - 35
DOUKY (France)
  E.D.F., Paris
    Series 505 (6) Big Skirt   12 - 14   14 - 16
    Others   12 - 14   14 - 16
DUDOVICH, MARCELLO (Italy)
  Early Deco Series   50 - 60   60 - 75
  Lovers Series (in car; picnic)   30 - 35   35 - 40
  Others   30 - 35   35 - 40
DUNCAN, F.
  M. & B.
    Series 1415 (6) On Train-his Hat 10 - 12   12 - 14
ELLETTI
  "Celesque" Series National Ladies   15 - 20   20 - 25
ELLIOTT, KATHRYN (U.S.A.)
  G.O.M.
    Series 1986   10 - 12   12 - 15
FABIANO
  M.L.E., Paris
    Series 63 At the Beach   15 - 18   18 - 22
FAINI (Italy)   10 - 12   12 - 14
FRANZONI, ROBERTO (Italy)
  Uff. Rev. Stampa;
  Dell, Anna & Gasparini

Mauzan, Uff. Rev. Stampa 80-5
No Caption

T. Corbella, Uff. Rev. Stampa 162-5
No Caption

Montedoro, Early Period Art Deco

Series 44 (6) Heads	12 - 14	14 - 18
Series 78 (6) Hands/Head	12 - 15	15 - 18
Series 4358 (6) Fashion - Windy Day	15 - 18	18 - 20
Ladies/Fashion	12 - 15	15 - 18
Erotic/Semi-Nudes	18 - 20	20 - 22
Golf/Tennis	18 - 20	20 - 22

GILLEY
  Paris Gravure

Series 1961, 1971 Semi-nudes	12 - 14	14 - 16

GOBBI, D. (Italy)
  Majestic

Series 2546, Chinese Dragon	15 - 18	18 - 22
Ladies	22 - 25	25 - 28
Gondola/Lovers	18 - 20	20 - 25
Series 1216	12 - 15	15 - 18
Series 2474 Harlequins	18 - 22	22 - 26
Series 2477	15 - 18	18 - 22
Series 2479	12 - 15	15 - 18
Series 2494	15 - 18	18 - 22
Series 2530, 2556, 2560	20 - 25	25 - 28

  Elite

Series 2631	12 - 15	15 - 18
Series 2550	18 - 20	20 - 22
Series 2631	12 - 15	15 - 18

GRANDE

Mauzan, Uff. Rev. Stampa 45-5
No Caption

Nanni, Uff. Rev. Stampa 206-2
No Caption

A. Terzi
Dell Anna & Gasperini 399-5

L. Usabal
No Publisher

D.A.G.
  Series 409 (6) In oval-sitting   8 - 10   10 - 12
GRAF, MARTE or MG
  Deco Silhouettes Series 733-758   8 - 12   12 - 15
  Other Deco Silhouettes   10 - 12   12 - 15
GROSZE, MANNI See Silhouettes
  Deco Silhouettes
  Deco Series 2041 Nudes   15 - 18   18 - 22
  PFB (In Diamond)
    Series 2042, Nudes   15 - 18   18 - 22
    Series 3339, Nudes   18 - 20   20 - 22
    Series 2052, Dancing   12 - 15   15 - 18
  Others   12 - 15   15 - 18
GUARNIERI, E. (Italy)
  Ladies   15 - 18   18 - 22
GUERZONI, G. (Italy)
  Ladies/Heads/Fashion   7 - 9   9 - 12
  Ladies/Animals   8 - 10   10 - 15
  Erotic/Semi-Nudes   10 - 12   12 - 18
HARBOUR, JENNIE   12 - 15   15 - 18
HARDY (GB)
  Ladies   8 - 10   10 - 12
  Ladies/Animals   10 - 12   12 - 15
  Harlequins   12 - 14   14 - 18

Erotic/Semi-Nudes	15 - 18	18 - 22
ICART, LOUIS (France)		
Lady & Black Dog	40 - 50	50 - 60
Series 48		
"L'Eternal Feminin" (6)	100 - 110	110 - 125
Signed/HELLI	35 - 40	40 - 50
KASKELINE		
Deco Silhouette Ladies	12 - 15	15 - 18
KAVAL, M. (France)		
Lapina, Paris		
Series 5027, 5029, 5030 (6) Hats	12 - 14	14 - 16
Series 5031, 5032 (6) Hats	12 - 14	14 - 16
Series 5034, 5036 (6) Hats	12 - 14	14 - 16
KOEHLER, MELA (Austria)		
B.K.W.I. Series 620 (6)	35 - 40	40 - 45
Early Ladies	45 - 55	55 - 75
Ladies, after 1920	30 - 35	35 - 45
KOVIES, K.		
D.A.G.		
Series 474-1, 474-3, 474-4 (Skating)	12 - 15	15 - 18
KUANI, C. COLAN		
Ultra		
Series 2166 (6) Shoulders	10 - 12	12 - 14
KURT, E. MAISON		
Fantasy Dolls Series	15 - 18	18 - 22

Nanni, Uff. Rev. Stampa 258-2
No Caption

L. Usabal, SWSB 4711
"For Competition

A. Busi, Degami 2006
Unsigned

Bonora, Vista Rev. Stampa 1354
No Caption

Japanese Series	12 - 15	15 - 18
LARRONI		
S.W.S.B.		
Series 6733 (6) Lovers Kissing	8 - 10	10 - 12
LE DUCIS, A.		
Uff. Rev. Stampa		
Series 2039 (6) Hi Fashion	10 - 12	12 - 15
LENOLEM		
Meissner & Buch		
Series 219	18 - 20	20 - 25
LONGLEY, CHILTON (U.S.A.)		
A.G. & Co., Ltd.		
Series 422	18 - 22	22 - 26
Others	18 - 22	22 - 26
LUDSON		
Series 90 (6) Hats	10 - 12	12 - 14
MANNING, G.		
P.A.R.		
Series 144 (6) Coat-Hat	10 - 14	14 - 16
MG or MANNI GROSZE See Silhouettes		
MASTROIANNI, D. (Italy)		
Ladies	7 - 9	9 - 12
MAUZAN, L. (Italy)		
Uff. Rev. Stampa;		
Dell, Anna & Gasparini		

Series 386, 394 (6) Lovers-kissing	10 - 12	12 - 14
Series 462, 498 (6) Lovers-by the sea	10 - 12	12 - 14
Series 343, 424 (6) Couples	10 - 12	12 - 14
Series 248 (6) Roman "Lovers"	12 - 14	14 - 16
Series 42 (6) Sport	14 - 16	16 - 18
Series 301, 438 (6)	15 - 18	18 - 22
Series 279, 297 (6) Heads - Green tint	20 - 22	22 - 25
Series 145, 252 (6) Hat & Scarf	20 - 22	22 - 25
Series 46, 230 (6) Fashion	15 - 18	18 - 22
Series 83, 250, 174 (6) Walk, Traveling	20 - 22	22 - 25
Series 247, 298 (6) Beauties	20 - 22	22 - 25
Series 53 (6) Man sits on giant shoes	10 - 12	12 - 14
Series 43, 235 (6) Shoulders up	12 - 15	15 - 18
Series 321, 343, 414 (6) Fashion	15 - 18	18 - 20
Series 8, 14, 80 (6) Hi Fashion	15 - 18	18 - 22
Series 201, 202, 2050 (6) Walking	10 - 12	12 - 15
Series 126 (6) Waist-up, in Chair	18 - 20	22 - 25
Series 2, 10 (6) W/Cupid	12 - 15	15 - 18
Tennis/Golf	18 - 20	20 - 25
Erotic/Semi-Nudes	20 - 22	22 - 25
M.C.		
Beautiful Fashions	15 - 18	18 - 25
MELASSO		
Series 125 (6) Hats	12 - 15	15 - 18
MESCHINI, G. (Italy)		

Mela Koehler, BKWI
"Tennis Anyone"

Mela Koehler, BKWI
No Caption

G.T.M.
   Series 113 (4) High Fur Collars, Hats   30 - 35   35 - 40
Ditta A. Guarneri, Milano
   Ladies/Dogs Series   35 - 40   40 - 50
   Ladies   32 - 35   35 - 40
   Harlequins   30 - 35   35 - 40
   Lovers   30 - 32   32 - 36
METLIKOVITZ, LEOPOLDO or LM (Italy)
   Ladies/Fashion   10 - 12   12 - 14
   Bathing Beauties   10 - 12   12 - 15
   Couples   8 - 10   10 - 12
MIKKI (Finland)   8 - 10   10 - 12
MONESTIER (Italy)
  E.G. Falci
   Series 27 (6) Girl-mask, Harlequin   14 - 16   16 - 20
   Series 830 (6) Hats   14 - 16   16 - 20
   Others   8 - 10   10 - 12
MONTEDORO (Italy)
   Series A (6)   40 - 50   50 - 60
   Series B (6)   50 - 60   60 - 70
MUGGIANI (Italy)
   Ladies/Heads/Fashion   12 - 15   15 - 18
   Ladies/Animals   15 - 18   18 - 22
NANNI G. (Italy)
  Uff. Rev. Stampa &
  Dell, Anna & Gasparini
   Series 26-A, 597 (6) Couples Kissing   12 - 14   14 - 16
   Series 373 (6) Couples Kissing   14 - 16   16 - 18
   Series 225 (6) National Girls   15 - 18   18 - 22
   Series 529 (6) Pajamas, Smoking   15 - 18   18 - 22
   Series 206, 253, 256 (6) Hats   18 - 20   20 - 25
   Series 21, 304, 378 (6) Hats   18 - 20   20 - 25
   Series 162 (6) Hats and Ties   20 - 22   22 - 27
   Series 308, 376, 396 (6) Heads   14 - 16   16 - 18
   Series 283 (6) Fur Collar Hats   18 - 20   20 - 25
   Series 377, 521 Hats, Coats   14 - 16   16 - 18
   Series 337 (6) Playing Cards-Hats   18 - 20   22 - 25
   Series 372, 505 (6) Heads, Hi Fashion   12 - 14   14 - 16
   Series 480 (6) In Buggy   15 - 18   18 - 22
   Series 494 (6) W/Hat Boxes   20 - 22   22 - 25
   Series 445 (6) Lounging around   20 - 22   22 - 25
   Series 540 (6) Heads   22 - 25   25 - 28
  Couples   10 - 12   12 - 14
  Ladies/Animals   15 - 18   18 - 22
  Harlequins   18 - 22   22 - 25
  Soccer Series   18 - 22   22 - 25
  Erotic/Semi-Nudes   22 - 25   25 - 30
ORLANDI, V. (Italy)
  T.A.M.
   Series 7612 (6) Couples Hugging   8 - 10   10 - 12
PAGNOTTA (Italy)

Series 494 (6) Hi Fashion	8 - 10	10 - 12
PENTSY	8 - 10	10 - 12
PEPIN		
Delta, Paris		
Series 23 Hi Fashion	18 - 22	22 - 25
PINOCHI, E. (Italy)		
Series 206 (6) Hats	10 - 12	12 - 15
Series 172 (6) Lovers	10 - 12	12 - 15
Others	8 - 10	10 - 12
RAPPINI (Italy)		
Series 2016 (6) W/Hand Mirror	10 - 12	12 - 14
Ladies/Heads/Fashion	12 - 15	15 - 18
Ladies/Animals	15 - 18	18 - 22
Ladies/Sports	15 - 18	18 - 22
RICCO, LORIS (Italy)		
Ladies	18 - 22	22 - 26
Lovers	15 - 18	18 - 22
Harlequins	20 - 22	22 - 26
RODE, G.		
Uff. Rev. Stampa		
Series 6529 (6) On Chair	12 - 14	14 - 16
SALMONI, G. (Italy)	10 - 12	12 - 14
SALVADORI (Italy)		
Series 168 (6) "The Wolf" Fur	15 - 18	18 - 22
SANTINO, F. (Italy)		
Uff. Rev. Stampa		
Series 131 (6) Fashion Pose	12 - 15	15 - 18
SAN MARCO (Italy)		
P.A.R.		
Series 2037, 2082 Hats	12 - 15	15 - 20
Fantasy Series - Lady/Bubbles	15 - 18	18 - 25
Others	10 - 12	12 - 15
SCATTINI (Italy)		
Ladies	15 - 18	18 - 22
Harlequins	18 - 22	22 - 25
SCROCCHI (Italy)		
Series 4360 (6) Fashion	10 - 12	12 - 14
SENN		
Series 190	18 - 20	20 - 22
SIMONETTI, A. (Italy)		
Uff. Rev. Stampa		
Series 236 (6) Lovers Kissing	10 - 12	12 - 14
Others	12 - 14	14 - 16
SHAND, C.E.	20 - 25	25 - 30
TACCHI, E. (Italy)		
Series 494 (6) Hi Fashion	8 - 10	10 - 12
TERZI, A. (Italy)		
Uff. Rev. Stampa;		
Dell, Anna & Gasparini		
Series 287, 299 (6) Heads	10 - 12	12 - 15
Series 322 (6) Heads	15 - 18	18 - 22

Series 323 (6) Sitting	10 - 12	12 - 15
Series 486 (6) Fashion	10 - 12	12 - 15
Series 454 (6) Fashion	15 - 18	18 - 22
Series 482 (6) Small Images	8 - 10	10 - 12
Golf/Tennis	14 - 16	16 - 20
Couples	10 - 12	12 - 14
Ladies/Animals	12 - 14	14 - 18
TUHKA, A. (Finland)	10 - 12	12 - 14
USABAL, L.		
Erkal		
Series 324 (6) "Gypsy"	10 - 12	12 - 14
Series 363 (6) Butterfly Ladies	18 - 22	22 - 26
P.F.B. in Diamond		
Series 6073 (6) Beauties on Pillows	12 - 14	14 - 16
S.&G.S.i.B.		
Series 733 (6) Huge Flower Fantasy	14 - 16	16 - 20
S.W.S.B.		
Ser. 6378, 6379, 6381 (6) Dancing	10 - 12	12 - 15
Ser. 6382, 6384 (6) Dancing	10 - 12	12 - 15
Ser. 6387, 1071, 1091 (6) Dancing	10 - 12	12 - 15
Ser. 1058, 1330, 1333 (6) Dancing	10 - 12	12 - 15
Series 1207, 1208 (6) Dancing	12 - 14	14 - 16
Guner & Simon		
Series 2027 (6) Lovers Kissing	8 - 10	10 - 12
VASSALO, A. (Italy)	12 - 14	14 - 16
VENTURA, R.	10 - 12	12 - 15
VINCENT, R.	12 - 15	15 - 18
VINNOY		
Ladies	12 - 14	14 - 18
ZABCZINSKY		
C.B.B.		
Series 21-1 (6) Dancing	15 - 18	18 - 22
Series 21-2 (6) Standing	18 - 20	20 - 25
Series 21-3 (6) Dancing	15 - 18	18 - 22
Series 21-4 (6) Dancing	15 - 18	18 - 22
Series 21-5 (6) Dancing	15 - 18	18 - 22
Series 21-6 (6) Dancing	15 - 18	18 - 22
ZANDRINO, A. (Italy)		
Series 18 (6) Nude W/Wild Animals	20 - 25	25 - 30
Series 17 (6) Fans	12 - 15	15 - 17
Series 23, 24, 30 (6) Fashion	12 - 15	15 - 17
Series 94 (6) Hats	12 - 15	15 - 17
ZINI, M.		
Ladies	10 - 12	12 - 15

ART DECO CHILDREN

Many of the same Italian artists who painted the Art Deco Beautiful Ladies also did some great work illustrating children of the period. Although not as great as the ladies, they still have their niche with today's collectors of Art Deco. Bertiglia, Bompard, Busi, Chiostri, Mauzan, and, to a greater extent, Colombo, generated playful and colorful children that seem to come alive on cards that have survived.

Chloe Preston, Margaret Borris, Phyllis Cooper, and America's Margaret Ellen Price (MEP) were some of the non-Italian artists who contributed great work for those of us who love beautiful children. Additionally, some Art Deco children can be found on early American linen cards. Unfortunately, most all are unsigned.

ART DECO CHILDREN

AZZONI, N. (Italy)		
Dell Anna & Gasparini		
Series 517 (6)	12 - 14	14 - 16
BERTIGLIA (Italy)		
Series 155 & 1053 (6) Dutch Kids	8 - 10	10 - 12
Series 1010 (6) Playing War	12 - 14	14 - 18
Series 1069 (6)	7 - 8	8 - 10
Series 2034 (6) Kids in Big Cars	12 - 14	14 - 16
Series 2459 (6)	12 - 14	14 - 18
Series 2114 (6) W/Dolls	10 - 12	12 - 16
Series 2428 (6) Making Movies	12 - 15	15 - 18
Series 2444 (6)	8 - 10	10 - 12
Series 2461 (6)	10 - 12	12 - 15
BOMPARD, S. (Italy)		
Series 379 (6)	8 - 9	9 - 10
Series 454 (6)	8 - 9	9 - 10
Series 497 (6)	8 - 9	9 - 10
Series 523 (6)	8 - 10	10 - 12
Series 567 (6)	8 - 10	10 - 12
Series 906 (6)	8 - 10	10 - 12
Series 993 (6)	8 - 10	10 - 12
BONORA (Italy)		
Boy Scout Series 760	16 - 20	20 - 25
BORISS, M.		
Armag Co.		
"Occupation Series" (6)	6 - 8	8 - 10
BUSI, A. (Italy)		
Series 500 (6)	12 - 14	14 - 16
Boy Scout Series	16 - 20	20 - 25
CASTELLI, V. (Italy)		
Ultra		
Series 533 (6)	8 - 10	10 - 12
CENNI, E. (Italy)	5 - 6	6 - 7
CHIOSTRI, SOFIA (Italy)		

N. Azzoni
Dell Anna & Gasparini 517

Colombo, Ultra 2039
No Caption

Chloe Preston, Series E
"Puppchen"

Chloe Preston, Series E
"Kanone"

Ballerini & Fratini

Series 184 (6) Japanese	10 - 12	12 - 15
Series 188 (6)	10 - 12	12 - 15
Series 319	15 - 18	18 - 20

COLOMBO, E. (Italy)

Series 234 (6)	7 - 8	8 - 9
Series 454 (6)	8 - 9	9 - 10
Series 618 (6)	8 - 10	10 - 12
Series 665 (6) Child W/Dog	8 - 10	10 - 12
Series 960 (6)	8 - 10	10 - 12
Series 1764, 1905 (6)	8 - 10	10 - 12
Series 1964 (6)	8 - 10	10 - 12
Series 1968 (6)	10 - 12	12 - 14
Series 2007 (6)	6 - 8	8 - 10
Series 2033 (6)	8 - 10	10 - 12
Series 2044 (6)	8 - 10	10 - 12
Series 2140, 2141 (6)	6 - 8	8 - 10
Series 2181 (6)	8 - 10	10 - 12
Series 2223 (6)	10 - 12	12 - 14
Series 2252 (6)	6 - 8	8 - 10

G.M.D.

Series 1964 (6)	8 - 10	10 - 12

Ultra

Series 2039 (6)	8 - 10	10 - 12

COOPER, PHYLLIS (GB)

Raphael Tuck

Series 3463	8 - 10	10 - 12
CORBELLA, A.	8 - 10	10 - 12

GOLIA, E. (Italy)

Series 102 War-time Children	18 - 20	20 - 25
GRASSETTI (Italy)	6 - 8	8 - 10

GRILLI, S. (Italy)

GUASTA (Italy)	6 - 8	8 - 10
KOEHLER, MELA (Austria)	20 - 25	25 - 30

MAUZAN (Italy)

Series 45 W/dogs	10 - 12	12 - 15
NORFINI (Italy)	8 - 10	10 - 12
PIATTOLI, G. (Italy)	6 - 8	8 - 10
PINOCHI, E. (Italy)	6 - 8	8 - 10

PRESTON, CHLOE

B.R. Co.

Series E (Black background) (6)	12 - 15	15 - 18
PRICE, MARGARET EVANS (MEP) (U.S.A.)	8 - 10	10 - 12
ROWLES, L.	8 - 10	10 - 12
S.K.	8 - 10	10 - 12
SGRILLI (Italy)	8 - 10	10 - 12
ZANDRINO, ADELINA (Italy)	10 - 12	12 - 14

ART NOUVEAU

Art Nouveau postcards had their beginning at the turn of the century in Europe. Primarily, the movement began in Paris—where the great poster artists were congregated—and in Vienna. This new expression of decorative art was the rage of the era, and the poster and magazines such as *"Jugend," "Simplicissimus," "Le Rire," "La Plume,"* and *"The Poster,"* were used as a means to transmit this expression to the art lovers of the world.

The works of the great poster artists based in Paris, Alphonse Mucha (who was the most famous), Steinlen, Jules Cheret, Paul Berthon, Villon, Toulouse-Lautrec, Grasset, and many others, were also published in smaller format as beautiful and colorful postcards. Many were published in "The Collection of One Hundred" and "Salon of One Hundred" (Salon des Cent), all selected for their beauty and artistic greatness.

It was in Vienna, however, that the most beautiful and most artistic postcards were produced. Publishers, such as Philipp & Kramer and the Wiener Werkstaette, and artists of the "Secession" movement led by Koloman Moser, Karl Jozsa, and Oskar Kokoschka, produced thousands of beautiful cards that are treasured by collectors worldwide.

The values of some of these cards have reached unbelievable heights, as can be witnessed from auction reports throughout the world. As values of the more well-known artists, such as Mucha and Toulouse-Lautrec, spiral ever upward they also bring the values of the lesser publicized artist up with them.

Although cards of the Art Nouveau era are very costly and rare, many of these treasures can still be found in old albums and accumulations that have lain dormant for almost a century. Those who continue the quest may someday be rewarded.

	VG	EX
B.G.	40 - 45	45 - 50
ABIELLE, JACK	40 - 45	45 - 50
BASCH, ARPAD (Hungary)		
Series 769 (6)	175 - 185	185 - 200
Series 761 (6)	120 - 130	130 - 140
National Ladies (10)	120 - 130	130 - 140
"1900 Grand Femme" (6)	120 - 140	140 - 160
BRADLEY, W.H.	140 - 150	150 - 160
BRUNELLESCHI	70 - 80	80 - 100
CAUVY, L. (Denmark)	20 - 30	30 - 35
CHRISTIANSEN, HANS		
"Pari" Series, High Fashion Ladies	150 - 160	160 - 175

Karl Jozsa, A. Sockl Wien, Series 7, "Femme au Coeur"

Koloman Moser, Philipp & Kramer
Series 111/4

A. Mucha
"Cocorico"

"Twentieth Century Women"	140 - 150	150 - 160
Darmstadt Expo, 1902		
Lady vignettes (6)	140 - 150	150 - 165
COMBAZ, GISBERT (Belgium)		
Dietrich, Brussels		
"Elements" Series (12)	80 - 100	100 - 120
"Proverbs" Series (12)	80 - 100	100 - 120
"Sins" Series (12)	90 - 110	110 - 135
CRAFFONARA	40 - 50	50 - 60
DANIELL, EVA (GB)		
Raphael Tuck		
Unsigned		
"Art" Series 2524 (6)	150 - 160	160 - 175
"Art" Series 2525 (6)	125 - 130	130 - 140
DOCKER, F. (Austria)		
Raphael Neuber, Vienna		
Head Series 26	40 - 50	50 - 60
FRUNDT, H.	25 - 30	30 - 35
HAGER, NINI (Austria)	50 - 55	55 - 65
H.G.R.		
Series 316 (6)	25 - 30	30 - 35
HOCK, F.	30 - 35	35 - 40
HOFFMAN, J.	40 - 45	45 - 50
HOHENSTEIN, A. (Russia)		

Munier, "La Chic a Paree"

1901 Milano Int. Expo Series	25 - 30	30 - 35
JOZSA, KARL (Austria)		
A. Sockl, Wien		
"Femme au Coeur"	70 - 80	80 - 90
Others	50 - 60	60 - 70
KLAVITCH, RUDOLPH (Austria)	100 - 120	120 - 140
KEMPF, TH. (Austria)	20 - 25	25 - 30
KIENERK, G.		
"Cocorico"	150 - 160	160 - 175
KIEZKOW	70 - 75	75 - 80
KING, JESSIE M.	70 - 80	80 - 90
KIRCHNER, RAPHAEL		
H.M. & Co.		
"Angels" **Series 184**	80 - 90	90 - 100
M. Munk, Vienna		
"Continental" **Series 4003 (6)**		
"Sun Rays" or "Women in the Sun"	70 - 80	80 - 100
Series 1124 Japanese faces in flowers	70 - 80	80 - 90
"Geisha" **Series**	30 - 35	35 - 40
"Mikado" **Series**	30 - 35	35 - 40
"Les Cigarettes Du Monde" (6)	80 - 90	90 - 100
"La Favorite"	50 - 55	55 - 65
"Leda"	50 - 60	60 - 70
Pascalis Moss & Co.		
"Marionette" **Series 4140**	80 - 90	90 - 95
"Leda & the Swan" **(10)** (Uns.)	75 - 85	85 - 90
Raphael Tuck		
"Continental" **Series 4024 (6)**	125 - 150	150 - 175

KONOPA (Austria)	30 - 40	40 - 50
KOSA (Austria)	75 - 85	85 - 100
LAUDA, RICHARD (Denmark)	40 - 50	50 - 60
LIKARZ, MARIA (Austria)	150 - 160	160 - 175
LESSIEUX, LOUIS	40 - 50	50 - 60
MACDONALD, A.K.	40 - 50	50 - 60
MEUNIER, HENRI (Belgium)	200 - 225	225 - 250
"Four Seasons" (4)	60 - 70	70 - 80
"Inspiration"	100 - 110	110 - 120
"Zodiac"	60 - 70	70 - 80
MOSER, KOLOMAN		
Philipp & Kramer		
Series V	150 - 160	160 - 175
Philipp & Kramer		
Series 111	140 - 150	150 - 160
MUCHA, A. (Czechoslovakia)		
Waverley Cycles Adv. Card		
Sold for $13,500 in 1991		
Isaac H. Blanchard Co., N.Y.		
"Jeanne D'Arc" - with Maude Adams		
as Joan. Only 3 copies are known.		
It has been advertised at $15,000.		
Champenois, F., Paris		
Sarah Bernhardt Poster Cards	140 - 150	150 - 175
Months of the Year	150 - 160	160 - 170

Poster Card of Toulouse-Lautrec, "Moulin Rouge Bal la Goulue"

Four Seasons	225 - 250	250 - 275
Times of Day	175 - 185	185 - 200
"La Plume"	370 - 380	380 - 400
"La Fleur"	370 - 380	380 - 400
"L'Aurore"	370 - 380	380 - 400
"La Crepuscle"	370 - 380	380 - 400
"Primevere"	370 - 380	380 - 400
"Ages of Man"	250 - 260	260 - 275
"Cocorico" Girl with rooster	450 - 475	475 - 500
"Cocorico" With lilies	400 - 425	450 - 475
Souvenir "La Belle Jardiniere"	400 - 425	425 - 450
Series 502-505 Souv. "La Belle Jardiniere"	375 - 400	400 - 425
Czechoslovakian Designs	40 - 50	50 - 60
NOURY, GASTON (France)	40 - 50	50 - 60
PATELLA, B.	25 - 30	30 - 35
PELLON, A.		
"Ideal" Series (6)	80 - 90	90 - 100
RAUH, LUDWIG (Germany)	30 - 40	40 - 50
RYAN		
A 633 "Folly"	10 - 12	12 - 15
A 634 "Joy"	10 - 12	12 - 15
A 638 "So Lonesome"	10 - 12	12 - 15
A 677 "Dreaming of Days Gone By"	10 - 12	12 - 15
SCHIELE, EGON	80 - 90	90 - 100
SONREL, ELISABETH	200 - 225	225 - 250
STEINLEN, A.T. (Switzerland)		
Better Issues	200 - 210	210 - 225
Others	30 - 35	35 - 45
TOULOUSE-LAUTREC (France)		
"Cabaret Bruant"	360 - 400	400 - 450
"La Goulue au Moulin Rouge"	950 - 975	975 - 995

WIENER WERKSTAETTE

Author's note: I owe the following information and pricing of the beautiful and rare Wiener Werkstaette postcards to Mr. Detlef Hilmer of Munich, Germany. Mr. Hilmer, the leading authority and buyer/seller of WW cards, has the largest and finest postcard shop in Europe, and possibly the world. Beginning in 1983, I have spent at least two full days each spring and fall looking through his tremendous stocks of postcards of every type. The shop is located just outside the Munich railway station (*Haupt Bahnhof*) and is a treat for any traveling postcard enthusiast.

The postcards of the Wiener Werkstaette had their beginning in Vienna around 1908 during the "Secession-ist" art movement. The new art came about as around 50 artists began producing extremely beautiful works differing in style from those of their Art Nouveau predecessors. The WW series consisted of around 1000 different cards and production runs varied from a low of 200 to as many as 6000-7000 per card. Therefore, the number minted, plus the particular artist and the number that still exist influence the price structures.

All cards have the WW, WIENER WERKSTAETTE trademark in a box on top-left of the reverse side. Also, most all have the number of the card in the box, just below the trademark.

Some of the most affluent artists were Oscar Kokoshka, Egon Schiele, Rudolf Klavich, Moritz Jung, and Joseph Hoffmann. Others, such as Mela Koehler, Suzi Singer, and W. Hampel, are also well known for works by other publishers.

According to Mr. Hilmer, the cards sell in the following

Mela Koehler
473

Maria Likarz
557

ranges on top quality material. He also states that cards of less quality sell very well because collectors desire to obtain examples of the famed WW cards.

SCHIELE, EGON	$3000 - 4000
HOFFMANN, JOSEF	2000 - 3500
KLAVACH, RUDOLF So called Woodcuts	2000 - 3000
KOKOSHKA, OSCAR	1250 - 2000
JUNGNICKEL, L.	950 - 1250
JUNG, MORITZ	600 - 1250
KOEHLER, MELA	300 - 600
LIKARZ, MARIA	300 - 600
LOFFLER, BERTHOLD	300 - 600

MOTIFS

Architecture (Best selling at this time)	
SCHWETZ, KARL	200 - 300
Others	200 - 250
Christmas, New Year, Easter	300 - 950
Crazy Animals	300 - 400
Decorative	300 - 600
Jewish New Year Tapestry Greetings	30 - 90
Krampus	600 - 950

Moriz Jung
506

Karl Schwetz
211

Mela Koehler 482

Mode	300 - 600
Santas	600 - 950

Bold Colors and Heavy Colors sell best.
Crazy Motifs are more expensive.

Lowest-priced card is #12 @ $25-30.
Next is cards of **FRITZI LOW** @ $90.

Fritzi Low 808

5

BEAUTIFUL CHILDREN

	VG	EX
ALANEN, JOSEPH (Finland)		
Easter Witch Children	$ 8 - 10	$ 10 - 12
Miniature Easter Witch Children	15 - 18	18 - 20
ANDERSON, V.C. (U.S.A.)	5 - 6	6 - 7
ANTTILA, EVA (Finland)	6 - 8	8 - 10
ATWELL, MABEL LUCIE (GB)		
Early Period, Pre 1915	12 - 15	15 - 18
Middle Period, 1915-1930	10 - 12	12 - 15
1930's-1950 Period	6 - 8	8 - 10
Valentine & Sons		
Series 748 Golliwogs	18 - 20	20 - 25
Series A561 Golliwogs	15 - 18	18 - 22
Series A579 Golliwogs	18 - 20	20 - 25
Suffragette "Where's My Vote"	18 - 20	20 - 25
See Blacks		
AZZONI, N. (Italy) See Deco Children		
BARBER, C.W.		
Carlton Publishing Co.	6 - 8	8 - 10
BARHAM, S. (GB) See Fairies		
C.W. Faulkner		
Series 502	5 - 6	6 - 7
Series 701	5 - 6	6 - 7
Series 964	5 - 6	6 - 7
Series 1734		
"The Pied Piper of Hamelin"	10 - 12	12 - 14
BARROWS, ELIZABETH	5 - 6	6 - 7

Frances Brundage,
Postmarked 1900, Unsigned

Frances Brundage, R. Tuck 106
"Cupid's Sports"

BAUMGARTEN, FRITZ also FB		
Meissner & Buch	6 - 8	8 - 10
Other Publishers	6 - 8	8 - 10
BAYER, CHARLES A.	2 - 3	3 - 4
BEM (BOEHM) (Russia)		
Russian Alphabet Series	12 - 15	15 - 20
Russian Children	10 - 12	12 - 15
BERTIGLIA, A. (Italy) See Deco Children		
BIRCH, NORA	4 - 5	5 - 6
BLODGETT, BERTHA		
AMP Co.		
Series 209, Easter	6 - 7	7 - 8
Series 410, Christmas	6 - 7	7 - 8
Little Girls/Huge Hat Series	6 - 8	8 - 10
BOMPARD, S. (Italy) See Deco Children		
BORISS, MARGARET	6 - 8	8 - 10
BRETT, MOLLY See Fairies		
BRUNDAGE, FRANCES		
Sam Gabriel		
New Year		
Series 300, 302, 316 (10)	10 - 12	12 - 14
St. Patrick's Day		
Series 140 (10) (Unsigned)	8 - 10	10 - 12
Memorial Day		

Frances Brundage, Postmarked 1900, Unsigned

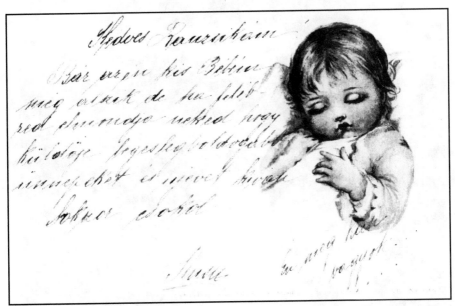

Frances Brundage, Theo Strofer 5475

Series 150   10 - 12   12 - 15
"In that instant o'er his..."
"Would I could duly praise..."
"Enough of Merit has each..."
"Brave minds, howe'er at war..."
"One Flag, one Land, one Heart..."
"By fairy hands their knell..."

Frances Brundage, Unsigned

Herzlichen Glückwunsch

zum neuen Jahre

Frances Brundage, Unsigned

Frances Brundage
Unsigned

Frances Brundage
Unsigned

Valentine's Day		
Series 413 (6)	8 - 10	10 - 12
Halloween		
Series 120, 121 (10)	15 - 18	18 - 22
Series 123 (10)	12 - 15	15 - 18
Series 125 (6)	15 - 18	18 - 20
Thanksgiving		
Series 130, 132, 133 (10)	8 - 10	10 - 12
Series 135 (6)	6 - 8	8 - 10
Christmas		
Series 200, 208, 219	10 - 12	12 - 15
Santas	15 - 18	18 - 22
Raphael Tuck		
New Year		
Series 601 (Unsigned)	8 - 10	10 - 12
Series 1036	10 - 12	12 - 15
Valentine's Day		
Series 11 (4) (Unsigned)	8 - 10	10 - 12
Series 20, 26 (Unsigned)	10 - 12	12 - 15
Series 100, 101 (6) (Unsigned)	10 - 12	12 - 14
Blacks	20 - 22	22 - 26
Series 102 (6)	12 - 15	15 - 18
Blacks	22 - 25	25 - 30
Series 115 (4)	8 - 10	10 - 12

Blacks	22 - 25	25 - 30
Series 118 (4)	10 - 12	12 - 14
Blacks	18 - 20	20 - 22
Easter		
Series 1049 (3)	8 - 10	10 - 12
Memorial Day		
Series 173 (12) (Unsigned)	8 - 10	10 - 12
Halloween		
Series 174 (12) (Unsigned)	12 - 14	14 - 16
Christmas		
Series 4 (12)	12 - 15	15 - 20
Series 165 (2)	10 - 12	12 - 15
Blacks	18 - 20	20 - 25
Series 1035 (2)	10 - 12	12 - 15
Series 2723 "Colored Folks" (6)	50 - 60	60 - 70
Series 4096 "Funny Folks" Blacks (4)	25 - 30	30 - 35

See Blacks
Early Foreign Publishers
Carl Hirsch, W.H.B., Theo Stroefer
(T.S.N.), Wezel & Naumann,
C. Baum, & Anon.

Large Images	25 - 30	30 - 40
Small Images	20 - 25	25 - 30
BURD, C.M. (U.S.A.)		
Rally Day Series	6 - 8	8 - 10

Frances Brundage,
Unsigned

Frances Brundage
Postmarked 1901, Unsigned

Frances Brundage, Wezel & Naumann 41-3
Unsigned

Birthday Series	6 - 8	8 - 10
BUSI, A. See Art Deco Children		
CARR, GENE		
Rotograph Co.		
Series 219 4th of July	8 - 10	10 - 12
C.B.T.	2 - 3	3 - 4
CASTELLI, V. See Art Deco Children		
CENNI, E.	5 - 6	6 - 7
CHAMBERLIN (U.S.A.)		
Campbell		
310 "Suffrage First"	60 - 70	70 - 80
312 "Let's Pull..." Suffrage	60 - 70	70 - 80
CHIOSTRI, S. (Italy) See A. Deco Children		
CLAPSADDLE, ELLEN H. (U.S.A.)		

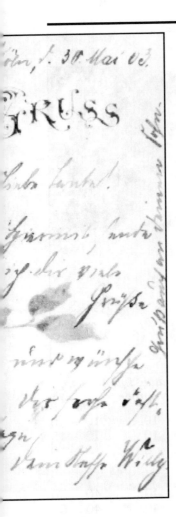

Frances Brundage, Wezel & Naumann
Unsigned

International Art Publishing Co.

Angels, Cherubs	4 - 6	6 - 8
Animals	4 - 5	5 - 6
Young Ladies, Women	5 - 6	6 - 8
Bells, Florals	2 - 3	3 - 4
Good Luck, Thanksgiving	2 - 3	3 - 4
Thanksgiving Children	5 - 6	6 - 9
Indians	6 - 7	7 - 10
Transportation	2 - 3	3 - 5
Christmas Children	7 - 9	9 - 12
Santas	10 - 12	12 - 18
Birthday Children	6 - 8	8 - 10
Easter Children	7 - 9	9 - 12
Valentine Greetings	5 - 6	6 - 7
Valentine Children		

Ellen Clapsaddle, Wolfe & Co.
"Love me, Love my Vote"

Ellen Clapsaddle, Int. Art Co.
No Number

Series 941, 942, 944	8 - 10	10 - 15
Series 952, 953	8 - 10	10 - 15
Series 1034, 1081 (Uns.)	6 - 8	8 - 10
Valentine Mechanicals		
Series 16190 (4)		
"To My Valentine"	35 - 40	40 - 50
"St. Valentine's Greeting"	35 - 40	40 - 50
"To My Sweetheart"	35 - 40	40 - 50
"Love's Fond Greeting"	35 - 40	40 - 50
Series 51810	20 - 25	25 - 30
Memorial Day		
Series 973, 2444, 4397 (6)	8 - 9	9 - 12
Series 2935 (6)	10 - 12	12 - 14
Washington's Birthday		
Series 16208, 16209 (4)	5 - 8	8 - 10
Series 16250 (6)	5 - 8	8 - 10
Series 51896 (6)	5 - 8	8 - 10
St. Patrick's Days	6 - 9	9 - 12
Independence Day		
Series 2443, 4398	8 - 12	12 - 14
Halloween		
Series 978 (6)	12 - 14	14 - 16
Series 1393	12 - 14	14 - 16
Series 1667	15 - 18	18 - 20
Others	12 - 14	14 - 16

Halloween Mechanicals
  Series 1236

"A Jolly Halloween" Black Child	175 - 200	200 - 225
"A Merry Halloween"	70 - 80	80 - 100
"A Thrilling Halloween"	70 - 80	80 - 100
"The Highest Expectations for H'ween"	70 - 80	80 - 100

Wolfe & Co.
Add $2-4 to Int. Art Pub. prices.
Add $8-10 to Halloween prices.
Suffragettes

"Love Me, Love My Vote"	60 - 70	70 - 80
"Women's Sphere is in the Home"	80 - 90	90 - 100

Foreign Publishers
Add $3-5 to above prices.

CLARK, A. (U.S.A.)	5 - 6	6 - 7
CLOKE, RENE (GB) See Fairies		
C.W. Faulkner Series (1930's)	8 - 10	10 - 12
Valentine's Series (1930's - 40's)	6 - 8	8 - 10
Salmon Bros. Series (1930's - 40's)	6 - 7	7 - 8
1950's Series	3 - 4	4 - 5
Medici Society Series (1950's - 60's)	1 - 2	2 - 3
COLBY, V.	2 - 3	3 - 4
CORBETT, BERTHA (U.S.A.)		
J.I. Austin		
Sunbonnet Children	8 - 10	10 - 15

Ellen Clapsaddle, Garre 1081
Unsigned

Ellen Clapsaddle, Garre 1034
Unsigned

CORY, F.Y.	2 - 3	3 - 4
CURTIS, E. (U.S.A.)		
Raphael Tuck		
Garden Patch 2	8 - 10	10 - 12
"Apple"		
"Beet"		
"Cantelope"		
"Carrot"		
"Peach"		
"Radish"		
"Red Pepper"		
"Watermelon"		
Raphael Tuck		
"**Valentine Maids**" **Series D12**		
PC 1 "School Slates" (12)	6 - 7	7 - 8
PC 3 "Love's Labors" (12)	6 - 7	7 - 8
PC 4 "From Many Lands" (12)	6 - 7	7 - 8
CZEGKA, B. (Polish)		
W.R.B. & Co.		
Series 22 (6)	8 - 10	10 - 12
DeGARMES	1 - 2	2 - 3
DEWEES, ETHEL (E.D.) (EHD) (U.S.A.)		
AMP Co.	6 - 8	8 - 9
Ernest Nister Series 2543	8 - 10	10 - 12

Ellen Clapsaddle, Int. Art Co. 2936
"Liberty and Union..."

Ellen Clapsaddle, Int. Art Co. 4398
"Days of Flags and Cannon..."

Frances Brundage
Unsigned, Anonymous

Frances Brundage
Unsigned, Anonymous

DEXTER, MARJORIE	4 - 5	5 - 6
DIXON, DOROTHY (U.S.A.)		
Ullman Mfg. Co.		
Sunbonnet Babies	8 - 10	10 - 12
DRAYTON, GRACE (WIEDERSEIM) (U.S.A.)		
Reinthal & Newman		
306 "A Button Sewed on..."	20 - 25	25 - 28
488 "Lambey Dear"	15 - 20	20 - 25
489 "Oh Dear Me"	15 - 20	20 - 25
492 "Gee up Dobbin" (unsigned)	15 - 20	20 - 25
493 Skipping Rope	15 - 20	20 - 25
495 Teacher & Children	15 - 20	20 - 25
496 "Do you, or don't you?"	15 - 20	20 - 25
497 "I Should Worry"	15 - 20	20 - 25
500 "More of All"	20 - 25	25 - 28
502 "Love at first sight"	20 - 25	25 - 30
503 "The Trousseau"	20 - 25	25 - 30
504 "The Wedding"	20 - 25	25 - 30
505 "The Honeymoon"	20 - 25	25 - 30
506	20 - 25	25 - 30
507 "Their New Love"	20 - 25	25 - 30
Raphael Tuck		
Series 223 (6) (Unsigned)		
Series 241 "Bright Eyes" (6) (Uns.)	20 - 25	25 - 30

"I'se Awful Sweet..."	20 - 25	25 - 30
"I'm Your Little Darling Boy..."	20 - 25	25 - 30
"The Boys About Me Rant..."	20 - 25	25 - 30
Others	20 - 25	25 - 30
Series 242 (6) (Unsigned)	15 - 20	20 - 25
Series 243 (6) "Love Message" (Uns.)	20 - 25	25 - 30
Series 1002 (6) "Happy Easter" (Uns.)	20 - 25	25 - 28
See Blacks		
Davis Co.		
34 Baby Girl in Sled	25 - 30	30 - 35
B.B. London (6) (Unsigned)	25 - 30	30 - 35
DULK, M.		
Gibson Art		
Series 252		
Fantasy Flower Girls, Birthday	10 - 12	12 - 16
"Daffodil"		
"Forget me Not"		
"Pansy"		
"Poppy"		
"Pussy Willow"		
"Red Rose"		
"Rose"		
"Sweet Pea"		
"Tulip"		
"Violet"		

Pauli Ebner, P/P.P.
Signed P.E.

Pauli Ebner, M. Munk 1129
Happy Birthday

Pauli Ebner, M. Munk 704
No Caption

Pauli Ebner, A.R. 1375

Pauli Ebner, A.R. 1453
Happy Easter

Pauli Ebner, A.R. 1453
Happy Easter

Valentine Series - Girls (6)	8 - 10	10 - 12
EBNER, PAULI (Austria)		
Early - Signed PE	15 - 18	18 - 22
Santas	18 - 22	22 - 25
M. Munk, Vienna		
Series 878 Toys	15 - 17	17 - 20
Series 1126 Victorian Children	10 - 12	12 - 14
Series 1129 Birthday	10 - 12	12 - 15
Series 403, 986, 1019 New Year	12 - 15	15 - 18
Series 550, 1136, 1269 New Year	15 - 17	17 - 20
Series 1044 Winter	12 - 14	14 - 16
Series 1158, 1263	12 - 14	14 - 16
Series 1106 Christmas	12 - 14	14 - 16
August Rokol, Vienna or AR		
Series 1428 Birthday	12 - 14	14 - 18
Series 1375, 1440 Toys	15 - 17	17 - 20
Series 2486, 1453 Easter	12 - 14	14 - 18
Series 1321	12 - 14	14 - 16
"Puppet Marriage Series"	18 - 22	22 - 26
E.F.D. or ELLEN F. DREW		
M.A.P. Co.	3 - 4	4 - 6
Ernest Nister	5 - 6	6 - 8
EGERTON, LINDA	6 - 8	8 - 10
ELLAM, WILLIAM (GB)	5 - 6	6 - 8

W. Fialkowski, AVM 1355
German Caption

HBG, L&E 2217
"To My Valentine"

HBG, L&E No Number, Thanksgiving Blessings

ELLIOTT, KATHRYN (U.S.A.)	4 - 5	5 - 6
Gibson Art Co.		
Halloween Series (10)	6 - 8	8 - 10
F.B. (not Brundage)	5 - 6	6 - 8
F.S.M.		
Heininger		
"Courtship & Marriage Series"	8 - 10	10 - 12
FEDERLEY, ALEXANDER (Finland)	5 - 6	6 - 8
FEIERTAG, K. (Austria)		
B.K.W.I.	5 - 6	6 - 8
FIALKOWSKI, WALLY (Germany)		
Large Comical Children	10 - 12	12 - 14
Small Children & Babies	6 - 8	8 - 10
Black Children	12 - 15	15 - 18
FLOWERS, CHARLES (U.S.A.)	5 - 6	6 - 7
FRANK, E.	5 - 6	6 - 7
GASSAWAY, KATHERINE (U.S.A.)		
Raphael Tuck		
Series 113, Bridal, Valentines (6)	6 - 8	8 - 10
Series 130 Easter Series (12)	6 - 7	7 - 8
Series 22495 "The New Baby" (6)	6 - 8	8 - 10
Rotograph Co.		
"Age" Series	6 - 8	8 - 10
117 "1 Year"		
118 "2 Years"		
119 "3 Years"		
120 "4 Years"		
121 "5 Years"		

"National Girls"

220 "America"	8 - 10	10 - 12
221 "Ireland"	7 - 8	8 - 10
222 "England"	7 - 8	8 - 10
223 "Germany"	7 - 8	8 - 10
224 "France"	7 - 8	8 - 10
225	7 - 8	8 - 10
226 "Italy"	7 - 8	8 - 10
227 "Sweden"	7 - 8	8 - 10
"American Kid" Series (6)	5 - 6	6 - 8
Black Children	8 - 10	10 - 15
Others	5 - 6	6 - 8
GEORGE, MARY ELEANOR		
Ernest Nister	15 - 18	18 - 22
GILSON, T. (U.S.A.)	4 - 5	5 - 6
Black Children Comics	8 - 10	10 - 15
GOLAY, MARY	3 - 4	4 - 5
GOODMAN, MAUDE		
Raphael Tuck		
Series 824-833	8 - 10	10 - 12
GOVEY, A. (GB)		
Humphrey Milford, London		
"Dreams and Fairies" Golliwogs	12 - 14	14 - 18
GREENAWAY, KATE and KG (GB)		

Kate Greenaway was one of the first well-known illustrators of children. Her earliest works were of Valentines, Birthday, and Christmas non-postcards. Later came her

Kate Greenaway, O.G. 1780, Unsigned

Kate Greenaway, Unsigned

famous children's books and almanacs. She did many fine illustrations that were used in the *"Mother Goose"* and *"Old Nursery Rhymes"* books printed by Rutledge and Sons.

Postcards were produced in very limited quantities from these early illustrations. They are indeed rarities, and are very hard to find in any condition. Kate died in 1901 before the great postcard era of 1905-1918 began. Her works that were adapted for postcards are signed "KG" and have undivided backs. They depict her well-known children types and each has a verse from the *"Mother Goose"* book which she illustrated. Various unsigned works have been found through the years that have been attributed to her.

KATE GREENAWAY
Multilingual backs, with verse	60 - 75	75 - 90
Without verse (Uns.)	30 - 40	40 - 50
From *Mother Goose*		
and *Old Nursery Rhymes* (B&W) *	60 - 75	75 - 95

    Signed KG, W/Verse
    "A diller, a dollar..."
    "As Tommy Snooks, and Bessie Brooks..."
    "Billie Boy Blue..."
    "Cross Patch, lift the latch..."
    "Elsie Marley has grown so fine..."

"Girls and boys come out to play..."
"Goosey, goosey, gander..."
"Hark!, Hark!, the dogs bark..."
"Here am I, little jumping Joan..."
"Humpty Dumpty sat on a wall..."
"Jack and Jill Went up the hill..."
"Johnny shall have a new bonnet...
"Little Betty Blue, lost her..."
"Little Jack Horner sat in the corner..."
"Little lad, little lad..."
"Mary, Mary, quite contrary..."
"Polly put the kettle on..."
"Ride a cock-horse, To Banbury-cross..."
"Ring-a-ring-a-roses..."
"Rock-a-bye baby..."
"There was an old woman..."
"Tom, Tom, the pipers son..."
Listing is incomplete
* From article by Don and Judy McNichol
in "What Cheer News," R.Island P.C. Club

GREINER, MAGNUS (U.S.A.)
 International Art Pub. Co.

Dutch Children Series 491 (6)	6 - 7	7 - 8
Dutch Children Series 692	6 - 7	7 - 8
"Molly & the Bear" Series 791	10 - 12	12 - 14

Maud Humphrey, Anonymous
(Her only signed card.)

John McCutcheon
"A Boy in Wintertime"

Rose O'Neill
"Votes for Our Mothers"

S.B. Pearse, M. Munk 728
Unsigned

See Blacks

GRIGGS, H.B. also H.B.G.

L & E (Leubrie & Elkus)

Christmas

Series 2224, 2264, 2275	6 - 8	8 - 10

New Years

Series 2225, 2266, 2276	6 - 8	8 - 10

Easter

Series 2226, 2254, 2271	6 - 8	8 - 10

Valentine's Day

Series 2218, 2243, 2244, 2267	8 - 10	10 - 12
Series 2217, 2219, 2248	10 - 12	12 - 14
Blacks	15 - 18	18 - 20

St. Patrick's Day

Series 2230, 2232, 2253, 2269	8 - 10	10 - 12

Thanksgiving

Series 2212, 2213, 2233, 2263, 2273	6 - 8	8 - 10

George Washington's Birthday

Series 2268	8 - 10	10 - 12

Halloween

Series 2214, 2216, 2262	10 - 12	12 - 14
Series 2263, 2272	12 - 14	14 - 16
Series 2231, 7010	15 - 16	16 - 18

Birthday

Series 2232	6 - 8	8 - 10

Anon. Publisher Series		
Series 2215, 7010	12 - 14	14 - 16
GRIMBALL, META		
Gutmann & Gutmann	12 - 15	15 - 20
Reinthal & Newman	12 - 15	15 - 18
FOREIGN ISSUES		
Novitas		
Series 20607		
1 "He Won't Bite" W/German caption	22 - 25	25 - 30
Series 10726		
"Puppen Mutterchen's Einkauf"	22 - 25	25 - 30
"Storenfried"	22 - 25	25 - 30
Series 10930		
"Say Das Nicht Noch Mal!"	22 - 25	25 - 30
"Kinderdieb"	22 - 25	25 - 30
GROSS, O.	2 - 3	3 - 4
GUARINO, ANTHONY	3 - 4	4 - 5
GUTMANN, BESSIE PEASE (U.S.A.)		
Also BESSIE COLLINS PEASE		
Gutmann & Gutmann		
No Number "Sweet Sixteen"	18 - 22	22 - 26
501 "Senorita"	18 - 20	20 - 22
502 "Waiting"	18 - 22	22 - 26
505 "I Wish You Were Here"	18 - 22	22 - 26
803 "Alice"	20 - 25	25 - 30
1201 "Seeing"	30 - 35	35 - 40
1202 "Smelling"	30 - 35	35 - 40

Rose O'Neill, Gibson Art Co., Unsigned Kewpie

Ethel Parkinson, M. Munk 531, No Caption

S.B. Pearse, M. Munk 728
Unsigned

S.B. Pearse, M. Munk 563
Unsigned

1203 "Hearing"	30 - 35	35 - 40
1204 "Feeling"	30 - 35	35 - 40
Novitas		
10726 "Naschkatzchen"	40 - 45	45 - 50
10930 "Zwietracht"	40 - 45	45 - 50
10966 "Delighted"	35 - 40	40 - 45
15727 "Rosebuds"	35 - 40	40 - 45
20608 "My Bruzzier had a fever..."	35 - 40	40 - 45
Series 20360 "The Bride"	35 - 40	40 - 45
"The Debutante"	35 - 40	40 - 45
"The Baby"	35 - 40	40 - 45
"Off to School"	35 - 40	40 - 45
"The Mother"	35 - 40	40 - 45
Series 20361 "Sunshine"	35 - 40	40 - 45
20556 Images in Water	40 - 45	45 - 50
20558 Mother on Knees Kisses Boy	35 - 40	40 - 45
20607-4 "The First Lesson"	35 - 40	40 - 45
20607-6 "The New Love"	35 - 40	40 - 45
20608 "Music Hath Charm"	35 - 40	40 - 45
"All is Vanity"	35 - 40	40 - 45
"Feeling"	35 - 40	40 - 45
"Delighted"	20 - 25	25 - 30
"The Foster Mother"	35 - 40	40 - 45
"Guess Who?" (Uns.)	20 - 25	25 - 30
"Love is Blind"	35 - 40	40 - 45

"Margaret"	35 - 40	40 - 45
"Stolen Sweets" (Uns.)	20 - 25	25 - 30
"Strenuous"	20 - 25	25 - 30
Russian		
155 With many dolls (Unsigned)	40 - 50	50 - 60
Others	35 - 40	40 - 45
HALLOCK, RUTH	5 - 6	6 - 8
HARDY, FLORENCE (GB)		
C.W. Faulkner & Co.	8 - 9	9 - 10
Dancing Series 914 (6)	12 - 14	14 - 16
M. Munk, Vienna		
Series 352 (6)	8 - 10	10 - 12
Others	6 - 8	8 - 10
HAYS, MARGARET G. (U.S.A.)		
Ernest Nister		
Series 2749 Big Eyes	25 - 30	30 - 35
Series 2751 "Miss Polly Pigtails"	25 - 30	30 - 35
2748 Dressed in Pink		
2749 Dressed in Green		
2750 Dressed in Purple		
2751 Dressed in Red		
2752 Dressed in Yellow		
2753 Dressed in Blue		
Series 3059 Valentine Children	15 - 17	17 - 20

Margaret E. Price, Stecher 1403-F
"Valentine Greetings"

R.R., M. Munk 1030
The Nurse

Series 3061 (6) Large Images	15 - 17	17 - 20
The Rose Co.		
Christmas Series (6)	15 - 17	17 - 20
Anonymous		
Paper Doll Series 3 (6)	65 - 75	75 - 90
Paper Doll Series 6 (6)	65 - 75	75 - 90
HEINMULLER, A.		
International Art Pub. Co.		
Series 1002 Halloween (6)	8 - 10	10 - 12
Series 1003 St. Patrick's Day (6)	4 - 6	6 - 7
Series 1004 Thanksgiving (6)	4 - 5	5 - 6
Series 1620 Valentine's Day (6)	5 - 6	6 - 7
HUMMEL		
Earlier Period	12 - 15	15 - 18
Late Period	5 - 6	6 - 7
HUMPHREY, MAUD		
V.O. Hammon Pub. Co.		
579 "Washington's Courtship"	60 - 70	70 - 90
Others	60 - 70	70 - 90
Gray Lithograph Co. (Unsigned)		
43, 44, 45, 46, 47, 48, 49, 50	12 - 15	15 - 20
Rotograph		
Series F457	12 - 15	15 - 20
HUMPHREYS, L.G.	2 - 3	3 - 4
HUTAF, AUGUST (U.S.A.)		
Ullman Mfg. Co.		
"A Little Odd Fellow"	6 - 8	8 - 10
"A Little Shriner"	6 - 8	8 - 10
Others	6 - 8	8 - 10
Other Publishers	4 - 6	6 - 8
I.M.J.		
M. Munk		
Children Series	6 - 7	7 - 8
JOHNSON, J.	5 - 6	6 - 7
K.V.		
LP Co.		
Kewpie-like Children	8 - 10	10 - 12
Black Children, or mixed	10 - 12	12 - 16
KASKELINE, F.		
Silhouette Series 9033 (6)	6 - 8	8 - 9
Others	6 - 7	7 - 8
KEMBLE, E.B. See Blacks		
Comic Children	3 - 4	4 - 5
KER, MARY SIGSBEE	4 - 5	5 - 6
KIRK, M.L.		
National Art Co.		
Birthday Signs (7)	8 - 10	10 - 12
KNOEFEL		
Illuminated Appearance		
Novitas		
Series 664 (6)	6 - 8	8 - 12

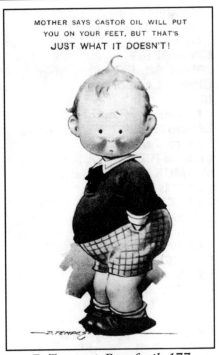

M. Sowerby, R&N 2001
"Phyllis"

D. Tempest, Bamforth 177
"Mother Says..."

Series 656 With phones (6)	10 - 12	12 - 14
Series 15834, 20887 (Mother-Child)	8 - 10	10 - 12

KOEHLER, MELA   See Art Deco Children
LeMAIR, H. WILLEBEEK (GB)
  Augener, Ltd.

Children's "Pieces of Schumann"	12 - 15	15 - 18

  "Catch Me if You Can"
  "Dreaming"
  "First Loss"
  "Melody"
  "The Merry Pheasant"
  "Perfect Happiness"
  "The Poor Orphan"
  "Romance"
  "Roundelay"
  "Sicilienne"
  "Soldier's March"
  "Vintage"

"The Children's Corner" (12)	6 - 7	7 - 8
"Little Songs of Long Ago" (12)	10 - 12	12 - 15

  See Nursery Rhymes
LEVI, C.
  Suffragette

Series 210, 3308 "Komical Koons"	20 - 22	22 - 25

LEWIN, F.G.

Bamforth Co.		
"Black Kids" Comics	10 - 12	12 - 15
Others	6 - 8	8 - 10
LINDEBERG		
Head Studies	6 - 8	8 - 10
KINSELLA, E.P.	6 - 8	8 - 10
LD		
Meissner & Buch	6 - 8	8 - 9
LANDSTROM, B. (Finland)		
Fairy Tales	6 - 8	8 - 10
LEE, ALICE (U.S.A.)	2 - 3	3 - 4
MAILICK, R. (Germany)		
Angels, Children	8 - 10	10 - 15
MALLET, BEATRICE (GB)		
Raphael Tuck		
"Cute Kiddies" Oilette Series		
3567, 3568,3628, 3629 (6)	8 - 9	9 - 10
MARCELLUS, IRENE		
E. Nister		
Child's head in pie, mittens, etc.	14 - 15	15 - 18
MARSH, H.G.C. (GB)		
BD		
Child and Teddy Bear	10 - 12	12 - 15
"Wee Willie Winkle"	8 - 10	10 - 12
"Curly Locks"	7 - 8	8 - 10

D. Tempest, Bamforth 142
"Luck What's Here"

Grace Wiederseim
Campbell Soup Co.

McCUTCHEON, JOHN T. (U.S.A.)	4 - 6	6 - 8
M.E.P. see MARGARET EVANS PRICE, MP		
M.D.S. (U.S.A.)		
Black Children (See Blacks)		
Others	6 - 7	7 - 8
M.M.S.		
G.K. Prince		
Series 421	5 - 6	6 - 8
MITCHELL, SADIE	4 - 5	5 - 6
NASH, A. (U.S.A.)		
Heckscher		
Series 704	6 - 8	8 - 10
NOSWORTHY, FLORENCE (GB)	6 - 8	8 - 10
NUMBER, JACK		
PFB (in Diamond) German captions		
Series 2068 (4)	8 - 10	10 - 12
Series 2070 (4)	8 - 10	10 - 12
Series 2076 (4)	8 - 10	10 - 12
NYSTROM, JENNY (Sweden)	10 - 12	12 - 16
See Fairy Tales		
NYSTROM, KURT (Sweden)	6 - 7	7 - 10
O'NEILL, ROSE (U.S.A.)		

One of the most popular of all the signed artists is Rose O'Neill, who created and drew the lovable Kewpie doll. The Kewpies delighted children and adults alike during the period after World War 1 through the Great Depression of the thirties.

Rose's first works were for advertising and inside and cover illustrations for some of the leading magazines. All showed the adorable Kewpies in various activities. The Gibson Art Company published O'Neill's designs on postcards for most all of the holiday greetings. Her best and most popular were those of Christmas.

The Edward Gross Co. published a great set of six large image Kewpies, while Campbell Art and National Woman Suffrage each issued a card on Women's Suffrage that have become the most famous of all her works. She also did two series of blacks that were published by Raphael Tuck. They are very scarce and would be a prize for any collection.

The Campbell Art Klever Cards are die-cut so that the card can be folded in half and the Kewpies "stand up." Rose O'Neill's wonderful Kewpie cards continue to be among the

favorites in the deltiological field, and are avidly pursued
by many collectors.

ROSE O'NEILL

Gibson Art Co.		
Greetings with Kewpies	30 - 35	35 - 40
Edward Gross, N.Y.		
Large Image Kewpies (6)	45 - 55	55 - 65
Campbell Art Co.		
Klever Kards		
Dated 1914 (26)	30 - 35	35 - 40
Dated 1915 (20)	30 - 35	35 - 40
228 "Votes for Women"	120 - 130	130 - 150
National Woman Suffrage		
"Votes for our Mothers"	225 - 250	250 - 275
Raphael Tuck		
Series 2482 Oilettes Blacks		
"High Society in Coontown"	100 - 110	110 - 120
Black Series "Coontown Kids"	80 - 90	90 - 100
Rock Island Line, advertising	45 - 50	50 - 60
Parker-Bruaner Co., Ice Cream adv.	40 - 45	45 - 50
OUTCAULT, R. (U.S.A.) See Comics		
Ullman Mfg. Co.		
Series 76 "Darktown" Blacks	12 - 14	14 - 18
Others	8 - 10	10 - 12
PALMER, PHYLLIS (U.S.A)	2 - 3	3 - 4
PARKINSON, ETHEL		
BC		
Series 745 (6)	8 - 10	10 - 12
BD		
Series 475 (6)	10 - 12	12 - 14
C.W. Faulkner		
Series 951	12 - 14	14 - 16
M. Munk, Vienna		
Series 132, 380, 488 (6)	10 - 12	12 - 15
Series 232, 502, 554 (6)	8 - 10	10 - 12
Series 191, 234 (6)	8 - 10	10 - 12
Series 531 (6)	8 - 10	10 - 12
Days of the Week (Dutch Children)	12 - 15	15 - 18
Others	8 - 10	10 - 12
PARLETT, HARRY (COMICUS) (GB)	5 - 6	6 - 7
PATERSON, VERA	6 - 7	7 - 8
PEARSE, S.B. (SUSAN)		
M. Munk, Vienna		
Series 563, 727 (6)	8 - 10	10 - 12
Series 635 (6) Dolls	14 - 18	18 - 22
Series 679, 712, 713 (6)	10 - 12	12 - 14
Series 758 (6) Dancing	12 - 14	14 - 18
Series 844, 922, 925 (6)	12 - 14	14 - 18

Bernhardt Wall, Bergman 620

Bernhardt Wall, Bergman 620

Bernhardt Wall, Bergman 620

Bernhardt Wall, Bergman 620

Bernhardt Wall, Bergman "Votes for Women"	Grace Wiederseim, R&N 177 "And What Did Mama's Boy..."	
Series 856 (6) With toys	14 - 18	18 - 22
Series 925 (6)	10 - 12	12 - 15
Series 958 (6) Dancing	12 - 15	15 - 18
Series 728 (6) (Uns.)	10 - 12	12 - 15
Others	8 - 10	10 - 12
PEASE, BESSIE COLLINS		
See Bessie Pease Gutmann		
PETERSEN, HANNES	5 - 6	6 - 8
PITTS, JOHN E. and JEP (U.S.A.)	5 - 6	6 - 8
POWELL, LYMAN	5 - 6	6 - 8
PRESTON, CHLOE (GB)	6 - 7	7 - 8
See Art Deco Children		
PRICE, MARGARET EVANS M.E.P. & MP		
Stecher Litho Co.		
Series 417 (6) Christmas	6 - 7	7 - 8
Series 656, 657, 749 (6) Christmas)	8 - 9	9 - 12
Series 517, 628, 821 (6) Valentine's	8 - 9	9 - 12
Series 503 (6) Easter		
Series 400, 1239 (6) Halloween	10 - 12	12 - 14
Series 98 (6) Flower Children	8 - 10	10 - 12
Series 403 (6) St. Patrick's	6 - 8	8 - 10
Girl Scouts	12 - 15	15 - 18

Note: Many of the Stecher Series were reprinted in the 40's & 50's.

Agnes Richardson, Charles Hauff, No Number, "The Quarrel"

R.R.
M. Munk, Vienna		
Series 1030	8 - 10	10 - 12
RICHARDSON, AGNES (GB)		
Charles Hauff		
No No. Series	8 - 10	10 - 12
C.W. Faulkner		
Series 126, 6126 (6)	10 - 12	12 - 14
Raphael Tuck		
Series C3609	12 - 15	15 - 18
Series 8670 (6)	12 - 14	14 - 16
M. Munk Vienna		
Series 706 (6)	8 - 10	10 - 12
Others	8 - 10	10 - 12
International Art Co.		
1958 "My Love is Like..."	6 - 8	8 - 10
1959 "I'll Take Care of Mummy"	6 - 8	8 - 10
Raphael Tuck		
Series C3609 (6)	8 - 10	10 - 12
Series 8670 (6)	8 - 10	10 - 12
Series 1262 "Art" (6) Golliwogs	15 - 18	18 - 22
Series 1281 "Art" (6) Golliwogs	15 - 18	18 - 20
Series 1282 "Rescued" (6) Golliwogs	18 - 20	20 - 22
Series 1397 (6) Golliwogs	18 - 20	20 - 25
Valentine & Sons		
Series C2006 (6) Golliwogs	15 - 18	18 - 20
Others	8 - 10	10 - 12
See Blacks		

ROBINSON, ROBERT (U.S.A.)
  Edward Gross

Series 205 Boy Ball Player	15 - 20	20 - 25

RUSSELL, MARY LaFENETRA (U.S.A.)
  Sam Gabriel Co.

Children	4 - 6	6 - 8
Halloween	8 - 10	10 - 12

SANFORD, H.D. (GB) See Blacks
SANFORD, M. (GB)
  Raphael Tuck

Black Series	8 - 10	10 - 14
SAUNDERS, E.H. (E.H.S.)	5 - 6	6 - 8

SMITH, JESSIE WILCOX (U.S.A.)
  Reinthal & Newman

"Garden" Series 100	12 - 15	15 - 18

  "Among the Poppies"
  "Five O'Clock Tea"
  "The Garden Wall"
  "The Green Door"
  "In the Garden"
  "The Lily Pool"
SOWERBY, MILLICENT (GB)

Amy Millicent Sowerby was an English artist who illustrated wonderful and delightful children's books. Her most famous were Lewis Carroll's *"Alice in Wonderland,"* and Robert Lewis Stevenson's *"A Child's Garden of Verse."* Her illustrations also appeared on beautifully printed picture postcards that were intended for children.

Sowerby's cards all have very precise detail, colors are exceptionally bright, and the lithography is excellent. It is no wonder that more and more collectors each year join in the search for her cards.

Since most of her cards were published in England and Europe, and for that particular market, they are more abundant there. The American Post Card Co. and Reinthal & Newman, of New York, published several series for distribution in the U.S., but these seem to be rather elusive.

AMY MILLICENT SOWERBY
  Reinthal & Newman

Unnumbered Series	10 - 12	12 - 16

  "Cold"
  "Cloudy"
  "Dry"

"Dull"		
"Fair"		
"Wet"		
Series 2001	12 - 14	14 - 18
"Peggy"		
"Phoebe"		
"Phyllis"		
"Priscilla"		
No Publisher		
"Little Jewels" Series	12 - 15	15 - 18
"Amethyst"		
"Emerald"		
"Pearl"		
"Ruby"		
"Sapphire"		
"Turquoise"		
"Woodland Games" (6)	10 - 12	12 - 15
See Fairies		
See Nursery Rhymes		
SPARK, CHICKY	5 - 6	6 - 8
SPURGIN, FRED (GB)	4 - 5	5 - 6
See Blacks		
STENBERG, AINA (Sweden)	12 - 15	15 - 18
STOCKS, M.		
H.K. & Co.		
"Jack in the Box" (Golliwogs)	12 - 14	14 - 18
SURR, RUTH WELCH (U.S.A.)	2 - 3	3 - 4
R.T.	2 - 3	3 - 4
TARRANT, MARGARET (GB)	6 - 8	8 - 12
TEMPEST, D. (GB)		
Bamforth Co.		
Comic Kids and Animals (30's)	3 - 4	4 - 6
Black Kid Comics	8 - 10	10 - 12
TWELVETREES, C. or C.T. (U.S.A.)		
Ullman Mfg. Co.		
"National Cupid" Series 75		
1877 "United States"	8 - 10	10 - 12
1878 "England"	6 - 8	8 - 10
1879 "Ireland"	6 - 8	8 - 10
1880 "Scotland"	6 - 8	8 - 10
1882 "Mexico"	6 - 8	8 - 10
1883 "Holland"	6 - 8	8 - 10
1884 "Spain"	6 - 8	8 - 10
1885 "Canada"	8 - 10	10 - 12
1887 "China"	6 - 8	8 - 10
1888 "Italy"	6 - 8	8 - 10
Edward Gross, N.Y.		
Comical Kids	6 - 7	7 - 8
"Wedding Series"	8 - 10	10 - 12
"Infant Series" 1050	6 - 7	7 - 8

"Am I crying..."
"I'm a war baby, but..."
"I'm the family darling..."
"Folks all say..."
"Our baby can't talk..."
  "Watch your step..."
National Art
  "Days of the Week" Series   6 - 7   7 - 8
  "Morning-Noon-Night" Series   6 - 8   8 - 10
UPTON, FLORENCE K.
  Raphael Tuck
    Golliwog Series
    Series 1791, 1792   22 - 25   25 - 28
    Series 1793, 1794   20 - 25   25 - 30
VOIGHT, C.A.   3 - 4   4 - 5
VON HARTMAN, E.   2 - 3   3 - 4
WALL, BERNHARDT C. (U.S.A.)
  Ullman Mfg. Co.
    "Overall Boys"
    92 "Young America"   6 - 8   8 - 10
    93 "Me & Jack"   6 - 8   8 - 10
    94 "Leap Frog"   6 - 8   8 - 10
    95 "A Rough Rider"   6 - 8   8 - 10
    "The Senses"
    1716 "Feeling"   6 - 8   8 - 9

Ellen Clapsaddle, Wolfe Co.
Unsigned

Ellen Clapsaddle, Foreign
Unsigned

1717 "Smelling"	6 - 8	8 - 9
1718 "Tasting"	6 - 8	8 - 9
1719 "Hearing"	6 - 8	8 - 9
1720 "Seeing"	6 - 8	8 - 9

Bergman
  Suffragettes
  "Votes for Women" Series   30 - 35   35 - 40
    See Sunbonnet Babies, Children
  Anonymous Publisher
  Animated Fruit & Vegetable Series   7 - 8   8 - 9
    "Apple"
    "Cabbage"
    "Karat"
    "Potato"
    "Pair"
    "Cucumber"
    "Pine"
    "Lemon"
    "Peach"
    "Pumpkin"
    "Ears"
    "Turnip"
    "Onion"
    "Melon"
  See Nursery Rhymes
  See Blacks

WIEDERSEIM, GRACE also GRACE DRAYTON
  Reinthal & Newman
    No Numbers

"A button sewed on..."	15 - 20	20 - 25
"Blow"	15 - 20	20 - 25
"I think I'd rather..."	15 - 20	20 - 25
"The more I see..."	15 - 20	20 - 25
"You're going to get..."	15 - 20	20 - 25
98 "Nothing doing"	15 - 20	20 - 25
99 "Where's oo hanky"	15 - 20	20 - 25
110 "What you don't know..."	15 - 20	20 - 25
112 "No Ma'am, we ain't..."	15 - 20	20 - 25
113 "So near & yet so far"	15 - 20	20 - 25
115 "Curfew shall not..."	15 - 20	20 - 25
116 "I'm so discouraged..."	15 - 20	20 - 25
117 "Courage"	15 - 20	20 - 25
120 "I hate a spanking..."	15 - 20	20 - 25
121 "Stung!"	15 - 20	20 - 25
174 "Here's How"	15 - 20	20 - 25
175 "Don't wake me up..."	15 - 20	20 - 25
176 "I wish I was somebody..."	15 - 20	20 - 25
177 "And what did Mamma's boy..."	15 - 20	20 - 25
249 "Gee! but this is..."	15 - 20	20 - 25
250 "Wanted! Somebody..."	15 - 20	20 - 25
308 "I'd rather say Hello..."	15 - 20	20 - 25

Ellen Clapsaddle, Wolfe Co.   *Ellen Clapsaddle, Int. Art Co.*
No Caption   *"A Happy Halloween"*

493 Skipping Rope	15 - 20	20 - 25
496 "Do you or don't you"	15 - 20	20 - 25
Raphael Tuck		
"In Arcady"	25 - 30	30 - 35
Series 200		
"Cunning Cupids"	25 - 28	28 - 32
Series 224, 240, 243 (Uns.)	15 - 18	18 - 25
A.M. Davis, Boston		
Series 34		
"Christmas Messages"	15 - 20	20 - 25
Series 143		
"Birthday Messages"	15 - 20	20 - 25
Series 357		
"Easter Messages"	15 - 20	20 - 25
Anonymous		
Series 38 "Days of Week" (Uns.)	15 - 20	20 - 25
Campbell Art Co.	30 - 35	35 - 40
Campbell Soup Co.		
Campbell Soup Kids		
Copyright, Large Images	70 - 80	80 - 90
Copyright, Small Images	40 - 50	50 - 60
SWIFT & CO.		
With ads on reverse side (6)	30 - 35	35 - 40

Schweizer Co.
Series 10596
Boy/Girl under Mistletoe   30 - 33   33 - 38
"Beware of Dog" sign   30 - 33   33 - 38
"Choose Me"   30 - 33   33 - 38
"Help the Poor"   30 - 33   33 - 38
"You mustn't kiss me!"   30 - 33   33 - 38
WHITE, FLORA   See Fairy Tales
Salmon & Co.
"Birthday Signs" Series   8 - 10   10 - 12

NURSERY RHYMES

BARNES, G.L.
Cats - Fairy Tale/Nursery Rhymes 12 - 14   14 - 16
"Little Boy Blue"
"Red Riding Hood"
"Tom, Tom, Pipers Son"
Others
BRETT, MOLLY
The Medici Society, Ltd., London
Series 145, 147, 155, 178 (6)   5 - 6   6 - 8
Series 178, 179, 185 (6)   5 - 6   6 - 8
FOLKARD, CHARLES
A & C Black
"Nursery Rhymes & Tales"
   Series 91 (6)   10 - 12   12 - 15
"Beauty & the Beast"
"Cinderella"
"Little Bo Peep"
"Tom, Tom, the Piper's Son"
"Red Riding Hood"
"Sleeping Beauty"
JACKSON, HELEN
Raphael Tuck
Series 6749 (6)   8 - 10   10 - 12
KENNEDY
C.W. Faulkner
Series 1633 (6)   8 - 10   10 - 12
LeMAIR, H. WILLIBEEK (GB)
Our Old Nursery Rhymes (12)   10 - 12   12 - 15
"Baa Baa Black Sheep"
"Dickery, Dickery, Dock"
"Georgy Porgy"
"Here We Go Round the Mulberry Bush"
"I Love Little Pussy"
"Little Bo Peep"
"Mary Had a Little Lamb"
"Oranges and Lemons"
"O Where is My Little Dog Gone"
"Pat a Cake"

Ellen Clapsaddle, No Publisher, Foreign, Unsigned

"Pussy Cat, Pussy Cat"
"Sing a Song of Sixpence"
Old Rhymes With New Pictures (12)　10 - 12　　　12 - 15
"Humpty Dumpty"
"Little Boy Blue"
"Little Miss Muffet"
"Luck Locket"
"Jack & Jill"
"Little Jack Horner"
"Polly Put the Kettle On"
"Three Blind Mice"
"Twinkle, Twinkle Little Star"
"Yankee Doodle"
Little Songs of Long Ago (12)　　　8 - 10　　　10 - 12
"Dame Get Up and Bake Your Pies"
"I Had a Little Nut Tree"
"I Saw Three Ships a'Sailing"
"Little Polly Flinders"
"Little Tom Tucker"
"London Bridge has Broken Down"
"Old King Cole"
"Over the Hills and Far Away"
"There Came to My Window"
"The North Wind Doth Blow"
"Young Lambs to Sell"
"Simple Simon"
Little People (6)　　　　　　　8 - 10　　　10 - 12
"Evening Prayer"
"In the Garden"

"Good Evening, Mr. Hare"
"Little Culprit"
"In the Belfrey"
"Time to Get Up"

More Old Nursery Rhymes (12)	10 - 12	12 - 15

"A Frog He Would a Wooing Go"
"A Happy Family"
"Bed Time"
"Curley Locks"
"Girls and Boys Come Out to Play"
"Hush-a-by Baby"
"Ride a Cock Horse"
"The Crooked Man"
"There Was a Little Man"
"Three Little Kittens"

Old Dutch Nursery Rhymes	8 - 10	10 - 12

"Follow the Leader"
"Our Baby Prince"
"Polly Perkin"
"The Little Sailor"
"The Marionettes"
"The Tiny Man"
"Turn Round, Turn Round"

Small Rhymes for Small People (12)	8 - 10	10 - 12

"Dance-a-Baby Ditty"
"Dance to Your Daddy"
"Goosey Gander"
"Lavender Blue"
"Lazy Sheep"
"Little Jumping Joan"
"See Saw, Margery Daw"
"Sleep, Baby, Sleep"
"The Babes in the Woods"
"Three Mice Went to a Hole to Spin"

The Children's Corner	6 - 8	8 - 10

"Baby's Fright"
"Dreadfully Busy"
"Fishing Boats"
"Greedy"
"Hair Cutting"
"Last Year's Frock"
"Out of the Snow"
"Preserving Dickey"
"Poor Baby"
"Queen of the Birds"
"The Dove's Dinner Time"
"The Garden City"
"The Invalid's Birthday"

NIXON, K.
  C.W. Faulkner

"Alice in Wonderland" (6)	10 - 12	12 - 15

NOSWORTHY, F.E.
  F.A. Owen
    Series 160   10 - 12   12 - 14
SOWERBY, AMY MILLICENT
  Humphrey Milford, London
    "Nursery Rhymes" Series (6)   12 - 15   15 - 18
    "Little Bo-Peep"
    "Little Jack Horner"
    "Little Miss Muffet"
    "Mistress Mary"
    "The Piers's Son"
    "Wee Willie Winkle"
    "Favorite Nursery Stories" (6)   10 - 12   12 - 15
TARRANT, MARGARET   6 - 8   8 - 12
WALL, BERNHARDT
  Ullman Mfg. Co.
    Sunbonnet Girls
    "Nursery Rhymes" Series (Uns.)   6 - 8   8 - 10
    1664 "Little Bo Peep"
    1665 "To Market, To Market"
    1666 "Rain, Rain Go Away"
    1667 "See Saw, Marjorie Daw"
    1668 "Goosey, Goosey, Gander"
    1669 "Come, let's go to Bed"
    "Mary and Her Lamb" Sunbonnets
    1759-1762   8 - 10   10 - 12
PUBLISHERS, Anonymous Artists
Jules Bien Series 40 (6)   6 - 8   8 - 10
C.S. Clark Series 2   6 - 8   8 - 10
F.H.S. Co. Series 9 (6)   6 - 8   8 - 10
F.A. Owen Series 161   7 - 8   8 - 10
P.F.B. Series 6943 (6)   12 - 14   14 - 16
  Series 8666 (6)   12 - 15   15 - 18
Raphael Tuck
    "Little Nursery Lovers" Ser. 9 (12)   8 - 10   10 - 15
    "Nursery Don'ts" Ser. 12 (12)   8 - 10   10 - 15
    "Nursery Rhymes" Ser. 3376 (6)   10 - 12   12 - 18
    Series 3328, 3379, 3488 (6)   10 - 12   12 - 18
WHEELER, DOROTHY
  Humphery Milford
    "Snow Children" Series (6)   8 -10   10 - 12

SUNBONNET GIRLS

CORBETT, BERTHA
  J.I. Austin
    Sunbonnet Children   8 - 10   10 - 15
DIXON, DOROTHY
  Ullman Mfg. Co.
    Sunbonnet Babies   8 - 10   10 - 12

WALL, BERNHARDT
Ullman Mfg. Co.

Month's of the Year (Unsigned)		
1633-1644	8 - 9	9 - 12
Days of the Week (Unsigned)		
1408-1410, 1491-1494	10 - 12	12 - 15
Sunbonnet Seasons		
1901 Spring	10 - 12	12 - 14
1902 Summer	10 - 12	12 - 14
1903 Autumn	10 - 12	12 - 14
1904 Winter	10 - 12	12 - 14
Sunbonnet Twins		
1645 "Give us this Day..."	10 - 12	12 - 14
1646 "The Star Spangled Banner..."	12 - 14	14 - 18
1647 "Should Auld Acquaintance..."	10 - 12	12 - 14
1648 "A Good Book is..."	10 - 12	12 - 14
1649 "Now I Lay Me Down..."	10 - 12	12 - 14
1650 "Be It Ever So Humble..."	10 - 12	12 - 14
Sunbonnet Girls Nursery Rhymes		
1664 "Little Bo Peep"	10 - 12	12 - 15
1665 "To Market, to Market"	10 - 12	12 - 15
1666 "Rain, Rain, Go Away"	10 - 12	12 - 15
1667 "See Saw, Marjorie Daw"	10 - 12	12 - 15
1668 "Goosey, Goosey, Gander"	10 - 12	12 - 15
Sunbonnet Girls		
"Mary & Her Lamb" Series		
1759-1762	8 - 10	10 - 12
Sunbonnet Girls		
1765 "6 A.M., Milking-time"	8 - 10	10 - 12
1766 "7 A.M., Breakfast-time"	8 - 10	10 - 12
1767 "10 A.M., Mowing-time"	8 - 10	10 - 12
1768 "12 N., Noon-time"	8 - 10	10 - 12
1769 "3 P.M., Haying-time"	8 - 10	10 - 12
1770 "6 P.M., Home, Sweet Home"	8 - 10	10 - 12
Bergman Co.		
Sunbonnet Series (Unnumbered)	8 - 10	10 - 12
U through Z	20 - 22	22 - 25

FANTASY

Fantasy, according to **Webster,** means imagination or fancy; wild visionary fancy; an unnatural or bizarre mental image; illusion, phantasm; an odd notion, whim, caprice; a highly imaginative poem, play; mental images as in a daydream. All of these definitions come to life on beautiful and wonderful fantasy postcards!

Most of the fantasies bring to life the days of our youth...of fairies and fairy tales, of frog kings and sleeping princesses, of dolls and teddy bears and dressed animals doing people things; of mermaids and sea creatures, of vixens and voluptuous nudes...which came later. These make a wonderful fantasy world for us all!

Before the influx of foreign cards to the U.S. in the late 70's and 80's, collectors of fantasy had to be content with the works of Dwig and a handful of other artists, a few nursery rhymes and fairy tales, some exaggerations of big fish, mosquitos and farm produce, etc.—not too great for a fantasy collector.

Slowly the beautiful and desirable imports began appearing in auctions and finally in dealer stocks, and now everyone has discovered them. Price have spiraled upward and most all types are in great demand. The most desirable are listed in these pages. Have a Fantasy time!

FAIRIES

The Fairy family includes Brownies, Elves, Gnomes, Goblins, Fairies, Leprechauns, Pixies, and Sprites.

	VG	EX
BARHAM		
C.W. Faulkner		
Series 1859 (6) "Fairies"	$10 - 12	$12 - 14
BAUMGARTEN, FRITZ (Germany)		
Opel & Hess, Jena		
Series 1509	10 - 12	12 - 15
Other Series	10 - 12	12 - 15
Other Publishers	10 - 12	12 - 15
BERGER		
Series 116 (B&W)	15 - 20	20 - 25
CLOKE, RENE (GB)		
Valentine & Sons		
"Fairies" (6)	15 - 18	18 - 22
Series 1002 (6)	12 - 15	15 - 18
Series 1183 (6)	12 - 15	15 - 18
Series 1848 (6)	15 - 18	18 - 22
J. Salmon		
Series 4626 (6)	10 - 12	12 - 15
Series 4627 (6)	10 - 12	12 - 15
COWHAN, H. (GB)		
C.W. Faulkner		
"The Fairy Glen" Series (6)	10 - 15	15 - 18
DAUSTY		
C. & P. & Co.		

Thomas Maybank, R. Tuck 6683, "A Few Lines"

F. Wiesbauer
"Neckerei"

F. Baumgarten, Opel & Hess 1484
No Caption

Series 704 (6) "Nymphs"	8 - 10	10 - 12
GIRIS, CESAR		
Raphael Tuck		
Series 2365 (6) "Madame Butterfly"	18 - 20	20 - 25
MARSHALL, ALICE (GB)		
Raphael Tuck		
Series 3490 (6) "Fairyland Fancies"	15 - 18	18 - 25
Series 3489 (6)	18 - 20	20 - 26
MARSH, HGC (GB)		
C.W. Faulkner		
Series 1510 (6)	12 - 15	15 - 18
MAUSER, PHYLLIS (GB)		
P. Salmon		
Series 5159 (6) "Brownies and Fairies"	10 - 12	12 - 15
MAYBANK, THOMAS (GB)		
Raphael Tuck		
Series 6683 (6) "Midsummer Dreams"	20 - 22	22 - 26
MILLER, HILDA (GB)		
C.W. Faulkner		
Series 1690 "Fairies"	12 - 15	15 - 18
Series 1693 "Fairies"	12 - 15	15 - 18
Series 1822 "Peter Pan"	15 - 18	18 - 20
MULLER, PAUL LOTHAR (German)		
Oscar Heierman, Berlin		
Series 550 "Gnomes"	8 - 10	10 - 12

F. Baumgarten, Opel & Hess 1485
No Caption

F. Baumgarten, Opel & Hess 1486
"Der Gratulant"

OUTHWAITE, IDA R. (GB)
  A & C Black, London

Series 72 "Elves & Fairies"	18 - 20	20 - 25
Series 76 "Elves & Fairies"	18 - 20	20 - 25
Series 79 "Elves & Fairies"	18 - 20	20 - 25
Mermaid - "Playing With Bubbles"	20 - 25	25 - 30

SCHULZ, E. (Austria)
  B.K.W.I.

Series 391 (6)	18 - 20	20 - 25

  M. Munk, Vienna

Series 1363 (6)	15 - 18	18 - 22
Series 1364 (6)	18 - 20	20 - 25
Series 1365 (6)	18 - 20	20 - 25
Series 435 (6) Uns. Andersen's F. Tale	18 - 20	20 - 25

SOWERBY, MILLICENT (GB)
  Humphrey Milford, London

"Woodland Games" (6) Fairies	18 - 20	20 - 25
"Fairies Friends" Series (6)	22 - 25	25 - 28
"Flowers & Wings" (6) Elves	15 - 18	18 - 22
"Merry Elves" (6)	15 - 18	18 - 22
"Favorite Children" (6)	10 - 12	12 - 15
"Flower Children" (6)	12 - 15	15 - 18
"Old Time Games" (6)	10 - 12	12 - 15
"Sky Fairies" (6)	18 - 20	20 - 25

STEELE. L.R. (GB)		
Salmon & Co.		
Series 5050-5055 "Famous Fairies"	8 - 10	10 - 12
TARRANT, MARGARET (GB)		
Medici Society		
PK 120 "The Fairy Troupe"	8 - 10	10 - 12
PK 184 "The Enchantress"	8 - 10	10 - 12
Others	8 - 10	10 - 12
UNTERSBERGER, ANDREAS (Germany)		
Emil Kohn, Munchen		
Fairy & Gnome Series (12)	12 - 14	14 - 18
WATKINS, DOROTHY (GB)		
Bamforth Co.		
Series 1 (6) "Fairy Secret"	8 - 10	10 - 14
WEIGAND, MARTIN		
Gnomes, Mushroom Series (12)	15 - 18	18 - 22
Raphael Tuck		
Oilette Series 6683 (6)	15 - 20	20 - 25
"Mid Summer Dreams" (6)	15 - 20	20 - 25
Valentine & Sons		
Series 108 (6)	10 - 12	12 - 15
ANONYMOUS		
Elves	5 - 8	8 - 15
Fairies	8 - 10	10 - 15
Gnomes	6 - 8	8 - 12
Goblins (usually Halloween)	8 - 10	10 - 15
Leprechauns	5 - 7	7 - 12
Pixies	8 - 10	10 - 15
Sprites	7 - 8	8 - 10

FAIRY TALES

ANDERSEN, HANS		
"The Little Mermaid"	15 - 20	20 - 25
BARHAM		
Series 1734		
"The Pied Piper of Hamelin"	10 - 12	12 - 14
BAUMGARTEN, FRITZ (FB)		
Series 1487, 1516	10 - 12	12 - 14
BORISS, MARGARET		
"Hansel and Gretel" (6)	8 - 10	10 - 12
"Pied Piper of Hamelin" (6)	8 - 10	10 - 12
"Puss in Boots" (6)	8 - 10	10 - 12
COMMIEHAU, A.		
Series 48	6 - 8	8 - 10
HERRFURTH, OSCAR (Germany)		
UVA Chrom, Stuttgart		
Brothers Grimm Fairy Tales (6 per series)		
125 "Hansel & Gretel"	6 - 7	7 - 8
128 "Rotkappchen" (Red Riding Hood)	7 - 8	8 - 9
139 "Frau Holle" (Lady Hell)	4 - 5	5 - 6

140 "Dornroschen" (Sleeping Beauty)	7 - 8	8 - 9
147 "Schneewittchen" (Snow White)	7 - 8	8 - 9
154 "Aschenbrodl" (Cinderella)	6 - 7	7 - 8
223 "Der Gestiefelte Kater" (Puss-in-Boots)	5 - 6	6 - 7
241 "Die Gansemagd" (The Goose Maid)	5 - 6	6 - 7
242 "Der Rattenfanger von Hameln" (Pied Piper)	7 - 8	8 - 9
252 "Der Schweinhirt" (The Pig Herdsman)	5 - 6	6 - 7
254 "Siebenschon" (Seven Lovelies)	5 - 6	6 - 7
264 "Der Wolf und die Sieben Geisslein" (The Wolf and the Seven Goats)	4 - 5	5 - 6
266 "Marienkind"	4 - 5	5 - 6
267 "Tischlein deck dich"	4 - 5	5 - 6
268 "Die Seiben Schwaben"	5 - 6	6 - 7
269 "Bruderchein und Schwesterchen"	6 - 7	7 - 8
285 "Die Bremer Stadtmusikanten"	5 - 6	6 - 7
298 "Hans im Gluck" (Jack & Jill)	5 - 6	6 - 7
299 "Das Tapfere Schneiderlein"	5 - 6	6 - 7
311 "Der Kleine Daumling" (Tom Thumb)	6 - 7	7 - 8
319 "Hase und Igel-Das Lumpengesindel"	5 - 6	6 - 7
320 "Die Sieben Raben" (The Seven Ravens)	6 - 7	7 - 8
324 "Munchausen I"	4 - 5	5 - 6
325 "Munchausen II"	4 - 5	5 - 6
354 "Das Schlaraffenland" (Milk & Honey Land)	4 - 5	5 - 6

O. Kubel, FRG 14
"Dornroschen"

E. Schulz, Schulverine 321
"Rotkappchen"

E. Schulz, Schulverein 905
"Der Rattenfanger"

E. Schulz, Schulverein 564
"Aschenbrödel"

355 "Der Frosch Konig" (The Frog King)	6 - 7	7 - 8
363 "Die Heinselmannchen"	5 - 6	6 - 7
369 "Till Eulenspiegel" (12 cards)	4 - 5	5 - 6

Tales or Sagen (6 card series)

Sage - A fantastic or incredible tale

127 "Die Nibelungen - Sage"	6 - 7	7 - 8
141 "Parsival" (Parsifal)	7 - 8	8 - 9
157 "Rubezahl I"	4 - 5	5 - 6
161 "Rubezahl II"	4 - 5	5 - 6
158 "Wilhelm Tell" (12 cards)	5 - 6	6 - 7
239 "Die Tristan - Sage"	6 - 7	7 - 8
247 "Die Parsival - Sage I"	6 - 7	7 - 8
JUCHTZER	7 - 8	8 - 10
KUBEL, O.		
Brothers Grimm Tales	10 - 12	12 - 14
KUTZER, E.		
Der. Sudmark		
253 "Die Parsival - Sage II"	12 - 15	15 - 18
248 "Walther von der Vogelweide"	6 - 7	7 - 8
258 "Die Lohengrin - Sage"	7 - 8	8 - 9
259 "Die Tannehaüser - Sage"	7 - 8	8 - 9
263 "Aus der Zeit der Minnesanger"	6 - 7	7 - 8
361 "Der Lichtenstein" (12 cards)	4 - 5	5 - 6

Johanna Bedman, Grift., Potsdam,
Red Riding Hood

E. Schulz, BKWI 885-3
"Der Rattenfanger"

LANDSTROM, B. (Finland)	6 - 8	8 - 10
LEETE, F. (Germany)		
H.K. & M. Co.		
"Siegfried" (6) Poster cards	8 - 10	10 - 12
MUHLBERG	8 - 10	10 - 12
NYSTROM, JENNY (Sweden)		
Signed issues	20 - 22	22 - 25
Unsigned issues	10 - 12	12 - 14
PAYER, E.	7 - 8	8 - 10
PINGGERA		
Posters	12 - 15	15 - 18
240 "Sneewittchen"		
245 "Aschenpuitel"		
251 "Jung Frau"		
"Rubezahl"		
SCHIRMER	8 - 10	10 - 12
SCHULZ, E. (Austria)		
B.K.W.I.		
Poster Cards		
Series 435 (6) "Andersen's Fairy Tales	15 - 18	18 - 22
Deutscher Schulverein		
Poster Cards		
319 "Rumpelstilzchen"	15 - 18	18 - 25
320 "Schneewittchen" (Snow White)	18 - 20	20 - 25
321 "Rotkappchen" (Red Riding Hood)	18 - 20	20 - 22

322 "Die Sieben Raben" (The 7 Ravens)	15 - 18	18 - 22
564 "Aschenbrodel" (Cinderella)	20 - 22	22 - 25
653 "Der Frosch Konig" (The Frog King)	20 - 22	22 - 25
862 "Dornroschen" (Sleeping Beauty)	18 - 20	20 - 22

WAIN, LOUIS (GB)

Raphael Tuck

Series 3385 "Paper Doll Cats"   225 - 250   250 - 300

"Aladdin"

"Beauty and the Beast"

"Cinderella"

"Dick Whittington"

"Little Red Riding Hood"

"Robinhood"

WALL, BERNHARDT

Ullman Mfg. Co.

"Red Riding Hood" Series   8 - 10   10 - 12

1752 "Take some cakes..."

1753 "On the Way to Grandmother's..."

1754 "Arrives at Grandmother's..."

1755 "Comes to Bed..."

1756 "Innocently lied down in bed..."

1757 "Hears the Wolf say..."

WHITE, FLORA (GB)

Ilfracombe Mermaid "Who are You?"   20 - 25   25 - 30

Poster Series   12 - 15   15 - 20

"Cinderella"

"Dick Whittington"

"Goose Girl"

"Hop-O-My-Thumb"

Anonymous, Red Riding Hood ("Rotkappchen")

"Peter Pan"
"Puss-in-Boots"
P.F.B.
  Fairy Tale Series   15 - 18   18 - 22
    "Cinderella"
    "The House of Sweets"
    "Little Red Riding Hood"
    "Sleeping Beauty"
    "Snow White"
    "Tom Thumb"
Ullman Mfg. Co.

1752-1757 "Little Red Riding Hood"	8 - 10	10 - 12
1759-1762 "Mary & Her Lamb"	8 - 10	10 - 12
WINKLER	7 - 8	8 - 10

ANONYMOUS
Paper Doll Cut-outs

Series 3382 "Little Bo-Peep"	40 - 45	45 - 55
Series 3383 "Little Boy Blue"	40 - 45	45 - 55

FANTASY NUDES

BENDER
  "La Femme" (Snakes)   12 - 15   15 - 18
BOCKLIN, A.
  Bruckmann A.G.

21 "Triton & Nereide" (Merman)	10 - 12	12 - 15
6 "The Nereid" (Snake)	12 - 15	15 - 18

BRAUNE, E.
  Amag Kunst

63 "Walkure" (Horse)	10 - 12	12 - 15

CABANEL, A.
  Salon J.P.P.

2206 "Nymph & Faun" (Man-Goat)	12 - 15	15 - 18

COURSELLES-DUMONT
  Lapina

564 "In der Arena" (Lion)	12 - 15	15 - 18

DUSSEK, E.A.
  J.K.

69 "Froschkonigs Braut" (Frog)	15 - 18	18 - 22

FISCHER-COERLINE
  M.K.

2475 "Salome" (Severed head)	12 - 15	15 - 18

GEIGER, C.A.
  Marke J.S.C.

6109 "Liebeskampf" (Man-Sea Beast)	15 - 18	18 - 22
6112 "Salome" (Severed Head)	12 - 15	15 - 18

GIOVANNI, A.
  ARS Minima

119 "Salome" (Severed head)	12 - 15	15 - 18

GLOTZ, A.D.
  B.K.W.I.

E. Schulz, BKWI 165-4 | *E. Schulz, BKWI 165-2*

1009 "Lebensluge" (Ghost of Dead)	10 - 12	12 - 15
HIRSCH	10 - 12	12 - 14
HOESSLIN, GEORGE		
NPG		
491 "Die Schaumgebstene" (Nude in Shell)	10 - 12	12 - 15
KELLER, F.		
Russian		
076 "Finale" (Death Head)	12 - 15	15 - 18
KOMINEL	10 - 12	12 - 14
KORPAL	10 - 12	12 - 15
LAMM	10 - 12	12 - 15
LEETE, F.		
Munchener Kunst		
3113 "Nidre und Wasserman" (Water Creature)	10 - 12	12 - 15
3114 "Gefangene Nymphe" (Dwarfs)	10 - 12	12 - 15
3117 "Triton Belaufde Nereide" (Merman)	10 - 12	12 - 15
LENOIR, CH.		
Lapina		
5112 "Victory" (Octopus)	15 - 18	18 - 22
LEOPAROVA		
KV		
1183 "Salome" (Severed head)	10 - 12	12 - 15
MANDL, J.		
Minerva		
177 "Printemps" (Wings)	10 - 12	12 - 15

Schivert, Arthur Rehn
"Die Hexe"

C.A. Geiger
Marke J.S.C. 6109, "Liebeskampf"

MASTAGLIO
Galerie Munchener Meister
380 "Duell" (Nudes fencing)   10 - 12   12 - 15
MASTROIANNI, C.
188 "Fievre d'Amore" (Waterfall)   10 - 12   12 - 15
MEUNIER, S.
Marque L.E.
Series 64 (6) (Nudes and snakes)   28 - 32   32 - 36
MUHLBERG
Nude Riding a Seahorse   12 - 15   15 - 18
MULLER-BAUMGARTEN
FEM
161 "Faun & Nymphe" (Man-Goat)   8 - 10   10 - 12
MUTTICH, C.V.
V.K.K.V.
2077 "Sulejka" (Peacock)   10 - 12   12 - 15
NORMAN, E.P.   10 - 12   12 - 14
PENOT, A.
Lapina
1340 "Red Butterfly" (Red-winged Nude)   12 - 15   15 - 18
PIOTROWSKI, A.
Minerva
1028 "Salome" (Severed Head)   10 - 12   12 - 15
Manke JSC
6082 "Charmeuse de Serpents" (Snake)   15 - 18   18 - 22

REINACKER, G.
  PFB
  6302 "Schlangen-Bandigerin" (Snake)   12 - 15   15 - 18
ROWLAND, FR.
  SVD
  379 "Sirenen" (Snakes)   12 - 15   15 - 18
RUTHAUG
  LP
  2815 "Pan and Psyche" (Man-Beast)   15 - 18   18 - 22
ROYER, L.
  Salon de Paris
  374 "La Sirene" (Death head)   12 - 15   15 - 18
SAMSON, E.
  A.N., Paris
  243 "Diane"   (Wolf Dogs)   10 - 12   12 - 15
SCALBERT, J.
  S.P.A.
  48 "Leda and the Swan"   10 - 12   12 - 15
SCHMUTZLER
  Russian
  Richard
  245 "Salome" (Severed head)   12 - 15   15 - 18
SCHIFF, R.
  W.R.B. & Co.
  22-74 "Leda and the Swan"   15 - 18   18 - 22

Fischer-Coerlin, Modener Kunst
"Salome"

Ed. Adrian Dussek, J.K. 69
"Froschkönigs Braut"

SCHIVERT, V.
  Arthur Rehn & Co.
    "Die Hexe"   15 - 18   18 - 22
SCHULZ, E.
  Poster Cards
  B.K.W.I.
    41 "The Frog King" (Big Frog)   15 - 18   18 - 22
    885 Goethe's "Der Fischer" (Mermaid)   25 - 30   30 - 35
    885 "God & the Baiadere"   18 - 20   20 - 25
    979 "Die Forelle" (Mermaid)   25 - 28   28 - 32
    205 Wagner's "Parsival"   15 - 18   18 - 22
    557 "Lotusblume" (Nude in flower)   18 - 20   20 - 25
    Series 165 (6) (Nudes on giant flowers) 18 - 20   20 - 25
SOJKA, J.   10 - 12   12 - 15
STELLA, EDUARD
  BRW
    354 "Diane" (Dogs)   18 - 20   20 - 22
STUCK   10 - 12   12 - 14
STYKA, JAN
  Lapina
    810 "Good Friends" (Horse)   10 - 12   12 - 15
SZYNDIER, P.
  Mal. Polske
    22 "Eve" (Snakes)   20 - 22   22 - 25
SOLOMKO
  T.S.N.
    Nude in Peacock feathers   18 - 20   20 - 22
WACHSMUTH, M.   10 - 12   12 - 14
WARZENIECKI, M.
  WILSA

Anonymous, M.N. ©1910

90 "Une Nouvelle Esclave" (Death)	10 - 12	12 - 15

WOLLNER, H.
B.W.K.I.

1101 "Sadismus" (Death head)	10 - 12	12 - 15

VEITH, E.
B.K.W.I.

"Teasing" (Man-Goat)	10 - 12	12 - 15

ZANDER
SSWB

4790 "Sieg der Schonheit" (Tiger)	10 - 12	12 - 15

ZATZKA, H.
Panphot, Vienna

1284 "La Perle" (Nude in Oyster Shell)	12 - 15	15 - 18

MERMAIDS

ATWELL, MABEL LUCIE
Valentine & Sons

951 With Black Doll	15 - 18	18 - 22

BENEZUR

"Der Kampf"	16 - 18	18 - 22

BOCKLIN, A.
F. Bruckmann AG

"Play of Naiads"	12 - 15	15 - 18

E. Schulz, BKWI 885-5
"Der Fischer"

E. Schulz, BKWI 979-5
"Die Forelle"

Chiostri, Ballerini & Fratini 238
No Caption

Chiostri, Ballerini & Fratini 317
No Caption

R. Tuck Series 6822, "Mermaid"

Kurt Agthe, C.L., Hamburg 1028, "Blessee"

"Im Spiel der Wellen"	12 - 15	15 - 18
CARTER, REG.		
Max Ettinger & Co.		
Series 4453 (6) Diver Series	15 - 20	20 - 25
CHIOSTRI, S.		
Ballerini & Fratini		
Series 238 (6) Deco	40 - 45	45 - 55
Series 317 (6) Deco	40 - 42	42 - 50
GILLAUME		
Art Moderne		
Series 764 "Seetrift"	15 - 18	18 - 22

E. Schulz, Schubert, BKWI 766-2, "Der Fischer"

GOHLER, H.
  Richard
    "Du Nixlein Wunderhold..."   15 - 18   18 - 22
KASPARIDES
    "Bath of Water Fairy"   15 - 18   18 - 22
LEETE, F.
  Munchener Kunst
    3116 "De Taufe des Fawn"   12 - 14   14 - 18
LIEBENWEIN, M.
  B.K.W.I.
    1028 "Der Verrufene Weiher"   15 - 18   18 - 22
OUTHWAITE
  A & C Black, London
  Series 73
    "Playing with Bubbles"   22 - 26   26 - 30
SAGER, XAVIER
    Big Letter Card
    "Un Baiser D'Ostende"   22 - 25   25 - 30
SCHMUTZLER, L.
  Hanfstaengl Co.   12 - 15   15 - 18
SCHULZ, E.
  B.K.W.I.
    Poster Cards
    391-3 Heine's "Der Mond ist..."   20 - 22   22 - 26
    434-1 Andersen's Marchen   20 - 22   22 - 26
    766-2 Shubert's "Das Wasser..."   25 - 28   28 - 32
    885-5 Goethe's "Der Fischer"   28 - 30   30 - 35
    979-5 Schubert's "Die Forelle"   28 - 30   30 - 35
    203 "Flame of Love"   15 - 18   18 - 22
SOLOMKO, S.
  T.S.N.
    93 "The Tale"   15 - 18   18 - 25
WHITE, FLORA
  W.E. Mack, Hampstead
    Poster - "The Little Mermaid"   18 - 20   20 - 25
PUBLISHERS
  S. Hildeshimer & Co.
    Andersen's "The Little Mermaid"   20 - 25   25 - 30
  MN Co., 1910
    Unsigned and Unnumbered (10)   20 - 22   22 - 28
  M.&L.G.
    National Series, untitled
    Art Nouveau W/Seashell   25 - 30   30 - 35
  Raphael Tuck
    Series 6822 (6) Mermaid Series   25 - 30   30 - 35
    Series 694 (6) Wagner Series
    "The Rheingold"   20 - 25   25 - 28
ANONYMOUS
  Art Nouveau Series 643 (6)   50 - 55   55 - 65

SUPERIOR WOMEN/ LITTLE MEN FANTASY

The advent of Women's Suffrage started many changes affecting the relationships of men and women. None show these upcoming changes better than postcards illustrating the superiority of beautiful ladies over the opposite gender. Most tend to picture the men as being very small weaklings who are totally ruled by a beautiful girl or by his mate.

Puppets-on-a-string, being manipulated by the beautiful lady, little men being chastised because of money problems, or being attracted to a beauty like bees are to honey, are some of the dominant topics.

COLLINS
  "Little Men" Series — 10 - 12 — 12 - 15
FASCHE
  M. Munk, Vienna
    "Diabolo" (6) — 12 - 15 — 15 - 18
KYOPINSKI
  Little Men   (6) — 10 - 12 — 12 - 15
KUDERNEY
  M. Munk, Vienna
    Series 606 (6) — 12 - 15 — 15 - 18
    Series 699 (6) — 12 - 15 — 15 - 18
  N.F.
    Series 160-165 — 8 - 10 — 10 - 12
MAUZAN
  Series 83 (6) Little Men — 15 - 18 — 18 - 22
PENOT, A.
  Lapina
    Little Men Series (6) — 15 - 18 — 18 - 22
SAGER, XAVIER
  Series 43 (6) Soldiers/Women — 18 - 20 — 20 - 25
SCHONPFLUG
  B.K.W.I.
    Series 4132 (6) — 10 - 12 — 12 - 15
PUBLISHERS
  B.G.W.
    Series 123/1233 (6) — 8 - 10 — 10 - 12
  J. Marks
    Series 155 (8) "Summer Girl" — 10 - 12 — 12 - 14
  B.K.W.I.
    Series 136 (6) — 8 - 10 — 10 - 12
  WBG
    Series 123 (6) — 7 - 8 — 8 - 10

W. Scheuermann   Durch die Lupe
      Prooving his hearts — Par la loupe

W. Scheuermann, SWSB 6582, "Proving His Hearts"

KRAMPUS

Krampus was the impish devil, with one cloven hoof, who joined forces with St. Nicholas as he distributed toys, gifts and fruits to children at Christmas. While traveling with St. Nick he was good to the children who had been good, but those who knew they had been bad quickly scurried away.

Krampus chased them and would put them in the bucket or basket on his back. He would usually switch them with the big bundle of switches he always carried. The crying children were later released after promising to be good during the next year.

He was very suave and debonair around the pretty ladies, and many cards imply that they liked his advances toward them. However, to the older and ugly ladies he was very mean, and usually threw them into the burning flames.

Krampus cards, being part of a fantasy world, are very collectible. Cards of the early 1900's, especially those signed by artists and without the red backgrounds, command very high prices. Cards by artists of the Wiener Werkstaette and any Art Nouveau renderings are especially in demand, as are those with both Krampus and St. Nicholas on the same card.

It must be noted that many artists signed only their initials on the early Krampus cards and most of the red background cards are unsigned, making them less desirable. Krampus cards are still being produced for the Christmas season, so collectors must be sure of the era they are buying.

B.F.	12 - 14	14 - 16
BRUAT	20 - 25	25 - 28
DOCKER, F.	18 - 20	20 - 25
Krampus/St. Nicolo Series	22 - 25	25 - 30
ENDRODI	12 - 15	15 - 18
GELLARO	20 - 25	25 - 30
FG	15 - 18	18 - 22
G.L.	18 - 20	20 - 25
GEL, H.	18 - 20	20 - 25

H.G.		
C.H., Wien	20 - 25	25 - 30
H.		
Series 234 W/Old Ladies	20 - 22	22 - 25
H.M.S	15 - 20	20 - 25
HARTMANN, A.		
C.H., Wien		
Series 2490	25 - 30	30 - 35
HATZ	15 - 18	18 - 22
KRATZER		
Series 3236 (6)	15 - 18	18 - 22
KUTZER, E.	10 - 12	12 - 15
LASTMANN	20 - 25	25 - 30
MAILICK	20 - 25	25 - 30
MILAN, G.	10 - 12	12 - 14
O.W.	18 - 20	20 - 25
OHLER, C.	18 - 20	20 - 25
PAYER	15 - 18	18 - 25
R.	12 - 15	15 - 18
ROSTEN F.	10 - 12	12 - 15
SASULSKI, K.		
Polish card, "Pocztowki" 269	35 - 40	40 - 45
SCHEINER		
Czech card	20 - 25	25 - 30

K. Sasulski, Polish
"Gruss Vom Nikolo!"

Scheiner, Czech.
Czech. Caption

A. Hartmann, C.H., Wien
"Gruss vom Krampus"

C.B., Georg W. Agrandl
Russian Krampus

H.G., C.H., Wien
"Gruss vom Krampus"

SCHUBERT		
Series 22-244	25 - 30	30 - 35
SCHONPFLUG	25 - 30	30 - 35
SINGER, SUZI (Wiener Werkstaette)	70 - 80	80 - 90
Other Wiener Werkstaette		80 - 300

TEDDY BEARS

Since Teddy Bears are so much in demand by collectors, we are listing both artist-signed and those not signed by artists. Many great sets and series were unsigned and, because of inadequate records by early publishers, the artists have not been identified.

BUSY BEARS

J.I. Austen Co.	7 - 8	8 - 12

  427 Monday - Hanging the Wash
  428 Tuesday - Ironing
  429 Wednesday - Sweeping
  430 Thursday - Mopping
  431 Friday - Baking
  432 Saturday - Darning
  433 Learning to Spell

Fred Cavally, Thayer Pub. Co.
"Multiplication is Vexation"

Rose Clark, Rotograph Co.
"The Bride"

D.P. Crane, H.G.Z. & Co.
"Saturday"

Ellam, R. Tuck 9794
"Teddy Bears at Play"

D.P. Crane, H.G.Z. & Co.
"February"

M. Greiner, Int. Art Co. 791
No Caption

Harry Roundtree, Williston Press
"I am Collecting"

434 "Playing Leap Frog"		
435 "Off to School"		
436 "Getting it in the Usual Place"		
437 "Something Doing"		
438 "Vacation"		
BUSY BEARS, DAYS OF THE WEEK		
BERNHARDT WALL	6 - 8	8 - 10
1905 Sunday		
1906 Monday		
1907 Tuesday		
1908 Wednesday		
1909 Thursday		
1910 Friday		
1911 Saturday		
CRACKERJACK BEARS		
Rueckheim & Eckstein		
1 At the Lincoln Zoo	20 - 25	25 - 30
2 In Balloon	20 - 25	25 - 30
3 Over Niagara Falls	20 - 25	25 - 30
4 At Statue of Liberty	20 - 25	25 - 30
5 At Coney Island	20 - 25	25 - 30
6 In New York	20 - 25	25 - 30
7 Shaking Teddy's Hand (Roosevelt)	30 - 35	35 - 40
8 At Jamestown Fair	20 - 25	25 - 30

9 To the South	20 - 25	25 - 30
10 At Husking Bee	20 - 25	25 - 30
11 At the Circus	30 - 35	35 - 40
12 Playing Baseball	30 - 35	35 - 40
13 Cracker Jack Time	20 - 25	25 - 30
14 Making Cracker Jacks	20 - 25	25 - 30
15 At Yellowstone	20 - 25	25 - 30
16 Away to Mars	20 - 25	25 - 30
17-32	30 - 35	35 - 40

ROSE CLARK BEARS
ROSE CLARK

Rotograph Co., N.Y.	10 - 12	12 - 14

307 "Bear own Cadet"
308 "Is That You Henry?"
309 "Henry"
310 "The Bride"
311 "The Groom"
312 "A Bear Town Spot"
313 "A Bear Town Dude"
314 "I'm Going a Milking"
315 "I Won't be Home..."
316 "C-c-come on in"
317 "Fifth Avenue"
318 "Hymn No. 23"

M.D.S., Ullman Mfg. Co. 88
"Romantic Bears"

Cracker Jack Bears
Rueckheim Bros. & Eckstein 7

Bernhardt Wall, Ullman Mfg. Co.
1977, "This Little Bear…"

Bernhardt Wall, Ullman Mfg. Co.
1908, "Wednesday"

DOGGEREL DODGER BEARS

WHEELAN, A.

Paul Elder Co.	6	-	8	8	- 10

CRANE BEARS

CRANE, D.P.

H.G.Z. Co.

"Days of the Week"	12	-	15	15	- 18
"Months of the Year"	12	-	15	15	- 18

ELLAM BEARS

Raphael Tuck

Series 9794 (6)	12	-	15	15	- 18

HEAL DAYS OF THE WEEK

HEAL, WILLIAM S.	6	-	8	8	- 10

HILLSON DAYS OF THE WEEK

HILLSON, D.	6	-	8	8	- 10
KENNEDY, A.E.	12	-	15	15	- 18

LITTLE BEARS

Raphael Tuck

Series 118 (12)	12	-	15	15	- 18

"A Morning Dip"
"A Very Funny Song"
"Breaking the Record"
"Kept in School"

"Missed Again"
"Oh! What a Shock"
"Once in the Eye"
"The Cake Walk"
"The Ice Bears Beautifully"
"The Jolly Anglers"
"Tobogganing in the Snow"
"Your Good Health"

McLAUGHLIN BROS. BEARS
  McLaughlin Bros.   6 - 8   8 - 10
MOLLY & TEDDY BEARS
  GREINER, M.
  International Art
    Series 791 (6)   8 - 10   10 - 12
MOTHER GOOSE'S TEDDY BEARS
  CAVALLY, FRED (16)   10 - 12   12 - 15
OTTOMAN LITHOGRAPHING BEARS
  Ottoman Lithographing Co., N.Y.   8 - 10   10 - 12
    "Come Birdie Come"
    "Good Old Summertime"
    "Is Marriage a Failure?"
    "Many Happy Returns"
    "Never Touched Me"
    "Please Ask Pa"

C. Twelvetrees, Nat. Art 271
"It's Up to You"

M.D.S., Ullman Mfg. Co. 1929
"On the Links"

"Right Up-To-Date"
"Well, Well, You never can Tell"
"Where am I at?"
"Will She get the Lobster"
ROMANTIC BEARS
M.D.S.
Ullman Mfg. Co.
  Series 88 (4)

1950 "Too Late"	6 - 8	8 - 10
1951 "Who Cares?"	6 - 8	8 - 10
1952 "The Lullaby"	6 - 8	8 - 10
1953 "A Letter to My Love"	6 - 8	8 - 10

ROUNDTREE, HARRY
Williston Press   15 - 18   18 - 22
SPORTY BEARS
M.D.S.
Ullman Mfg. Co.
  Series 83

1923 "Love All"	12 - 14	14 - 16
1924 "Here's for a Home Run"	12 - 14	14 - 16
1925 "Out for a Big Game"	10 - 12	12 - 14
1926 "King of the Alley"	8 - 10	10 - 12
1927 "A Dip in the Surf"	8 - 10	10 - 12
1928 "An Unexpected Bite"	8 - 10	10 - 12
1929 "On the Links"	12 - 14	14 - 16

TWELVETREES BEARS
TWELVETREES, C.
National Art Co.   8 - 10   10 - 12
206 "Little Bear Behind"
207 "Stung"
208 "The Bear on Dark Stairway"
209 "How can you Bear this Weather?"
210 "A Bear Impression"
211 "The Seashore Bear"
271 "It's Up to You"   10 - 12   12 - 15
ROOSEVELT BEARS   20 - 25   25 - 30
  1 "At Home"
  2 "Go Aboard the Train"
  3 "In Sleeping Car"
  4 "On a Farm"
  5 "At a Country School"
  6 "At the County Fair"
  7 "Leaving the Ballroom"
  8 "At the Tailor's"
  9 "In the Department Store"
10 "At Niagara Falls"
11 "At Boston Public Library"
12 "Take an Auto Ride"
13 "At Harvard"
14 "On Iceberg"
15 "In New York City"

16 "At the Circus"
17 "Shooting Firecrackers"   30 - 35   35 - 40
20 "Dancing"
22 "In New York"
25 "Swimming"
29 "Go Fishing"
30 "Bears on a Pullman"
31 "Hunters"
There may be others.

ST. JOHN BEARS
ST. JOHN
Western News Co.   8 - 10   10 - 12
161 "Spring"
162 "Summer"
163 "Autumn"
164 "Winter"

TOWER TEDDY BEARS
Tower M. & N. Co.   8 - 10   10 - 12
"Beary Well, Thank You"
"But We are Civilized"
"Did You Ever Wear..."
"Don't Say a Word"
"Hurrah for - Eagle"
"Hurrah for the..."
"I'm Waiting for You"
"Our Birth, You Know"
"We Wear Pajamas"
"You Don't Say"

TP & CO. TEDDY BEARS
T.P. & Co.   8 - 10   10 - 12
"Out for Airing"
"I Wonder if He Saw Me?"
"Isn't He a Darling"
"How Strong He is"
"Oh! My! - He's Coming!"
"Off for the Honeymoon"
"Little Girl with Teddy"
"Dolly Gets an Inspiration"
"Lost, Strayed, or Stolen"

WALL, BERNHARDT
Ullman Mfg Co.
  "Busy Bears" Series   10 - 12   12 - 15
  "Little Bears" Series   10 - 12   12 - 15

REAL PHOTO TEDDY BEARS
W/Children (Large Bears)   20 - 25   25 - 35
W/Children (Small Bears)   12 - 18   18 - 25
W/Ladies (Large Bears)   18 - 22   22 - 28
W/Ladies (Small Bears)   12 - 15   15 - 18
Bears alone (Large)   15 - 20   20 - 25
Bears alone (Small)   12 - 14   14 - 16
Bears and Movie Stars   10 - 12   12 - 15

OTHER ARTIST-SIGNED TEDDY BEARS

W/Children (Large Bears)	10 - 15	15 - 20
W/Children (Small Bears)	8 - 12	12 - 15
W/Ladies (Large Bears)	10 - 12	12 - 18
W/Ladies (Small Bears)	8 - 12	12 - 15

WAGNER OPERA FIGURES

AIGNER

Series 259	6 - 8	8 - 10

BAUFCHILD

"Lohengrin" (6)	8 - 10	10 - 12

BERGMULLER, C.W. | 6 - 8 | 8 - 10

DOUBEK

Ackerman	8 - 10	10 - 12

ERLANG. P.V. | 7 - 8 | 8 - 9

E.S.D.

German Series

Series 8157 Die Walkure (6)	12 - 15	15 - 18
Series 8158 Siegfried (6)	12 - 15	15 - 20
Series 8159 Das Rheingold (6)	15 - 20	20 - 22
Series 8160 Gotterdammerung (6)	15 - 18	18 - 22
Series 8161 Die Meistersinger (6)	12 - 15	15 - 18
Series 8162 Tristan Und Isolde (6)	15 - 18	18 - 22
Ser. 8163 Der Fliegende Hollander (6)	12 - 15	15 - 18
Series 8164 Lohengrin (6)	15 - 18	18 - 22

GLOTZ, A.D.

"Parsival"	10 - 12	12 - 15
Series 22	8 - 10	10 - 12

GOETZ

M. Munk, Vienna

Series 861

"Die Feen"	8 - 10	10 - 12
"Die Meistersinger"	8 - 10	10 - 12
"Die Walkure"	8 - 10	10 - 12
"Gotterdammerung"	10 - 12	12 - 14
"Lohengrin"	8 - 10	10 - 12
"Parsival"	10 - 12	12 - 14
"Rienzi"	8 - 10	10 - 12
"Rheingold"	10 - 12	12 - 14
"Siegfried"	8 - 10	10 - 12
"Tannhaüser"	8 - 10	10 - 12
Series 982 (12)	6 - 8	8 - 10
Series E984 (12)	6 - 8	8 - 10

KUTZER, E.

Poster Cards

Vercides Sudmark

Series 245-256	15 - 20	20 - 25

245 "Die Meistersinger von Nürnberg"
246 "Die Meistersinger von Nürnberg"
247 "Die Meistersinger von Nürnberg"

248 "Lohengrin"
249 "Tristan und Isolde"
250
251
252 "Tannhaüser"
253 "Die Walkure"
254 "Das Rheingold"
255 "Siegfried"
256 "Siegfried"

LEETE, F.
Poster Cards
L. Pernitzch

Wagner's "Heldengestalten" (24)	12 - 15	15 - 18

LUDVIG

Series 718	6 - 8	8 - 10

NOWAK, OTTO
B.K.W.I.

Series 1412 "Parsival"	8 - 10	10 - 12
Series 2352	8 - 10	10 - 12

PETER, O.

Series 399	8 - 10	10 - 12

PILGER

"Tannhaüser" W/Music	8 - 10	10 - 12

H. Pinggera, Bund der Deutschen
249, "Parsifal"

E. Schulz, BKWI 438-5
"Wagner Rienzi"

Poster Cards
Deutches un Niederosterrich
   Series 242-252   12 - 15   15 - 18
    242 Siegfried
    248 Herrolof
    250 Tannhaüser
    750 Gotterdammerung
    751 Walkure
    752 Tannhaüser
   Series 258   8 - 10   10 - 12
SCHLIMARSKI
   Series 420   8 - 10   10 - 12
SCHULZ, E.
  B.K.W.I.
   Series 438 Posters   16 - 20   20 - 25
    "Der Fiegende Hollanders"
    "Tristan & Isolde"
    "Rienzi"
    "Lohengrin"
  Others
SPIELZ, A.
  Series 247
    "Parsival"   10 - 12   12 - 14
PUBLISHERS
  B.K.W.I.
   Series 438 (6)   12 - 15   15 - 18
  M. Munk, Vienna

E. Kutzer, Das Tapfere... Schneiderlien 147

Wagner's Series 28

Ladies in Wagner's Operas	10 - 12	12 - 14

T.S.N.

Series 141 (6) "Lohengrin"	8 - 10	10 - 12

Raphael Tuck
"Wagner" Series

Series 690 (6) "Siegfried"	12 - 15	15 - 20
Series 691 (6) "Lohengren"	12 - 15	15 - 20
Series 692 (6) "Gotterdammerung"	10 - 14	14 - 18
Series 693 (6) "Tristan and Isolde"	12 - 15	15 - 18
Series 694 (6) "The Rheingold"	15 - 20	20 - 25
Series 695 (6) "The Flying Dutchman"	10 - 14	14 - 18
Series XX, 1219 (6) "Modern Meister"	12 - 15	15 - 18

Ottmar Ziehr

Wagner's Operas (6)	25 - 28	28 - 32

DEATH FANTASY

CIEZKIEWKZ, E.

"Girl in Red"	8 - 10	10 - 15
"Woman & Skull"	8 - 10	10 - 12

CHOPIN, FR.
Series 116

"Playing Death"	8 - 10	10 - 12

LAMM, E.

Death in the Field	8 - 10	10 - 12

MANDL, JOSEPH

"The End"	8 - 10	10 - 12

PETER, O.

400 Burning Nudes	10 - 12	12 - 14

PODKOWINSKI

Nude on Fiery Horse	12 - 14	14 - 16

WACHSMUTH
PFB

"Die Beute"	10 - 12	12 - 14

WOLFF, H.
PFB

4480 Death Rides a Horse	10 - 12	12 - 15

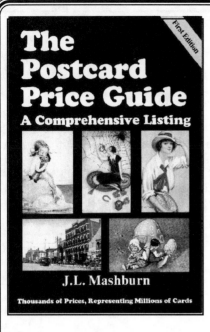

7

FRENCH GLAMOUR

While artists in America and other countries were busy illustrating the faces, the big hats, and the mode of dress of their beautiful women, their French counterparts were equally busy showing her other bodily attributes as well as her face. The mystique of the scantily and colorfully dressed beauties, showing lingerie, silk stockings, pajamas--and mostly nothing at all--made them the rage of the era. The French publishing firms of **Marque L-E** and **Delta** employed a varied and illustrious group of talented artists to glorify the maiden form.

Probably the most prolific and most popular of these was Suzanne Meunier with her renditions of numerous series of exotic nudes and semi-nudes. Jean Tam, with his saucy and sometimes comical ladies, also has become a favorite of many collectors. Louis Icart and Umberto Brunelleschi, better known for their works in the Art Deco field, each contributed a series in this glamorous field.

For some unknown reason, most all of the different series by **Delta** had 5 cards and **Marque L-E** contained 7 cards where normally there are 6, 8, 10, or 12 by other publishers. The highest priced and most desirable series is number 31 by Brunelleschi, but it contains only 6 cards.

Delta Series are noted. The other publisher, not listed, is

Marque L-E. It should be noted that some sets are duplicated by both publishers.

	VG	EX
BRUNELLESCHI, UMBERTO		
Series 31 (6)	80 - 90	90 - 110
CHARLET		
Delta Series 4	15 - 18	18 - 20
CHERUBINI	15 - 18	18 - 22
CREMIEUX, ED.		
Delta Series 44	15 - 18	18 - 22
Series 27	15 - 18	18 - 20
FABIANO		
Delta Series 5	12 - 15	15 - 18
Series 7, 11, 15	18 - 22	22 - 28
Series 32, 59, 63	15 - 18	18 - 22
FONTAN, LEO		
Series 17, 80	20 - 25	25 - 30
Series 23, 95, 5016	15 - 18	18 - 22
GALLAIS, P.		
Semi-Nude Series	20 - 22	22 - 26
GAYAC		
Series 290	18 - 20	20 - 25
GERBAULT		
Series 36	15 - 18	18 - 22

A. Bertiglia, Marque L.E. 60
No Caption

Cherubini, Delta Series
No Caption

Fabiano, Marque L.E. 63-1
No Caption

M. Millere, Marque L.E. 65-4
No Caption

Xavier Sager, Noyer 690
"Peaceful Shells"

Jean Tam, Marque L.E. 47
No Caption

HEROUARD		
Series 55, 300	20 - 25	25 - 30
ICART, LOUIS		
Series 48 (6)	60 - 70	70 - 80
JARACH, A.		
Delta Series 156, 158	18 - 20	20 - 22
Series 18	18 - 20	20 - 25
KIRCHNER, RAPHAEL		
Series 1, 5	35 - 40	40 - 50
KOISTER		
Delta Series 71	15 - 18	18 - 22
KUCHINKA, JAN (Czech.)		
H. Co. Semi-Nudes	25 - 30	30 - 35
LAFUGIE		
Series 45	15 - 18	18 - 22
LEONNEC		
Series 8	20 - 22	22 - 25
MANUEL, HENRI		
Series 51, 55	18 - 20	20 - 25
MEUNIER, SUZANNE		
Series 11, 20, 22	18 - 22	22 - 26
Series 26, 42, 77	22 - 25	25 - 35
Series 29, 32, 35	20 - 25	25 - 30
Series 56, 74	18 - 22	22 - 26
Series 24, 52, 60	18 - 22	22 - 26

L. Vallet, Lapina 2559
"La Douche" (Face)

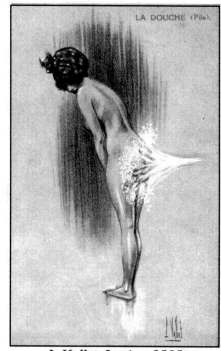

L. Vallet, Lapina 2505
"La Douche" (Tail)

Series 64, 96, 98	25 - 30	30 - 35
Series 99	18 - 22	22 - 26
Delta Series 90	20 - 22	22 - 26
MILLIERE, M.		
Series 6, 21, 30, 37	18 - 22	22 - 26
Series 34, 54, 65	20 - 25	25 - 30
NEY		
Delta Series 24	20 - 25	25 - 30
PELTIER		
Delta Series 28	20 - 25	25 - 28
PENOT, A.		
Series 10, 28	18 - 22	22 - 26
Series 16, 25	18 - 20	20 - 25
Series 97, 98, 109	15 - 18	18 - 22
PEPIN		
Delta Series 16, 21, 30	20 - 25	25 - 30
Series 23	22 - 26	26 - 32
PERAS		
Series 68	15 - 18	18 - 22
SAGER, XAVIER		
Noyer		
Series 131 - Pajamas	15 - 18	18 - 22
Series 138 - Lingerie	18 - 22	22 - 25
Series 156 - Lesbian Dancers	22 - 27	27 - 35
Series 690 - "Peaceful Shells"	20 - 25	25 - 30
Other Glamour Series	18 - 22	22 - 25
Erotic/Nudes	20 - 25	25 - 30
TAM, JEAN		
Series 39, 47, 50	18 - 22	22 - 25
Series 57, 67	20 - 25	25 - 30
Series 70, 78, 81	18 - 22	22 - 25
VALLET, L.		
Lapina		
Nude "La Douche" Series	18 - 22	22 - 25

COLOR NUDES

For many years, color nudes were completely neglected by the American postcard collector. The only issues available were those of the Great Masters' reproductions of paintings housed in the big museums and art galleries throughout he world. Most of these were done by the Stengel Art Co. of Dresden, Germany.

This gave color nudes a bad impression and repressed their growth until it was finally realized that there were hundreds of beautifully painted and very colorful nudes and semi-nudes that **were not museum reproductions.**

During the Golden Years of postcards, European artists—especially the French and Germans--painted classical nudes relating to mythical, historical, Biblical, fairy tale, and fantasy motifs that were adapted to postcards. These have become highly collectible and are pursued by many American deltiologists.

As there was no demand here in the states from 1900 to 1920, color nudes by American artists are very rare. Therefore, most all of those listed in this publication are those published in Europe. Most cards by the artists were issued as single entities and there are very few sets or series available.

	VG	EX
ALLEAUME, L.		
Lapina		
59 "In the Rose"	12 - 15	15 - 18
201 "Offering"	10 - 12	12 - 15
ASTI, A.		
JL & W		
36/25 No caption, unsigned	12 - 15	15 - 18
Salon 1897		
"Songeuse"	15 - 18	18 - 22
AUER, R.		
Salon J.C.Z.		
1 "Delight"	10 - 12	12 - 15
4 "Tender Flower"	12 - 15	15 - 18
AXENTOWICZ, T.		
ANCZYC		
10 "Noc"	20 - 25	25 - 30
110 "Noc"	18 - 20	20 - 25
DN		
29 "Studjum"	18 - 20	20 - 22
BARBER, COURT		
S.& G.S.i.B.		
1283 "Nach dem Bade"	12 - 15	15 - 18
1284 "Der Golden Schal"	12 - 15	15 - 18
BEAUFEREY, M. LOUISE		
Salon de 1914		
292 "Young Woman at her Dressing"	10 - 12	12 - 14
BENDER, S.		
H.M.		
"La Femme" Series	15 - 18	18 - 22

S. Bender, A.H. 1219, "La Femme"

M.L. Beaufrey, Salon de 1914 292
"Young Woman Dressing"

Calderera, No Pub. 3241-11
No Caption

BECAGLI, P.
  Salon de Paris
    "Paressguse"   12 - 15   15 - 18
BERNHARD
    "Bachante"   10 - 12   12 - 15
BESNARD
  Musee de Luxembourg
    500 "Woman Warming Herself"   8 - 10   10 - 12
BIESSY, GABRIEL
  Salon de Paris
    "The Model"   10 - 12   12 - 15
BORRMEISTER, R.
  Hermann Wolff
    1093 "Wald Marchen"   10 - 12   12 - 15
    1128 "Morgengruss"   10 - 12   12 - 15
BOTTINGER, H.
  J.P.P.
    1074 "Marchen"   12 - 15   15 - 18
BOULAND, M.
  A.N., Paris
    446 "Femme a l'echape"   12 - 15   15 - 18
BRICHARD, X.
  A.N., Paris
    404 "After the Bath"   12 - 15   15 - 18

BUBNA, G.
Hermann Wolf
1135 "Ein Neugierger"   10 - 12   12 - 15
BUKOVAC, V.
Minerva
21 No Caption   10 - 12   12 - 15
28 "Koketa"   10 - 12   12 - 15
BUSMEY, S.
Lapina
825 "The Dream of Love"   10 - 12   12 - 15
BUSSIERE
Salon de Paris
744 "Salome"   10 - 12   12 - 15
CAYRON, J.
Lapina
5433 "Repose"   12 - 15   15 - 18
CHANTRON, A.J.
Salon de Paris
933 "The Bind Weed"   12 - 15   15 - 18
CHAPIN
Stengel Art Co.
29920 "Souvenirs"   8 - 10   10 - 12
CHERY
"The Source"   10 - 12   12 - 14
COLLIN, R.
Lapina
408 "Floreal"   8 - 10   10 - 12
COMERRE, LEON
Palais des Beaux Arts
"The Golden Rain"   10 - 12   12 - 15
A.N., Paris
164 "While the Artist..."   8 - 10   10 - 12
Musee de Luxembourg
411 "The Spider"   8 - 10   10 - 12
COURTOIS, G.
Lapina
526 "La Lecture"   8 - 10   10 - 12
CROZAT
Galerie d'Art
117 "Apres le bal"   12 - 15   15 - 18
CUNICEL, EDW.
O.F.Z.-L
"Coquetry"   8 - 10   10 - 12
CZECH, E.
Apollon Sophia
70 "Temptation"   8 - 10   10 - 12
DE BOUCHE
E.K.N.
1050 "The New Ornament"   8 - 10   10 - 12
DERVAUX, G.
Lapina

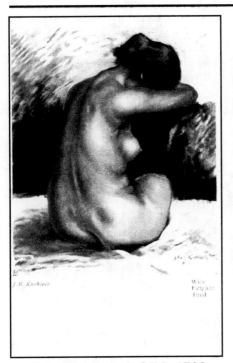

J.R. Knobloch, O.G.Z.L. 1700
"Tired"

Knoefel, Novitas 668
No Caption

5412 "Naughty"	10 - 12	12 - 15
DEWALD, A.		
Emgre-Sabn		
229 "Eve"	10 - 12	12 - 15
DOLEZEL-EZEL, P.		
F.H. & S.		
5221 No caption	10 - 12	12 - 15
DUPUIS, P.		
Hanfstaengel		
199 "The Wave"	12 - 15	15 - 18
DUSSEK, ED. ADRIAN		
KPHOT		
JK51 "In Gedanken"	15 - 18	18 - 22
JK52 "Im Atelier"	20 - 22	22 - 25
JK53 "Studie"	20 - 22	22 - 25
JK54 "Das Model"	12 - 15	15 - 18
JK55 "The Hat"	15 - 18	18 - 22
JK56 "Studie"	18 - 20	20 - 25
JK57 "The Model"	12 - 15	15 - 18
JK58 "The Hat"	15 - 18	18 - 22
JK59 "In Gedanken"	15 - 18	18 - 22
JK60 "Schwuller Tag"	12 - 15	15 - 18
JK61 "Kotetterie"	15 - 18	18 - 22
JK62 "Die Gold Gube"	15 - 18	18 - 22

JK63 "Vertraumt"	15 - 18	18 - 22
JK64 "Jugendstil Akstudie"	18 - 20	20 - 22
JK65 "Im Avendlicht"	15 - 18	18 - 22
JK66 "Halbakt"	25 - 28	28 - 32
JK67 "Erwachen"	18 - 22	22 - 25
JK68 "Blonder Akt"	20 - 22	22 - 25
JK69 "Frosch Koenigs Braut"	22 - 25	25 - 28
JK70 "Gross Toilette am Land"	12 - 15	15 - 18
JK18 "Das Neue Model"	10 - 12	12 - 15
JK25 "Modelpause"	12 - 15	15 - 18

EICHER, MAX
  O.G.Z.-L

291 "Nach Dem Bade"	10 - 12	12 - 15

EINBECK

"Nana"	10 - 12	12 - 15

ENJOLRAS, E.
  Lapina

718 "Repose"	12 - 15	15 - 18
"Ruth"	10 - 12	12 - 15
"Rest"	8 - 10	10 - 12

EVERART, M.
  A.N., Paris

7 "The Woman With Ribbons"	10 - 12	12 - 15

  SPA, Paris

4059 "The Woman With Lamp"	10 - 12	12 - 15
76 "Young Woman at Mirror"	12 - 15	15 - 18

FAR-SI
  A.N., Paris

"Oriental Perfume"	12 - 15	15 - 18

FEIKL, S.
  J.K.P.

236 "Akt"	10 - 12	12 - 15

FENNER-BEHMEL, H.
  Hanfstaengel's

194 "Ysabel"	15 - 18	18 - 22

FERRARIS, A.
  B.K.W.I.

"Leda"	12 - 15	15 - 18

FOURNIER

"Woman Bathing"	10 - 12	12 - 15

FREAND, E.
  Lapina

5415 "Familiar Birds"	8 - 10	10 - 12

FRIEDRICH, OTTO
  B.K.W.I.

1541 "Eitelkeit"	10 - 12	12 - 15

FRONTE, M.
  Lapina

"Woman Lying Down"	12 - 15	15 - 18

FUCHS, RUDOLPH
  W.R.B.& Co.

738 "Blaue Augen"	10 - 12	12 - 15
GALAND, LEON		
Salon de Paris		
"A Sleeping Woman"	12 - 15	15 - 18
GALLELLI, M.		
P. Heckscher		
143 "The First Pose"	10 - 12	12 - 15
GEIGER, C. AUG.		
NPG		
453 "Eva"	10 - 12	12 - 15
GERMAIN		
"First Session"	12 - 15	15 - 18
GERVEX, H.		
Palais des Beaux-Arts		
261 "Birth of Venus"	10 - 12	12 - 15
GITTER, H.		
Galerie Munchen Meister		
"Morgen"	8 - 10	10 - 12
"Tag"	6 - 8	8 - 10
GLUCKLEIN, S.		
Hanfstaengel's		
202 "Reposing"	10 - 12	12 - 15
GODWARD, J.W.		
Richard (Russia)		
295 "A Fair Reflection"	10 - 12	12 - 15

 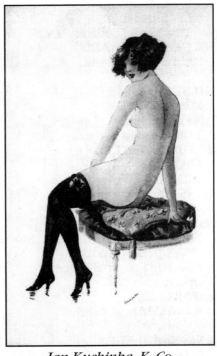

H.C. Kosel, BKWI 181/3
"Kungtgeschichte"

Jan Kuchinka, K. Co.
No Caption

GOEPFART, FRANZ
301 "Ruhender Akt"   10 - 12   12 - 15
GOROKHOV
N.P.G., Berlin
"Wassernixe"   12 - 15   15 - 18
GRENOUILLOUX, J.
Lapina
"The Fair Summer Days"   12 - 15   15 - 18
"The Nymph with Flags"   12 - 15   15 - 18
Apollon
78 "Speil der Wellen"   8 - 10   10 - 12
GUETIN, V.
Lapina
799 "Das Bad"   8 - 10   10 - 12
GUILLAUME, R.M.
Lapina
1400 "The Repose of the Model"   8 - 10   10 - 12
1083 "Rapid Change"   10 - 12   12 - 15
Soc. des Artistes
58 "The Fly"   8 - 10   10 - 12
A.H.
K.th W.II
636 "Lybelle"   10 - 12   12 - 15
HERVE, G.
Lapina
44 "Resting"   12 - 15   15 - 18
813 "Farniente"   12 - 15   15 - 18
"My Model and My Dog"   8 - 10   10 - 12
HEYMAN, RICHARD
Heinrich Hoffman
"Psyche"   10 - 12   12 - 15
HILSER
Minerva
83 No Caption   10 - 12   12 - 15
1130 "Siesta"   10 - 12   12 - 15
JANUSZEWSKI, J.
ANCZYC
185 "Akt"   8 - 10   10 - 12
455 No Caption   8 - 10   10 - 12
KASPARIDES, E.
B.K.W.I
161-4 "A Warm Summer Morning"   8 - 10   10 - 12
164-3 "The Airbath"   10 - 12   12 - 15
164-10 "Forest Silence"   8 - 10   10 - 12
Others   8 - 10   10 - 12
KIESEL, C.
A.R.&C.i.B.
"Salome"   8 - 10   10 - 12
KNOBLOCH, J.R.
O.G.Z.-L
700 "Tired"   8 - 10   10 - 12

KNOEFEL
  Novitas
  668 Illuminated Nudes   (4)   15 - 18   18 - 22
KLIMES
  Minerva
  1227 "Nymphe"   10 - 12   12 - 15
KORPAL, T.
  ANCYZ
  16 Bather "Au Ete"   10 - 12   12 - 15
KOSEL, H.C.
  B.K.W.I.
  181-3 "Kungstgeschlichte"   8 - 10   10 - 12
  181-8 "Nach im Bade"   8 - 10   10 - 12
  181-9 "Lekture"   8 - 10   10 - 12
  181-10 "Skaoin"   10 - 12   12 - 15
KRENES, H.
  C1-12 "Danse"   8 - 10   10 - 12
KRIER, E.A.
  Salon de Paris
  5379 "Folly at Home"   8 - 10   10 - 12
KUTEW, CH.
  First
    Series 90-8 No caption   8 - 10   10 - 12
    Series 90-10 No caption   12 - 15   15 - 18
  A.F.W.
    111-2 "Ondine"   10 - 12   12 - 15
    "Nymph"   12 - 15   15 - 18
LANZDORF, R.
  R.&J.D.
  501 "Young Bedouin Girl"   8 - 10   10 - 12
LAUREN, P.A.
  Lapina
  2032 "Didon"   8 - 10   10 - 12
LEEKE, F.
  Munchener Kunst
  3114 "Bad de Bestalin"   12 - 15   15 - 18
  Hans Koehler & Co.
  76 "Bacchantalin"   12 - 15   15 - 18
LEDIR
  P. Heckscher
  366 "Die Zofe"   8 - 10   10 - 12
LEFFEBURE, J.
  Musee de Luxembourg
  500 "Woman Warming Herself"   6 - 8   8 - 10
LENOIR, CH
  Lapina
  853 "Stream Song"   12 - 15   15 - 18
  A.N., Paris
  19 "Tanzerin"   8 - 10   10 - 12
L'EVEIL
  Salon 1914

304 "The Awakening"	12 - 15	15 - 18
LIEBERMAN, E.		
Emil Kohn		
890 "At the Window"	8 - 10	10 - 12
LINGER, O.		
G. Liersch & Co.		
537 "Susses Nichtshen"	10 - 12	12 - 15
LUCAS, H.		
Lapina		
890 "Happy Night"	10 - 12	12 - 15
MAKOVSKY, C.		
539 Russian Card "Dans ie Boudoir"	8 - 10	10 - 12
MALIQUET, C.		
Lapina		
"Voluptousness"	10 - 12	12 - 15
Salon de Paris		
56 "At the Hairdresser"	10 - 12	12 - 15
MANDL, JOSEPH		
Salon J.P.P.		
2056 "L'Innocence"	8 - 10	10 - 12
MARECEK		
KV		
1335 "Nach dem Bad"	8 - 10	10 - 12
VKKA		
1201 "Toileta"	6 - 8	8 - 10
MARTIN, F.		
AR & CiB		
395 "Vom dem Spiegel"	8 - 10	10 - 12
MARTIN-KAVEL		
Lapina		
"Nude on Tiger Rug"	8 - 10	10 - 12
934 "Surprised"	8 - 10	10 - 12
MAX, G.		
Apollon Sophia		
68 "Bacchante"	10 - 12	12 - 15
MENZLER, W.		
NPG		
512 "Akt"	8 - 10	10 - 12
MERCIER		
Art Moderne		
748 "Nymphe Endormie"	10 - 12	12 - 15
"Nymph Reclining"	10 - 12	12 - 15
MERLE, K.		
Moderner Kunst		
2355 "After the Bath"	8 - 10	10 - 12
MIASSOJEDOW, J.		
224 Russian "Arabian Tanzerin"	10 - 12	12 - 15
MOHN, ROTER		
Moderner Kunst		
245 "Feuerlilien"	8 - 10	10 - 12
246 No caption	8 - 10	10 - 12

Jan Kuchinka, K. Co.
No Caption

G. Rienacker, PFB 6034
"Die Favoritin"

MORIN
  Salon J.P.P.
    1124 "Feu Follet"   8 - 10   10 - 12
MULLER, RICH.
  Malke & Co.
    25 "My Models"   15 - 18   18 - 22
  SPGA
    251 "Gold Fish"   15 - 18   18 - 22
    252 "Der Rote Ibis"   15 - 18   18 - 22
    Others   15 - 18   18 - 22
NAKLADAATEL, J.
  J.P.P.
    Series 440-445 (6) Semi-nudes 15 - 18   18 - 22
NEJEDLY
  Salon J.P.P.
    "Erwachen"   10 - 12   12 - 15
NEMEJC, AUG.
  Polish "Tragedie"   8 - 10   10 - 12
NISSL, RUDOLF
  Novitas
    388 "Am im Mantel"   10 - 12   12 - 15
NONNENBRUCH, M.
  Salon J.P.P.
    2187 "La Sculpture"   10 - 12   12 - 15

O.G.Z.-L
1174 "After Dancing"   10 - 12   12 - 15
Hanfstaengel's
49 "Flora"   10 - 12   12 - 15
OSTROWSKI, A.J.
  Phillips
  Russian 2172 "The Model"   10 - 12   12 - 15
OTTOMAN
  Lapina
  "The Sleeping Courtesan"   8 - 10   10 - 12
PAPERITZ, G.
  Apollon Sophia
  84 "Boa Neuf"   12 - 15   15 - 18
  237 "Bayadere"   12 - 15   15 - 18
PAUSINGER
  Russian 063 "Salome"   12 - 15   15 - 18
PENOT, A.
  Lapina
  "Water Flower"   10 - 12   12 - 15
  "Bayadera"   8 - 10   10 - 12
  "A Young Girl"   10 - 12   12 - 15
  "The Charm of Spring"   12 - 15   15 - 18
  "Libelle"   10 - 12   12 - 15
  1340 "Red Butterfly"   12 - 15   15 - 18
  Salon de Paris
  229 "Repose"   10 - 12   12 - 15
PERRAULT
  Salon de Paris
  727 "Der Erste Mai"   10 - 12   12 - 15
PETER, O.
  S.V.D.
  292 "Das Kunstler Modell"   12 - 15   15 - 18
PRICE, J.M.
  Hanfstaengel's
  117 "Odaliske"   12 - 15   15 - 18
R.R.
  M. Munk
  Series 684 (6)   12 - 15   15 - 18
  Series 873 (6)   15 - 18   18 - 22
REINACKER, G.
  Marke JSC
  6054 "Am Morgen"   10 - 12   12 - 15
  6055 "Verkauft"   12 - 15   15 - 18
  6083 "Der Neue Schmuck"   12 - 15   15 - 18
  PFB
  6034 "Die Favoritin"   10 - 12   12 - 15
REIFENSTEIN, LEO
  Galzburger Kunst
  45 "Schonhut"   10 - 12   12 - 15
RETTIG, H.
  Munchener Meister

G. Seignac, A.N., Paris 507
"A Sprighty Girl"

V. Shivert, Arthur Rehn 360
"Die Rivalin"

568 "Im Spiegel"	10 - 12	12 - 15
RIESEN, O.		
A. Sch. & Co.		
7152 "Unschuld"	10 - 12	12 - 15
S.&G.SiB		
1471 "Am Morgen"	12 - 15	15 - 18
RITTER, C.		
Novitas		
397 "Im Gotteskleid"	10 - 12	12 - 15
ROUSSELET, E.		
Lapina		
1129 "Bathing"	12 - 15	15 - 18
"The Dream"	8 - 10	10 - 12
ROUSTEAUX-DARBOURD		
Salon 1912		
571 "Am Feuer"	10 - 12	12 - 15
SAIZEDE		
Lapina		
"A Woman and Statuette"	8 - 10	10 - 12
SALIGER		
Haus der D. Kunst		
"Die Sinne"	10 - 12	12 - 15
SCALBERT, J.		
A.N., Paris		
442 "The Shift"	8 - 10	10 - 12

Lapina
5158 "Hesitation"   10 - 12   12 - 15
SPA
30 "Satisfaction"   8 - 10   10 - 12
Salon de Paris
1570 "Five O'Clock Tea"   10 - 12   12 - 15
5085 "The Looking Glass"   10 - 12   12 - 15
SCIHLABITZ, A.
NPGA
30 "Akstudie"   10 - 12   12 - 15
SCHIVERT, V.
TSN
801 "Der Liebertraube"   6 - 8   8 - 10
NPG
237 "Susanne"   8 - 10   10 - 12
Munchener Kunst
193 No caption   12 - 15   15 - 18
199 No caption   12 - 15   15 - 18
PFB
42291 "Das Modell"   15 - 18   18 - 22
Arthur Rehn & Co.
"Die Quelle"   15 - 18   18 - 22
"Die Rivalin"   12 - 15   15 - 18
SCHLEMO, E.
TSN
888 "Schonheit is alles"   12 - 15   15 - 18
889 "Beauty"   10 - 12   12 - 15
SCHLIMARSKI, H.
B.K.W.I
1805 "Vanity"   10 - 12   12 - 15

R. Vallet, Lapina 2502, "Indolence"

H. Vasselon, Salon de Paris, "The Spring"

SCHMUTZLER, L.
O.G.Z.L.
364 "Courtezan"   15 - 18   18 - 22
E.N.
810 "Passion"   15 - 18   18 - 22
Others   12 - 15   15 - 18
SCHNEIDER, E.
"Die Windsbraut   10 - 12   12 - 15
NPGA
54 "Halbakt"   10 - 12   12 - 15
AMAG Kunst
51 "Bacchantin"   10 - 12   12 - 15
SCHULZ, E.
B.K.W.I.
885-1 Goethe's "Der Got und Baidere"   15 - 18   18 - 22
SEEBERGER, J.
A.N., Paris
446 "After the Bath"   10 - 12   12 - 15
470 "Smit with Love"   12 - 15   15 - 18
SEIGNAC, G.
A.N., Paris
"Gachucha"   8 - 10   10 - 12
597 "A Sprightly Girl"   10 - 12   12 - 15
760 "Indolence"   10 - 12   12 - 15
Lapina
"The Birth of Venus"   12 - 15   15 - 18
SEZILLE, D.E.
Lapina

913 "Annoying Accident"	12 - 15	15 - 18
SIEFERT, P.		
A.N., Paris		
"Diana"	15 - 18	18 - 22
SKALA		
Minerva		
1117 "Eva"	10 - 12	12 - 15
SOLOMKO, S.		
T.S.N.		
153 "Circe"	15 - 18	18 - 22
SOUBBOTINE		
NPG		
87 "Studie"	15 - 18	18 - 22
Granbergs		
Stockholm 577 "Im Harem"	15 - 18	18 - 22
STACHIEWICZ, P.		
Wydann. Salon		
152/23 "Kwiat Olean"	15 - 18	18 - 22
152/24 "Zloty Zawoj"	12 - 15	15 - 18
"Ruth"	12 - 15	15 - 18
STELLA, EDUARD		
BRW		
353 "Madame Sans Gene"	18 - 20	20 - 22
354 "Diana"	18 - 20	20 - 22
STEMBER, N.K.		
Phillips		
1078 "Elegie"	18 - 20	20 - 25
Hanfstaengels		
56 "Jugend" or "Youth"	18 - 20	20 - 25
STENGEL NUDES		
Various Artists	6 - 10	8 - 12
STYKA, TADE		
Lapina		
183 "Cinquecento"	6 - 8	8 - 10
SUCHANKE		
VKKA		
1336 "Fruhlingslied"	6 - 8	8 - 10
SYKORA, G.		
G.Z.		
032 "Der Necker"	8 - 10	10 - 12
TARDIEU, VICTOR		
Salon de Paris		
168 "Study in Nude"	10 - 12	12 - 15
URBAN, J.		
D.K. & Co.		
678 No caption	12 - 15	15 - 18
VACHA, L.		
Minerva		
1170 "Suzanne"	8 - 10	10 - 12
VALLET, L.		
Lapina		

M. Saizede, Salon de Paris 1120
"Frau mit Statuette"

Fr. Urban, J. Pichtel 45
No Caption

2498 "The Gourmet"	15 - 18	18 - 22
2506 "Luxury"	15 - 18	18 - 22
2507 "Pride"	15 - 18	18 - 22
Others	12 - 15	15 - 18
VASNIER, E.		
Lapina		
779 "The Toilet"	12 - 15	15 - 18
VASSELON, H.		
A. Noyer		
"The Spring"	12 - 15	15 - 18
VOLKER, ROB.		
Munchener Kunst		
385, 386 No caption	10 - 12	12 - 15
VOWE, P.G.		
MBK		
2546 No caption	8 - 10	10 - 12
WALLIKOW, F.B.		
GK.v., Berlin		
432 "Reifers Obst"	6 - 8	8 - 10
WEBER, E.		
B.W.K.I.		
2363 "Akt"	10 - 12	12 - 15
WITTING, W.		
S.V.D.		

358 "Auf Freier Hohe"	10 - 12	12 - 15
Dresdner KK		
"Jugend"	10 - 12	12 - 15
WOBRING, F.		
S.W.S.B.		
4771 "Morgentau"	8 - 10	10 - 12
ZIER, ED.		
Richard		
"La Siesta"	12 - 15	15 - 18
ZMURKO, FR.		
ANCZYC		
291, 297, 355, 448, 516	12 - 15	15 - 18
280, 347, 449, 510, 648	10 - 12	12 - 15
ZOPF, C.		
O.G.Z.-L		
865 "Curious"	8 - 10	10 - 12
ZWILLER, A.		
Salon de Paris		
"The Rest"	10 - 12	12 - 15

S. Bender, H.M. 1222
"La Femme"

BLACKS

	VG	EX
ATWELL, MABEL L.		
Valentine & Sons		
Series 745, A331 (6)	$ 10 - 12	$ 12 - 16
Series 614, 615 (6)	14 - 16	16 - 20
Series A550	8 - 10	10 - 12
Others		
Early Period, Pre-1915	14 - 16	16 - 20
Middle Period, 1915-1930	12 - 14	14 - 16
Late Period, 1930-1950	8 - 10	10 - 12
BRUNDAGE, FRANCES		
Raphael Tuck		
Series 2723 "Colored Folks" (6)	35 - 40	40 - 45
"Church Parade"		
"The Christening"		
"De Proof of de Puddin"		
"Don't took de las' piece"		
"The Village Choir"		
"You is a Chicken"		
Series 100, 102 (1), (2) (Unsigned)	20 - 22	22 - 26
Series 108 (4) (Unsigned)	25 - 30	30 - 35
Series 115 (Unsigned)	25 - 30	30 - 35
Series 118 (2) (Unsigned)	30 - 35	35 - 40
"Waiting fo' Mah Sweetheart"		
"To Greet Mah Valentine"		
Series 4096 "Funny Folk" (6)	30 - 35	35 - 40
Other Signed Brundage	15 - 18	18 - 22
Unsigned	12 - 15	15 - 18

W. Fialkowski, A.V.M. 1921

BUCHANAN, FRED		
Raphael Tuck		
Series 9309 (6)	10 - 12	12 - 15
CARTER, SYDNEY (GB)		
Hildesheimer & Co.		
Series 5232 "The Dance" Series	10 - 12	12 - 15
CLAPSADDLE, ELLEN		
International Art Pub. Co.		
Mechanical Series 1236		
"A Jolly Halloween" Black child	175 - 200	200 - 225
No Number Valentine	12 - 14	14 - 16
Girl sits on Box	10 - 12	12 - 14
Boy Offers Girl Ice Cream	12 - 14	14 - 16
Stewart & Woolf, London		
Black Boy Walking Left	20 - 25	25 - 30
Others	20 - 25	25 - 30
COCKRELL	6 - 8	8 - 10
COOK, A.M.		
ZAHC		
"In Erwartung"	12 - 15	15 - 18
CRANE	6 - 8	8 - 10
CURTIS, E.	6 - 8	8 - 10
DONADINI, JR.		
Series 454	12 - 15	15 - 18
FLC		
F.A. Moss	6 - 8	8 - 10
FYCH, C.D.		
Valentine & Sons	8 - 10	10 - 12

F.G. Lewin, Bamforth 179
"Alone at Last"

H.D. Sanford, R. Tuck 9457
"The Price of a Ride"

F.G. Lewin, Bamforth 13592, "Just we Two..."

Spar-Kuhl, AVM 636
No Caption

LIKE THE GERMANS I'M COMING OUT
IN MY TRUE COLOURS — BLACK
J'ai sorti mes couleurs pour faire comme tout le monde.

Fred Spurgin, Int. Art Co. 154
"Like the Germans..."

GASSAWAY, KATHERINE
  Rotograph Co.
  105 "I Scared I'll Get Sunburned"   8 - 10   10 - 12
  123 "I Wish I was in Dixie"   8 - 10   10 - 12
  Others   8 - 10   10 - 12
GILSON, T.
  E.J. Hey & Co.
  Series 262   10 - 12   12 - 14
  Series 410
  Mama and Child   10 - 12   12 - 14
  "Rats"   10 - 12   12 - 14
  Series 151
  "Le's 'av a puff"   8 - 10   10 - 12
  J. Salmon
  Series 2571   10 - 12   12 - 14
  British Manufacture Series   8 - 10   10 - 12
GREINER, MANGUS
  International Art
  Black Series 701-710
  701 "A Darktown Trip"   12 - 14   14 - 18
  702 "The Serenade"   12 - 14   14 - 18
  704 "A Lad & a Ladder"   12 - 14   14 - 18
  707 "A Darktown Idyl"   12 - 14   14 - 18
  708 "A Feast"   12 - 14   14 - 18
  709 "A Darktown Lover"   12 - 14   14 - 18

710 "A Darktown Philosopher"	12 - 14	14 - 18
HERMAN, H.		
Ullman Co.		
Series 106 (4)	12 - 14	14 - 16
HUTAF, AUGUST		
Ullman Mfg. Co.		
Series 113 "Blacktown Babies"	8 - 10	10 - 12
K.V.		
L.P.		
Series 206 Black Kewpies	10 - 12	12 - 15
KEMBLE, E. B.		
Black & White Comics	6 - 8	8 - 10
LEVI, C.		
Ullman Co.		
Series 165	8 - 10	10 - 12
Series 210, 3308 "Suffragette"	20 - 22	22 - 25
LEWIN, F.G.		
Artisque	12 - 16	16 - 18
Inter Art Co.	8 - 10	10 - 14
J. Salmon		
2756 "A Little Light on a Dark Subject"	10 - 12	12 - 14
"I's a waiting for you"	10 - 12	12 - 14
"Love will find a way"	10 - 12	12 - 14
2583 "I's is jus' Nuts on You"		
Boy, Girl near Tree Hut	8 - 10	10 - 12

D. Tempest, Bamforth 132
"Look me over, Buddy"

D. Tempest, Bamforth 807
"O, Honey! If ..."

Boy W/Flowers for Pickaninny Girl	10 - 12	12 - 14
Bamforth Co.	8 - 10	10 - 14
"Black Kid Comics"		
"Just We Two - in Our Little Canoe"	8 - 10	10 - 12
"I Love the Sea When You are in it"	8 - 10	10 - 12
"I's Just Bilin' ober..." Unsigned	6 - 8	8 - 10
"Two Lovin Hearts"	6 - 8	8 - 10
LONG, F.G.		
Kaufmann & Strauss, 1904	10 - 12	12 - 14
LUZE (France)	10 - 12	12 - 14
MAURICE, REG.		
Regent		
Series 4137	12 - 14	14 - 16
Series 501	12 - 14	14 - 16
M.D.S.		
Raphael Tuck		
Series 9049 "Happy Little Coons" (6)	12 - 14	14 - 16
Series 9093 "Curley Coons" (6)	14 - 16	16 - 18
Series 9227 "Happy Little Coons" (6)	12 - 14	14 - 16
Series 9228 "Happy Little Coons" (6)	12 - 14	14 - 16
Series 9229 "Happy Little Coons" (6)	14 - 16	16 - 18
McGILL, DONALD		
Bamforth Co.	6 - 8	8 - 12
D. Constance, Ltd.	6 - 8	8 - 12
MINNS, B.E.		
Carleton Publishing Co.		
"Glad Eye" Series (6)	10 - 12	12 - 15
O'NEILL, ROSE		
Raphael Tuck		
Series 2482 Oilettes		
"High Society in Coontown" (6)	100 - 110	110 - 120
"Coontown Kids" Series (6)	80 - 90	90 - 100
OUTCAULT		
Ullman Mfg. Co.		
Series 76 "Darktown"	12 - 14	14 - 18
Raphael Tuck		
Und/Back Valentines	10 - 13	13 - 18
Buster Brown & His Bubble - 3,6 & 8	20 - 25	25 - 30
RICHARDSON, AGNES	10 - 12	12 - 16
Celesque Series	12 - 14	14 - 18
RYAN	8 - 10	10 - 12
SANFORD, H. DIX or H.D. or H.D.S.		
Raphael Tuck		
Series 9428, 9489 (6)		
"Dark Girls & Black Boys"	10 - 12	12 - 15
Series 9318 "Seaside Coons" (6)	10 - 12	12 - 15
Series 9968, 9969 "Seaside Coons" (6)	10 - 12	12 - 15
Series 9427 "More Coons" (6)	10 - 12	12 - 15
Series 9457 "Happy Little Coons" (6)	10 - 12	12 - 15
Series 9050 "Sand Coons" (6)	10 - 12	12 - 15

Arth. Thiele, FED 306
No Caption

Arth. Thiele, FED 306
No Caption

Hildesheimer & Co.		
Series 5268 "Negroes"	8 - 10	10 - 12
SANFORD, M.		
Raphael Tuck Series	10 - 12	12 - 15
A.S.		
Hildesheimer & Co.		
Series 5268 No captions	8 - 10	10 - 12
SHEPHEARD, A. (GB)		
Raphael Tuck		
Series 9068 "Coon's Cooning" (6)	10 - 12	12 - 15
SPARKUHL		
AVM		
Series 636 White/Black	10 - 12	12 - 14
SPURGIN, FRED		
J & A Co.		
"Coon Series" 405		
"Am my nose still shiny?"	8 - 10	10 - 12
"Golly! You are looking pale"	10 - 12	12 - 14
"Things are looking Black"	10 - 12	12 - 14
TEMPEST, DAN		
Bamforth Co.		
"Look me over, buddy..."	8 - 10	10 - 12
"Oh, Honey! If..."	8 - 10	10 - 12
"I'se black all over..."	6 - 8	8 - 10

"Full on top--cooler than riding inside!"	8 - 10	10 - 12
"Here's a Quaint Coon"	8 - 10	10 - 12
"I'se Black all over"	6 - 8	8 - 10
Others	6 - 8	8 - 10

THIELE, ARTH.
FED

Series 306 Head Studies (6)	20 - 22	22 - 26
Series 871 Black Jockeys (6)	20 - 25	25 - 28

TWELVETREES, C.
Edward Gross

61 "Doe you tink..."	8 - 9	9 - 10
151 "She do, she don't"	8 - 10	10 - 12
864 Two Black Boys in Basket	6 - 7	7 - 8
"Woman - Kiss Me"	6 - 8	8 - 10

TYRELL
S.S. Porter

	8 - 10	10 - 12

USABAL, L.

Series 1295-1300	18 - 20	20 - 22

WALL, BERNHARDT
Ullman Mfg. Co.

Series 59 "Little Coons"	10 - 12	12 - 14
1660 "You all can hab de Rine"		
1661 "Deed, I didn't steal um"		
1662 "Who's dat say chicken"		
1663 "Just two Coons"		
Series 70 "Cute Coons"	10 - 12	12 - 14
1852 "A chip off the old Block"		
1853 "Whose Baby is OO?"		
1854 "He lubs me"		
1855 "I's so happy"		

WIEDERSEIM, GRACE
Raphael Tuck

Series 2723 "Colored Folks"	35 - 40	40 - 50
"Church Parade"		
"Don't Took the Last Piece"		
"The Christening"		
"De Proof of de Puddin"		

WUYTS
A. Noyer

Series 76 (6)	10 - 12	12 - 16

ZAHL
Poster Series

"Othello"	12 - 14	14 - 18
"Be'Jst Du?"	12 - 14	14 - 18

10

SPORTS

GOLF

	VG	EX
ATWELL, MABEL LUCIE		
Children Golfers	10 - 12	12 - 18
BARBER, COURT		
2023/5 "A Golf Champion"	12 - 15	15 - 18
CHRISTY, F. EARL		
Knapp Co.		
"Always Winning"	15 - 18	18 - 22
"Goodbye Summer"	15 - 18	18 - 22
R&N		
367 "The Day's Work"	15 - 18	18 - 22
FAS 200	20 - 25	25 - 28
Ill. P.C. Co. 572	10 - 12	12 - 15
P. Sander 198-1	15 - 18	18 - 22
Platinachrome	12 - 15	15 - 18
Ullman	10 - 12	12 - 15
Pain Karjalan Kirjap.		
"Love All"	35 - 40	40 - 45
CHRISTY, H.C.		
"The Golf Girl"	14 - 16	16 - 20
CORBELLA, T.		
Series 316 (6)	15 - 20	20 - 25
CROMBIE, C.		
Valentine & Sons		
"Etiquette," "Local Rule," etc. (6)	10 - 12	12 - 15
E.H.D.		
Golfing O'Possum	12 - 14	14 - 16

FISHER, HARRISON
  R&N
  103 "Fore"   18 - 22   22 - 25
  108 "Two Up"   18 - 22   22 - 25
GUNN, ARCHIE
  Anon. B&W (2)   12 - 14   14 - 18
  Anon. Color   15 - 18   18 - 22
  Lowney's Chocolates (6)   14 - 18   18 - 22
GUTTANY
  E. Gross
  "A Tee Party"   12 - 15   15 - 18
M.D.S.
  1929 "On the Links"   12 - 14   14 - 16
MAUZAN
  Series 10 (6)   16 - 18   18 - 22
NANNI
  Series 309 (6)   20 - 22   22 - 28
PILLARD
  Langsdorf
  "Teddy at Golf"   12 - 15   15 - 18
PRESTON, CHLOE
  A.R.&CiB.
  1587-4   12 - 15   15 - 18
QUINNELL
  "The Golf Girl"   12 - 15   15 - 18

F. Thundy, BKWI 237-1
No Caption

D. Tempest, Bamforth 129
Unsigned, "Anytime..."

"WHAT DID I GO ROUND IN YESTERDAY. CADDIE?"
"THE SAME CRAZY PANTS. MISTER!"

A. Taylor, Bamforth Co., "What Did I Go Round In..."

RELYA
  W.C.
    7, 8, 9, and 10   12 - 15   15 - 18
STUDDY
  "Bonzo" Various Series   12 - 15   15 - 18
THACKERAY, L.
  Raphael Tuck
    Series 9304, 9305 (6)   15 - 18   18 - 22
    Series 1627, 1628 (6)   15 - 18   18 - 22
THUNDY, F.   15 - 18   18 - 22
UNDERWOOD, C.
  M. Munk, Vienna
    "Lost"   10 - 12   12 - 15
  PUBLISHERS, Anonymous Artists
  Raphael Tuck
    Series 697 "Golf Hints" (6)   12 - 15   15 - 18
    Series 9499 "Humorous Golf" (6)   12 - 15   15 - 18
    Series 3600 "Golf Humor" (6)   12 - 15   15 - 18
    Series 9427 "More Coons" (1)   20 - 22   22 - 26

TENNIS

BUTCHER, ARTHUR
  A.R.i.B.
  1963   12 - 15   15 - 18
CASTELLI, V.
  Series 972 (6)   12 - 15   15 - 20
CHRISTY, F. EARL
  "The Girl I Like to Play With"   15 - 18   18 - 22

R&N
"Always Winning"	15 - 18	18 - 22
"Love All"	15 - 18	18 - 22

FAS 199 — 20 - 25 — 25 - 28
ILL. P.C. CO. 584 — 10 - 12 — 12 - 15
P. SANDER 198-4 "A Good Racquet..." — 14 - 16 — 16 - 20
COLOMBO
Series 479 (6)	18 - 22	22 - 26
Series 2098 (6)	18 - 22	22 - 26

CORBELLA
Series 316 (6)	15 - 18	18 - 22

FIDLER, ALICE L.
American Girl 73	15 - 18	18 - 22

FISCHER, PAUL (6) — 10 - 12 — 12 - 15
FISHER, HARRISON
R&N
No No. "A Tennis Champion"	15 - 18	18 - 25
834 "Her Game"	20 - 25	25 - 30
839 "A Love Score"	20 - 25	25 - 30

FRANZONI
B.K.W.I.
Series 368 (6)	15 - 18	18 - 22

GRAF, M.
Deco Silhouettes	15 - 18	18 - 22

Anonymous, R&N Series
"Love"

F. Earl Christy, Finnish
No Identification Series

Studdy (Bonzo), Valentine Series

F. Earl Christy, FAS 199
No Caption

GUNN, ARCHIE		
Bergman		
14 Tennis Girl	12 - 14	14 - 18
KENNEDY		
BDF		
Series 630 Dogs play tennis	12 - 14	14 - 18
KINSELLA, E.P. (6)	15 - 18	18 - 22
M.D.S.		
1923 "Love All"	12 - 15	15 - 18
NANNI		
Series 430 (6) Small Images	12 - 15	15 - 20
Series 434, 480 (6)	22 - 25	25 - 30
NAST, T. "Love Game"	15 - 18	18 - 20
PLANTIKOW	12 - 15	15 - 20
REYNOLDS, A. "The Lady Plays Tennis"	10 - 12	12 - 15
SCATTINI	20 - 25	25 - 30
SPURGIN, FRED		
"Deuce"	10 - 12	12 - 14
STUDDY		
"Bonzo" Various Series	12 - 14	14 - 18
TWELVETREES, C.		
77 Tennis-playing Hippo	12 - 15	15 - 20

UNDERWOOD, C.
  R.C. Co.

1443 "Victoria"	22 - 25	25 - 30
Others	12 - 14	14 - 16

USABAL

Series 336 (6)	15 - 18	18 - 22

F. Earl Christy, Platinachrome, No Caption

11

COMICS

	VG	EX
ANDERSON, M. (CYNICUS) (GB)	6 - 8	8 - 10
BAIRNSFATHER, BRUCE (GB)	6 - 8	8 - 10
BATEMAN, H.M. (GB)	4 - 5	5 - 6
BIGGAR, J.L. (GB)	4 - 5	5 - 6
BIANCO, T.	4 - 5	5 - 6
Political Comics	14 - 16	16 - 18
BISHOP, P. (U.S.A.)		
"Ginks" Series	8 - 10	10 - 12
Others	4 - 5	5 - 6
BRADSHAW, P.V. (GB)	6 - 8	8 - 9
BRILL, GEORGE (U.S.A.)	6 - 7	7 - 8
BROWNE, TOM (GB)		
Davidson Bros.		
Each Series contains 6 cards		
Series 2598 "Are We Downhearted..."	8 - 10	10 - 15
Series 2578 "Billiards made..."	8 - 10	10 - 12
Series 2618 "Baseball Ill."	8 - 10	10 - 12
Series 2619 "Baseball Ill."	10 - 12	12 - 15
Series 2637 "New Compensation Act"	8 - 10	10 - 12
Series 2585 "Amateur Photographer"	10 - 12	12 - 15
Series 2587 "Cycling"	10 - 12	12 - 14
Series 2594 "Kissing"	8 - 10	10 - 12
Series 2585 "Diabolo"	8 - 10	10 - 12
BUCHANAN, FRED (GB)	4 - 5	5 - 6
BULL, RENE (GB)	5 - 6	6 - 7
BUXTON, DUDLEY (GB)	4 - 5	5 - 6
CARMICHAEL		
T.P. Co.		
Series 668 "Anybody Here Seen Kelly?"	6 - 7	7 - 8

Tom Browne, Davidson Brothers 2627
"Diabolo"

Series 565 "I Love My Wife But..."	7 - 8	8 - 10
Series 261 "Would You?" (6)	6 - 7	7 - 8
Bamforth Co.		
Series 262 "If"	6 - 7	7 - 8
Others	6 - 7	7 - 8
CARR, GENE (U.S.A.)		
Rotograph Co, N.Y.		
4th of July Series	8 - 9	9 - 10
St. Patrick's Series	4 - 6	6 - 8
CARTER, REG (GB)		
Early Issues	4 - 6	6 - 8
After 1920 Issues	3 - 4	4 - 5
CARTER, SYDNEY (GB)	8 - 10	10 - 12
CAVALLY, F. (U.S.A.)	2 - 4	4 - 5
CHRISTIE, G.F. (GB)	3 - 4	4 - 6
COMICUS (HARRY PARTLETT) (GB)	2 - 3	3 - 4
COLBY, V.	1 - 2	2 - 3
CRUMBIE, CHARLES (GB)		
Valentines		
"Rules of Golf" Series	10 - 12	12 - 15
"Rules of Cricket" Series	6 - 8	8 - 10
"Humors of Fishing" Series	6 - 8	8 - 10
Others	4 - 6	6 - 8
DAVEY, GEORGE (GB)	4 - 5	5 - 6
DIRKS, GUS (GB) Comic Insects	4 - 6	6 - 8
DIRKS, R.		
American Journal Examiner		
Katzenjammer Kid	6 - 8	8 - 10

DISNEY, WALT

Foreign Issues

French, 30's era	15 - 20	20 - 25
German, 30's era	20 - 25	25 - 30
Czech., 30's era	20 - 25	25 - 30
Hungarian, 30's era	20 - 25	25 - 30
Other 30's era issues	15 - 20	20 - 25

DONADINI, JR.

Series 454 Black Comics (6)	12 - 15	15 - 18
Auto Driving Series (6)	10 - 12	12 - 15
Horse Racing Series (6)	10 - 12	12 - 15

DWIG (C.V. DWIGGINS) (U.S.A.)

C. Marks

Halloween Series 981 (12)	18 - 20	20 - 22

Raphael Tuck

"Cheer Up" Series (24)	6 - 8	8 - 10
"Don't" Series (24)	6 - 8	8 - 10
"Everytime" Series (24)	6 - 8	8 - 10
"Follies" Series (12)	6 - 8	8 - 10
"If" Series (24)	6 - 8	8 - 10
"Ophelia" (24)	6 - 8	8 - 10
"Help Wanted" Series (12)	6 - 7	7 - 8
"Never" Series (24)	6 - 7	7 - 8
"Jollies" Series (12)	6 - 8	8 - 10
"School Days" Series (24)	6 - 8	8 - 10
"Smiles" Series (24)	8 - 10	10 - 12
"Toast" Series (12)	8 - 10	10 - 12
"Zodiac" Series (12)	12 - 16	16 - 22

Charles Rose

"Baby" Series (6)	8 - 10	10 - 12

Carmichael, T.P. & Co. 668, "Anybody Here Seen Kelly?"

Dwig, R. Kaplan
Mirror Girl Series

Dwig, R. Tuck
New Year Series

Dwig, R. Kaplan
Mirror Girl Series

Dwig, R. Kaplan
Mirror Girl Series

"Moon" Series (6)	6 - 8	8 - 10
"Moving" Series (6)	8 - 10	10 - 12
"New York" Series (6)	8 - 10	10 - 12
"Oyster Girl" Series (6)	10 - 12	12 - 14
"Sandwich" Series (6)	8 - 10	10 - 12
"Superstition" Series (6)	8 - 10	10 - 12
"What are Wild Waves..." Series (6)	10 - 12	12 - 14
"The Wurst Girl" Series (6)	10 - 12	12 - 14
"The Frankfurter Girl" (6)	10 - 12	12 - 14
R. Kaplan		
"Fortune Teller" Series (12)	8 - 9	9 - 10
"How Can You Do It?" Series (24)	6 - 7	7 - 8
"Mirror Girl" Series (24)	8 - 10	10 - 12
Sam Gabriel		
"If's & And's" Series (24)	6 - 7	7 - 8
"Leap Year" Series 401 (12)	9 - 10	10 - 12
"Fortune Teller" Series 55 (12)	6 - 8	8 - 10
Edward Gross		
"What's the Use" (6)	6 - 7	7 - 8
FISHER, BUD		
Mutt and Jeff (Uns.)	12 - 15	15 - 20
GIBSON, CHARLES DANA (U.S.A.)		
Henderson Co.		
Sepia Comics (36)	5 - 6	6 - 7
GILL, ARTHUR	4 - 5	5 - 6
GOLDBERG, RUBE		
Albie the Agent	8 - 10	10 - 12
Barton & Spooner		
"Foolish Questions"	5 - 6	6 - 8
GOODYEAR, ARCHIE	4 - 5	5 - 6
GRIGGS, H.B. and HBG		
L & E		
Halloween Series		
Series 2231	12 - 15	15 - 18
Series 2262, 2263	12 - 15	15 - 18
Series 2214	12 - 15	15 - 18
Series 2231	15 - 18	18 - 20
Others	6 - 8	8 - 12
HARDY, DUDLEY (GB)	5 - 6	6 - 8
HORINA, H. and H.H. (U.S.A.)		
Illustrated Post Card Co.	5 - 6	6 - 8
HUTAF, AUGUST		
P.C.K.		
"Advice to Vacationists"	5 - 6	6 - 7
Illustrated Post Card Co.		
"Leap Year"	6 - 8	8 - 10
Other "Leap Year" Issues	6 - 8	8 - 10
F.L.		
"Comical Types" (The Strong Man, etc.)	6 - 8	8 - 10
Others	5 - 6	6 - 8
KYD, J.C.C (GB)		

Dickens Characters	9 - 10	10 - 12

LEWIN, F.G. See Blacks
MARTIN ABE (U.S.A.)

Illustrated Post Card Co.	5 - 6	6 - 7

MAY, PHIL (GB
  Raphael Tuck

Series 1295 (6)	8 - 10	10 - 12
Series 1775 (6) Drunks	6 - 8	8 - 10

McCAY, WINDSOR
  Raphael Tuck

"Little Nemo" Series	15 - 18	18 - 22

McGILL, DONALD (GB)

Blacks	6 - 8	8 - 10
Others	2 - 3	3 - 4

McMANUS, GEORGE (U.S.A.)

"Bringing Up Father" Series	20 - 25	25 - 30

MUNSON, WALT Linens of 30's & 40's

	1 - 2	2 - 3

OPPER, F. (U.S.A.)

"Happy Hooligan" Series	8 - 10	10 - 12
"Alphonse and Gaston" Series	6 - 8	8 - 10
"And Her Name was Maud" Series	6 - 8	8 - 10
Others	5 - 6	6 - 8

  Add $3 for Tuck Issues
OUTCAULT, R.F. (U.S.A.)
  The American Journal Examiner
    Buster Brown Series (8)

"Look at Santa Claus"	15 - 18	18 - 22
"Oh See the Sea Serpent"	12 - 15	15 - 18
"Resolved: Nothing Can Stop Us"	10 - 12	12 - 15
"Say! Mary Jane..."	12 - 15	15 - 18
"What Enormous Bill on Legs..."	10 - 12	12 - 15
"Who is Buster Posing?"	15 - 18	18 - 22
"Who is Buster Getting Away From?"	12 - 15	15 - 18
"Who is the Laugh On?"	12 - 15	15 - 18

  Bloomingdale Brothers, 1902

Buster Brown Adv. Series (6)	20 - 22	22 - 25

  Bloomingdale Brothers
    Buster Brown

Santa Claus card	25 - 28	28 - 35

  Brown Shoe Co., 1909
    Buster Brown

Blue Ribbon Shoes Mos. of Year (12)	15 - 20	20 - 25

  Burr-McIntosh, 1903
    Buster Brown & His Bubble (10)

"A Quiet Day in Town"	15 - 20	20 - 25
"Hands Up"	15 - 20	20 - 25
"Black or White" (Blacks)	20 - 25	25 - 30
"Looking for Trouble"	15 - 20	20 - 25
"A Good Bump"	15 - 20	20 - 25
"Over the Bounding Main" (Blacks)	20 - 25	25 - 30
"A Rise in Bear"	15 - 20	20 - 25

R.F. Outcault, R. Tuck 111
Valentine Series

D. Tempest, Bamforth 802
Good Luck Series

"A Smooth Bit of Road" (Blacks)	20 - 25	25 - 30
"The Constable"	20 - 25	25 - 30
"All Over"	15 - 20	20 - 25
Kaufmann and Strauss, 1903		
Advertising Cards w/various		
firms imprints (16+)	12 - 15	15 - 18
J. Ottmann, 1905		
Comic Series (40+)	10 - 12	12 - 15
J. Ottmann, 1906		
Christmas Card set (4?) (Unsigned)	12 - 15	15 - 18
F.A. Stokes, 1906		
Buster Brown		
Outcault Cartoon Lectures	15 - 18	18 - 22
"Come on Tige"		
"Gee, what's playing?"		
"Give it to Mary Jane Buddy"		
"If Tige would only go away"		
"Where are you going?"		
R.H. Tammer, 1906		
Buster Brown Series (Embossed) *	15 - 18	18 - 22
"Come and join us in a blowout"		
"I ain't got no time..."		
"Hurry back with the answer"		
"It was de Dutch"		

Arth. Thiele, Unsigned, "I Have My Hands Full"

"Way down in my heart..."
* Reduced series of above set, 1908	20 - 25	25 - 30

Raphael Tuck, 1903
Valentine Series (12)	10 - 12	12 - 15

Raphael Tuck, 1904
Valentine Scroll Series (6)	10 - 12	12 - 15

"Can you guess the one...?"
"Don't monkey with this heart of mine"
"Here's a wireless telegram..."
"I am perfectly willing..."
"Why don't someone ask...?"
"Won't you be my honey..."

Raphael Tuck
Obverse Trademark
Valentines (6)	10 - 12	12 - 15

"I adore you"
"I think I've made a lovely start..."
"O! Will I be your Valentine?"
"I want you to be my Valentine"
"Resolved that there's a certain party"
"Wouldn't that there's..."

Raphael Tuck
Series 106 Valentines (6)	10 - 12	12 - 15

Raphael Tuck
Valentine Series 111 (6)	10 - 12	12 - 15

Raphael Tuck
Valentine Series 112 (6)	10 - 12	12 - 15

"For you February 14th"
"Resolved that without my heart..."

"Still now"
"There's a certain person..."
"Will you be my Valentine..."

Raphael Tuck
New Outcault Series 7

Valentine Postcards	12 - 14	14 - 16

Raphael Tuck
Buster Brown Series 8

Valentine Postcards (10)	10 - 12	12 - 15
"Bear, bear, don't go away"	10 - 12	12 - 15
"Honey, how your eyes do shine..."	15 - 18	18 - 22
"I am perfectly willing..."	10 - 12	12 - 15
"I dreams erbout yo' eb'ry night..."	15 - 18	18 - 22
"Laugh, laugh and be merry..."	10 - 12	12 - 15
"Love me, and the world is mine"	10 - 12	12 - 15
"Now how do little birdies know..."	10 - 12	12 - 15
"Of all the days in the year..."	10 - 12	12 - 15
"Oh, maid, take pity..."	10 - 12	12 - 15
"Someone has asked someone..."	10 - 12	12 - 15

Raphael Tuck

Buster Brown Postcards	12 - 15	15 - 18

Raphael Tuck

Love Tributes Series 5	12 - 15	15 - 18

Ullman Mfg. Co., 1906

"Darktown" Series 76 (4)	12 - 14	14 - 18

"Darktown Doctors"
"Darkytown Dames"
"Deed, I dun eat no chicken"
"Koontown Kids"

Buster Brown Co., Chicago, 1906

Buster Brown 1906 Calendars	15 - 18	18 - 22
Buster Brown 1907 Calendars	15 - 18	18 - 22

Outcault Adv. Co., Chicago 1907

Buster Brown 1908 Calendars	15 - 18	18 - 22
Buster Brown 1909 Calendars	15 - 18	18 - 22
Buster Brown 1910 Calendars	15 - 18	18 - 22
Buster Brown 1911 Calendars	15 - 18	18 - 22

R.F. Outcault, New York, 1907

Little House Maid 1908 Calendars	12 - 15	15 - 18
Little House Maid 1909 Calendars	12 - 15	15 - 18
Little House Maid 1910 Calendars	12 - 15	15 - 18
Little House Maid 1911 Calendars	12 - 15	15 - 18
Mr. Swell Dresser 1908 Calendars	15 - 18	18 - 22
Mr. Swell Dresser 1909 Calendars	15 - 18	18 - 22
Mr. Swell Dresser 1910 Calendars	15 - 18	18 - 22

R.F. Outcault, N.Y., 1908-09-10-11

Bank Series 1909-10-11 Calendars	12 - 14	14 - 16

R.F. Outcault, N.Y. 1909

Banking Series 1912-13 Calendars	12 - 14	14 - 16

R.F. Outcault, N.Y., 1909

Rockford Watch 1909-10 Calendars	12 - 14	14 - 16

R.F. Outcault, N.Y., 1911
　　Yellow Kid 1910-11-12 Calendars   30 - 40   40 - 50
R.F. Outcault, N.Y., 1911
　　Yellow Kid 1913 Calendars   35 - 45   45 - 55
R.F. Outcault, Copyright
　　Blue Boy 1912-14 Calendars   12 - 15   15 - 18
R.F. Outcault, Copyright
　　Buster Brown 1912-1913 Calendars   12 - 15   15 - 18
　　Buster Brown 1914-1915 Calendars   12 - 15   15 - 18
　　Furniture 1912-1915 Calendars   12 - 15   15 - 18
　　Mary Jane 1911-1913 Calendars   12 - 15   15 - 18
　　Yellow Kid Look-a-Like
　　1914-1915 Calendars   12 - 15   15 - 18
PARLETT, HARRY
　Taylor's Orthochrome
　　Series 2830 (6) Roller Skating   8 - 10   10 - 12
PHIZ (H.K. BROWNE)   8 - 10   10 - 15
PIPPO
　Big Eyed Man Series   8 - 10   10 - 12
　Barber　　　　Blacksmith
　Cook　　　　　Gambler
　Doctor　　　　Musician
　Richman　　　　Sculptor
POULBOT, F. (France)   10 - 12   12 - 15
RAEMAKERS (Netherlands)   6 - 8   8 - 10
REZNICEK (Denmark)   12 - 15   15 - 18
ROBIDA (France)   10 - 12   12 - 15
SCHULTZ, C.E. and BUNNY
　　"Foxy Grandpa" Series   6 - 8   8 - 10

D. Tempest, Bamforth 124, "Just a Line..."

SHINN, COBB and TOM YAD (U.S.A.)		
See Art Nouveau		
H.A. Waters Co.		
"Foolish Questions" Series	3 - 4	4 - 5
"Ford Comics"	6 - 8	8 - 10
"Charlie Chapman" Cartoons	8 - 10	10 - 12
SPURGIN, FRED (GB)	5 - 6	6 - 7
See Blacks		
SWINNERTON		
American Journal Examiner	6 - 7	7 - 10
THACKERAY, L. (GB)		
Raphael Tuck		
"At the Seaside" (6)	8 - 9	9 - 12
"Game of Golf" (6)	12 - 14	14 - 18
THIELE, ARTH.		
L&P		
Fat Lady Series	8 - 10	10 - 12
Bathing Girls Series	10 - 12	12 - 14
WALL, BERNHARDT		
Many Sets and Series	5 - 6	6 - 10
WEAVER, E. (U.S.A.)		
Ford Comics	8 - 10	10 - 12
Others	1 - 2	2 - 3
WELLMAN, WALTER (U.S.A.)		
"Merry Widow Wiles"	5 - 6	6 - 8
"Life's Little Tragedies"	5 - 6	6 - 8
Linen Comics	1 - 1.50	1.50 - 2
WELLS, C.		
Lounsbury		
Series 2025 "Lovely Lilly"	6 - 7	7 - 8
WITT		
"Ford Booster" Comics	7 - 8	8 - 10
WOOD, LAWSON (GB)		
Chimps, Parrots, etc.	6 - 8	8 - 10
See Suffragettes		
Bauman		
Days of the Week - Ugly Girls Unsigned	6 - 8	8 - 9
Irwin Kline		
Masonic (No Numbers) (6)	6 - 7	7 - 8
YAD, TOM also Cobb Shinn	1 - 2	2 - 3
ZIM	4 - 5	5 - 6
P.F.B. UNSIGNED COMICS		
Series 5897 Mother-in-Law (6)	8 - 10	10 - 12
Series 6307 Comic Lovers (6)	8 - 10	10 - 12
Series 6538 Domestic Riot (6)	8 - 10	10 - 12
Many Others	6 - 8	8 - 12

Me enc;

12

ANIMALS

CATS

	VG	EX
ALDIN, CECIL (GB)	6 - 7	7 - 8
BARNES, G.L. (GB)		
Raphael Tuck		
Series 9301 "Cat Studies" (6)	8 - 10	10 - 12
Series 6495 "Cat Studies" (6)	8 - 10	10 - 12
Fairy Tale/Nursery Rhymes Series	10 - 12	12 - 14
"Little Boy Blue"		
"Red Riding Hood"		
"Tom, Tom, Piper's Son"		
Others		
BOULANGER, MAURICE (France)		
International Art Publishing Co.		
Series 472 Large Image	12 - 15	15 - 20
Series 473 Large Image	12 - 14	14 - 18
Raphael Tuck		
Series 122 "Merry Days" (6) Unsigned	6 - 8	8 - 10
BROWN, TOM		
Davidson Bros.		
Series 2509 (6) "Funny Cats"	8 - 10	10 - 12
Series 2528 (6) "Comic Cats"	8 - 10	10 - 12
CLIVETTE	6 - 8	8 - 10
COBBE, B. (GB)		
Raphael Tuck		
Series 9099, 9157 Oilettes (6)	10 - 12	12 - 14
Series 9436 Oilettes	10 - 12	12 - 14
DAWSON, LUCY	5 - 6	6 - 8

Feiertag, BKWI 47-2
Unsigned

Arth. Thiele, TSN 896
No Caption

ELLAM
  Raphael Tuck
    "Mixed Bathing" Series   8 - 10   10 - 13
    Series 9685 (6) "Tales of the Seaside"   8 - 10   10 - 12
  Illustrated P.C. Co.   8 - 10   10 - 12
FEIERTAG, K. (Austria)   4 - 6   6 - 8
FREES
  Rotograph Co.
    Real Photo Cat Comics   6 - 8   8 - 10
GEAR, MABEL
  Valentine & Sons   4 - 5   5 - 6
  Raphael Tuck   5 - 6   6 - 8
HOFFMAN, A.   5 - 6   6 - 8
KASKELINE
  SWSB Series 4370   5 - 6   6 - 8
LANDOR
  Raphael Tuck
    Real Photo Studies 5088, 7006 (6)   4 - 5   5 - 6
MAC or HENRY SHEPHEARD
  Valentine & Sons
    Cat Studies   10 - 12   12 - 15
SCHWAR
    Cat Studies   6 - 8   8 - 10
SPERLICH, T. (GB)   6 - 8   8 - 10
  German-American Novelty Co.
    Series 648 (6)   6 - 8   8 - 10

Langsdorf Co.		
Series 3047	8 - 10	10 - 12
STOCK, A.	5 - 6	6 - 8
STOCKS, M.	6 - 8	8 - 10
H.K. Co.		
Series 217, 327, 381 (6)	6 - 8	8 - 10
THIELE, ARTH.		
TSN		
Series 129 Dancing (6)	10 - 12	12 - 15
Series 134 Large Heads (6)	15 - 18	18 - 22
Series 710, 1015 (6)	15 - 18	18 - 22
Series 896 Large Heads (6)	20 - 22	22 - 25
Series 915 Comic Cats (6)	12 - 15	15 - 18
Series 995 Large Cupid Cats (6)	25 - 30	30 - 35
Series 1002 At Home (6)	10 - 12	12 - 15
Series 1007 Cat Families (6)	10 - 12	12 - 15
Series 1015, 1077, 1175 (6)	10 - 12	12 - 15
Series 1194, 1229 (6)	22 - 24	24 - 26
Series 1326 In Kitchen (6)	10 - 12	12 - 15
Series 1412 Large Image (6)	20 - 22	22 - 26
Series 1423 In School (6)	10 - 12	12 - 15
Series 1424 Large Image (6)	20 - 25	25 - 28
"Big Cleanup"		
"Big Washday"		
"Dressmaking"		
"Going to Bed"		
"Kitty Traveling"		
"Writing"		
Series 1602 Comical Cat Kids (6)	10 - 12	12 - 15
Series 1825, 1826 Cat Kids (6)	10 - 12	12 - 15
Series 1827, 1852 Cat Kids (6)	12 - 15	15 - 18
Series 1882, 2030 In School (6)	10 - 12	12 - 15
THOMAS, PAUL		
Raphael Tuck		
Series 1196 (6)	8 - 10	10 - 12
WAIN, LOUIS		
Raphael Tuck		
Oilette Series 3385		
Series 5 Paper Doll Postcards (6)	200 - 250	250 - 275
Calendar Series 298, 304 (6)	35 - 40	40 - 45
Series 331 (6)	30 - 35	35 - 40
Series 644 Japanese (6)	35 - 40	40 - 45
Series 1003 "Write Away" (6)	40 - 45	45 - 50
Oilette Series 1412, 6444 (6)	40 - 45	45 - 50
Series 8515, (6)	30 - 35	35 - 40
Series 6084, 6723, 6724 (6)	30 - 35	35 - 40
Series 6727 (6)	30 - 35	35 - 40
Series 9563 "Diabolo" (6)	35 - 40	40 - 45
Series 8819, 9396 (6)	30 - 35	35 - 40
Ettinger		
Series 5376 Santa (Unsigned)	80 - 90	90 - 110

Arth. Thiele, TSN Series 1412 (3)

C.W. Faulkner Series	30 - 35	35 - 40
National Series	30 - 35	35 - 40
E. Nister Series	30 - 35	35 - 40
J. Salmon Series	30 - 35	35 - 40
Wrench Series	25 - 30	30 - 35
Santa Claus Cats (6)	90 - 100	100 - 125

DOGS

BARTH, KATH	6 - 8	8 - 10
BUTONY		
BKWI		
Series 859 (6)	8 - 10	10 - 12
C.A.	6 - 8	8 - 10

Wer wagt es . . . .?

CORBELLA, T. (Italy)		
Series 378 (6)	12 - 15	15 - 18
Others	10 - 12	12 - 15
DONADINI, JR.		
Dog Studies (6)	10 - 12	12 - 15
Series 235 (6)	12 - 14	14 - 16
DRUMMOND, NORAH (GB)		
Raphael Tuck		
Series 9105 (6) "Sporting Dogs"	12 - 14	14 - 16
FEIERTAG (Austria)	4 - 5	5 - 6
Dressed, Doing People Things	8 - 10	10 - 12
FREES, H.W.		
Rotograph Co.		
Comic Dog Photos	4 - 6	6 - 7

GREINER, A.
    Series 726 Dog Studies (6)   8 - 10   10 - 12
    Series 727 (6)   8 - 10   10 - 12
GROSSMAN, A.   6 - 8   8 - 10
GROSSMAN, M.   8 - 10   10 - 12
HANKE, H.
    Series 4056 Dressed Dachshunds   10 - 12   12 - 15
HANSTEIN
  Raphael Tuck
    Series 4092 "Favorite Dogs" (6)   8 - 10   10 - 12
HARTLEIN, W.   6 - 7   7 - 8
HERZ, E.W. (Austria)   7 - 8   8 - 10
KENNEDY, A.E.
  C.W. Faulkner
    Series 1424   8 - 10   10 - 12
KIENE   10 - 12   12 - 15
KIRMBE
  Raphael Tuck
    Series 3586 "Racing Greyhounds" (6) 10 - 12   12 - 14
KLUGLMEYER (Austria)   6 - 8   8 - 10
MAC or HENRY SHEPHEARD
  Valentine & Sons
    "Tailwagger" Dog Series   10 - 12   12 - 14
MacGUIRE
    Head Studies (Pastels)   8 - 10   10 - 12

Studdy (Bonzo), Valentine's 1207
No Caption

Studdy (Bonzo), Valentine's 1077
"That Crusin' Feeling"

Arth. Thiele, TSN 843
No Caption

Louis Wain, R. Tuck
"A Dandy"

MAILICK, R.		
Dog Studies	10 - 12	12 - 15
MOODY, FANNIE	6 - 8	8 - 10
MULLER, A.		
Series 3956 (6) Dachshunds	12 - 15	15 - 18
Other Dressed Series	10 - 12	12 - 15
Others	6 - 8	8 - 10
OHLER, J.		
Comical Dogs	6 - 8	8 - 9
P.O.E. (Austria)	6 - 8	8 - 10
PANKRATZ		
Comical Dachshunds	10 - 12	12 - 15
REICHERT, C. (Austria)		
T.S.N.		
Series 923, 1280 (6)	7 - 8	8 - 10
Series 1336, 1337 (6)	8 - 10	10 - 12
Series 1851 (6)	8 - 10	10 - 12
SCHNOPLER, A. (Austria)		
Comical Dachshunds	10 - 12	12 - 18
SCHONIAN		
German American Art		
Series 529	8 - 10	10 - 12
T.S.N.		
Series 1961	8 - 10	10 - 12
SPERLICH	5 - 6	6 - 7

P. Sentsch, Mary Mull 1506

STOLZ, A. (Austria)		
Series 772 Dachshunds	8 - 10	10 - 12
STUDDY (GB)		
"Bonzo" Issues	8 - 10	10 - 12
With Tennis or Golf	12 - 14	14 - 18
With Black Dolls	12 - 15	15 - 18
THIELE, ARTH.		
Raphael Tuck		
Series 9799 (6)	15 - 18	18 - 22
T.S.N.		
Series 843 (6)	18 - 22	22 - 25
Series 1128, 1893 (6)	10 - 12	12 - 15
German American Novelty Co.		
Series 806 Large Image	18 - 22	22 - 25
THOMAS (GB)		
Raphael Tuck		
Series 6990 "French Poodles" (6)	10 - 12	12 - 14
WAIN, LOUIS (GB)		
Raphael Tuck		
Series 6401 Comical Dogs (6)	35 - 45	45 - 55
Series 6402 (6)	35 - 45	45 - 55
Series 9376 (6)	35 - 45	45 - 55
WATSON, MAUDE WEST (GB)		
Raphael Tuck		
"Dog Sketches"		
Series 3346, 8682, E8837, 9977 (6)	8 - 10	10 - 14
Series 3103 (6)	10 - 12	12 - 15
WEBER, E.		
Dachshund Comics	8 - 10	10 - 12

WOMELE
  M. Munk, Vienna
    Series 883   8 - 10   10 - 12
WUNDERLICH, A.
  Dachshunds   12 - 15   15 - 18

HORSES

ADAMS
  Meissner & Buch   8 - 10   10 - 12
BARTH, W.   8 - 10   10 - 12
BRAUN, LOUIS   8 - 10   10 - 12
CASTALANZA
  Series 342   8 - 10   10 - 12
CORBELLA
  Series 316 (6)   12 - 14   14 - 16
DONADINI, JR.
    Series 237 Racing Comics   10 - 12   12 - 15
DRUMMOND, NORAH
  Raphael Tuck
    Series 9065, 9138 (6)   8 - 10   10 - 12
    Series 9561 (6)   12 - 15   15 - 18
    Series 3109, 3194, 3603 (6)   8 - 10   10 - 12
FENNI (Racing Series)   10 - 12   12 - 14
FRIEDRICH, H.
    Series 464 (6)   6 - 8   8 - 10
HANSTEIN
  Raphael Tuck
    Series 810 (6) Steeple Chase   8 - 10   10 - 12

Paul Thomas, R. Tuck, "Circus Busch"

G. Koch, R. Tuck 588B
No Caption

HERMAN		
Raphael Tuck		
Oilette Series "The Horse" (6)	10 - 12	12 - 14
KOCH, A.		
B.K.W.I.		
Series 473 Trotters (6)	10 - 12	12 - 14
Series 377, 566 (6)	8 - 10	10 - 12
Series 660, 739, 865 (6), (6), (8)	10 - 12	12 - 14
Series 966 Circus Studies (6)	12 - 14	14 - 18
KOCH, LUDWIG		
B.K.W.I.		
Series 493, 948 (6)	10 - 12	12 - 15
Series 830, 865 (10)	12 - 14	14 - 16
Series 1447, 1470 (6)	10 - 12	12 - 15
Series 372, 377, 473 (6)	12 - 14	14 - 18
Series 566, 660, 739	12 - 14	14 - 16
O.F.Z.-L		
Series 280-285	10 - 12	12 - 15
KOCH, PROF. G.		
Raphael Tuck		
Series 588B (6)	10 - 12	12 - 15
KOLB		
Raphael Tuck		
Series 4084 Oilette (6)	10 - 12	12 - 14
KROMBACK	10 - 12	12 - 14
MATHEUSON	8 - 10	10 - 12
MAUZAN		
Series 383 (6)	10 - 12	12 - 14

MERTE, O.
  A.M.S.

Series 589, 599, 660 (6)	8 - 10	10 - 12
Series 623 Circus Horses (6)	10 - 12	12 - 15
Series 729 (6)	8 - 10	10 - 12

  Raphael Tuck

Series 9946 Circus Horses (6)	10 - 12	12 - 15

MULLER
  T.S.N.

Series 128, 133 (6)	8 - 10	10 - 12
Series 333, 411, 509 (6)	10 - 12	12 - 14

  SWSB

Series 6919 (6)	6 - 8	8 - 10

NANNI

Series 257, 307 (6)	8 - 10	10 - 12

PAYNE, HARRY

Raphael Tuck	10 -12	12 - 14

R.K.
  BKWI

Series 350, 380, 386 (6)	6 - 8	8 - 10

REICHERT, C.
  T.S.N.

Series 934, w/dogs (6)	8 - 10	10 - 12
Series 1359, 1605 (6)	8 - 10	10 - 12
Series 1606, w/dogs (6)	7 - 8	8 - 10
Series 1732, w/dogs (6)	8 - 10	10 - 12
Series 1782, 1870 (6)	10 - 12	12 - 14
Series 1422, Unsigned (6)	6 - 8	8 - 10

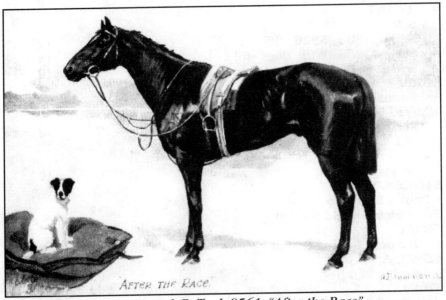

N. Drummond, R. Tuck 9561, "After the Race"

Paul Thomas, W. & L., Berlin 1182
No Caption

F. Schilling, R.R. & CiB 1136/1
No Caption

M. Munk, Vienna		
Series 268, 771 **(6)**	8 - 10	10 - 12
Series 1165 **(6)**	10 - 12	12 - 14
SCHILLING, F.	8 - 10	10 - 12
SCHONIAN		
T.S.N.		
Series 1838, 5826 **(6)**	10 - 12	12 - 15
Series 1935 With Dogs **(6)**	12 - 14	14 - 16
Series E1935 **(6)**	10 - 12	12 - 14
SCHULZ		
Series 972 **(6)**	6 - 8	8 - 10
Alfred Stiebel Co.		
Series 430, 438 **(6)**	10 - 12	12 - 15
SHILLING, F.		
A.R. & C.i.B.		
Series 1136 **(6)**	8 - 10	10 - 12
STOKES, VERNON		
Photochrom Co.		
"Celesque" Series **(6)**	7 - 8	8 - 9
TENNI		
Harness Racing Series	8 - 10	10 - 12
TERZI, A.		
Series 320 **(6)**	10 - 12	12 - 14
THAMSE		
Raphael Tuck	6 - 8	8 - 10

THOMAS, J.

Raphael Tuck		
Series 353, 529 **(6)**	10 - 12	12 - 14
Series 1182, 9254 **(6)**	12 - 14	14 - 16
Series 575-B Trotters **(6)**	10 - 12	12 - 15
Series 579 Steeplechase **(6)**	8 - 10	10 - 12
Racing Series	10 - 12	12 - 15
Series 9254 **(6)**	8 - 10	10 - 12
W&L, Berlin		
Series 1182	10 - 12	12 - 14
TRACHE, E.		
Series 464, 466, 788 **(6)**	8 - 10	10 - 12
Series E463, 1175 **(4)**	8 - 10	10 - 12
VELTEN		
A.B.D.		
Series 775	8 - 10	10 - 12
W.F.A.	7 - 8	8 - 10
WALKER		
Raphael Tuck		
Series 9544 **(6)** "Chargers"	8 - 10	10 - 12
WRIGHT, ALAN		
Series 12219 **(6)**	10 - 12	12 - 14
WRIGHT, GEORGE		
E.W. Savory, Ltd.		
Series 2118 **(6)**	8 - 10	10 - 12

W. Barth, BKWI 892
No Caption

O. Merté, ASM 589
No Caption

OTHER ANIMALS

BARNES-AUSTIN, EDGAR (GB)
  Raphael Tuck
    "Piggie-Wiggie" Series   10 - 12   12 - 14
BAUMGARTEN, FRITZ   Bunny Rabbits   8 - 10   10 - 12
CANTLE, J.M. (GB)   6 - 7   7 - 8
COBBS, B. (GB)
  Raphael Tuck
    Series 9539 (6) "Bunnies"   5 - 6   6 - 7
CRITE
  "Billy Possum" Series   12 - 15   15 - 20
DONADINI
  Animal Studies   8 - 10   10 - 12
DRUMMOND, NORAH (GB)
  Raphael Tuck
    Series 9507 (6) "Famous British Cattle"   7 - 8   8 - 10
    Series 3297 (6) "Faithful Friends"   7 - 8   8 - 12
EARNSHAW, HAROLD C.
  Millar & Lang   Comic Animals   4 - 6   6 - 8
  Gottschalk, Dreyfus & Davis   4 - 6   6 - 8
ELLAM
  Raphael Tuck
    Series 9684 (6) "Dressed Elephants"   15 - 18   18 - 22

Rose Clark, Rotograph 380
"Dew-Drop Frog"

Rose Clark, Rotograph 381
"Will B. Stout Frog"

Fritz Baumgarten, Erkal 4001

GEAR, MABEL (U.S.A.)	5 - 8	8 - 10
GREEN, ROLAND (GB)	5 - 6	6 - 7
HORINA, H.		
Ullman Mfg. Co.		
Series 91 (Jimmy Pig)		
1967 "This little pig went to market"	10 - 12	12 - 15
1968 "This little pig went bathing"	10 - 12	12 - 15
1969 "This little pig stayed home"	10 - 12	12 - 15
1970 "This little pig went to school"	10 - 12	12 - 15
1971 "This little pig went to a party"	10 - 12	12 - 15
1972 "This little pig went to war"	12 - 14	14 - 16
1973 "This little pig went fishing"	10 - 12	12 - 15
1974 "This little pig worked in garden"	10 - 12	12 - 15
1975 "This little pig went sailing"	10 - 12	12 - 15
1976 "This little pig was a drummer boy"	10 - 12	12 - 15
HUDSON, G.M.		
Raphael Tuck		
Series 8648 "Guinnepins"	8 - 10	10 - 12
JAMES, FRANK (GB)	4 - 5	5 - 6
KEENE, MINNIE (GB)	4 - 5	5 - 6
KENNEDY, A.E. (GB)	5 - 8	8 - 10
LANDSCER, SIR EDWIN (GB)	5 - 8	10 - 15
LESTER, A. (GB)	4 - 5	5 - 6
MAGUIRE, HELENA (GB)	5 - 6	6 - 7
Raphael Tuck		
Series 6713, 6714 (6) "Animal Studies"	7 - 8	8 - 1
MULLER, A. (Germany)	5 - 6	6 - 8

PERLBERG, F.
  Raphael Tuck

Art Series 991 **(6)**	6 - 7	7 - 8
POPE, DOROTHY (GB)	4 - 5	5 - 6
RANKIN, GEORGE (GB)	4 - 5	5 - 6
SCRIVENER, MAUDE (GB)	6 - 7	7 - 10
STEWART, J.A. (GB)	4 - 5	5 - 6

THIELE, ARTH
  German American Novelty Art Co.

Series 789 Pigs, Large Image	20 - 25	25 - 30

T.S.N.

Series 919 Dressed Ducks	15 - 20	20 - 25
Series 1165 Dressed Chicks	15 - 20	20 - 25
Series 1352 Dressed Chicks	12 - 15	15 - 18
Series 1452 Dressed Chicks	15 - 20	20 - 25
Series 1020, 1021 Dressed Bunnies	15 - 20	20 - 25
Series 781 Dressed Monkeys	20 - 22	22 - 26
VALTER, EUGENIE (GB)	5 - 6	6 - 7
WARDLE, ARTHUR (GB)	4 - 5	5 - 6
WEALTHY, R.J. (GB)	4 - 5	5 - 6
WEST, A.L. (GB)	5 - 6	6 - 7

13

MISCELLANEOUS

COWBOYS & INDIANS

CRAIG, CHARLES (U.S.A.)		
Williamson-Hafner		
Indian Series	6 - 8	8 - 10
CURTIS, E.S.		
Indian Series	16 - 18	18 - 25
DAVENPORT, R.A.		
Cowboys	6 - 7	7 - 9
FELLER, FRANK (U.S.A.)	8 - 10	10 - 12
GOLLINGS	7 - 8	8 - 10
GREGG, PAUL (U.S.A.)		
H.H. Tammen		
Cowboy Series	4 - 6	6 - 8
INNES, JOHN (U.S.A.)		
Western Art Series (6)	6 - 8	8 - 10

    "The Bad Man"
    "Pack Train"
    "The Portage"
    "Prairie Schooner"
    "Roping Bronco"
    "Warping the Fur Barge..."

MacFarlane Publishing Co.		
"Troilene Series"	6 - 8	8 - 10

    "Cattle Girl"
    "Warping the Air Barge Upstream"
    "Indians in a Snow Storm"
    "Indian Pony Race"
    "Roping a Steer"

"The Town Marshall"
"The War Canoe"
LARSEN, DUDE & DOT (U.S.A.)
Linens of 30' & 40's   1 - 2   2 - 3
MAY, KARL (Germany)
Cowboys and Indians   10 - 12   12 - 15
PAXON, E.S. (U.S.A.)
  McKee Printing Co.
  Indian Series   6 - 8   8 - 10
PAYNE, HARRY (GB)
  Raphael Tuck
  "The Wild West" Series   10 - 12   12 - 14
  "A Scamper Across the Prairie"
  "The Head of the Column"
  "Sounding the "Turn Out"
PETERSON, L. (U.S.A.)
  H.H. Tammen Co.
  "Indian" Series
  3420 "Chief Sitting Bull"   10 - 12   12 - 14
  3421 "Chief Geronimo"   10 - 12   12 - 14
  3422 "Chief Yellow Hawk"   8 - 10   10 - 12
  3423 "Chief Eagle Feather"   8 - 10   10 - 12
  3424 "Chief High Horse"   8 - 10   10 - 12
  3425 "Starlight"   8 - 10   10 - 12
  3426 "Chief Big Feather"   8 - 10   10 - 12

C.W. Russell, Ridgely Calendar Co.
"Lone Wolf–Piegan"

L. Peterson, H.H. Tammen
Chief Wolf Robe, Unsigned

Charles Craig, Detroit Pub. Co. 79014, "Apache War Party"

3427 "Sunshine"	8 - 10	10 - 12
3428 "Fighting Wolf"	8 - 10	10 - 12
3429 "Minnehaha"	10 - 12	12 - 14
3430 "Hiawatha"	10 - 12	12 - 15
3431 "Chief Red Cloud"	10 - 12	12 - 15
3432 "Eagle Feather and Squaw"	8 - 10	10 - 12
3433 "Chief Black Hawk"	10 - 12	12 - 14
Unsigned Series	8 - 10	10 - 12
"Cow Girl" Series	6 - 8	8 - 10
REISS, WINOLD	8 - 10	10 - 12
REMINGTON, FREDERIC (USA)		
Detroit Publishing Co.		
14179 "Evening on A Canadian"	35 - 45	45 - 55
14180 "His First Lesson"	30 - 35	35 - 40
14181 "A Fight for the Water Hole"	35 - 45	45 - 55
14182 "An Argument with the Marshal"	35 - 45	45 - 55
14183 "Calling the Moose"	30 - 35	35 - 45
REYNOLDS		
Cowboy Series 4400	5 - 6	6 - 8
Cowgirl Series 4406	5 - 6	6 - 8
RHINEHART, F.A. (U.S.A.)		
"Indian" Series		
"Rain in the Face" - Sioux	6 - 8	8 - 10
"Big Man"	6 - 8	8 - 10
"Chief Wolf Robe" - Cheyenne	9 - 10	10 - 12
"Chief Red Cloud" - Sioux	6 - 8	8 - 10
"Chief Sitting Bull" - Sioux	9 - 10	10 - 12
"Eagle Feather & Papoose"	6 - 8	8 - 10
"Two Little Braves" - Sioux & Fox	5 - 6	6 - 8

John Innes, Troilene Series, "Cow and Calf Roundup

"Chase-in-the-Morning"	6 - 8	8 - 10
"Hattie Tom" - Chiricahua Apache	9 - 10	10 - 12

RUSSELL, CHARLES M. (U.S.A.)

Ridgley Calendar Co.   20 - 25   25 - 30
   "Are You the Real Thing?"
   "Antelope Hunt"
   "A Touch of Western High Life"
   "The Buffalo Hunt"
   "Roping a Grizzly"
   "A Wounded Grizzly"
   "Roping a Wolf"
   "Blackfeet Burning..."
   "The Wild Horse Hunters"
   "Better than Bacon"
   "Waiting for a Chinook"
   "Where Ignorance is Bliss"
   "Lone Wolf - Piegan"
   "Red Cloud"
   Others   10 - 12   12 - 14

Raphael Tuck
Series 2171 "Indian Chiefs" (12)   10 - 12   12 - 14
Series 9131   10 - 12   12 - 16
   "Chief Charging Bear"
   "Chief Not Afraid of Pawnee"
   "Chief Black Chicken"
   "Chief Eagle Track"
   "Chief Black Thunder"
   "Chief White Swan"
Series 9011 "Hiawatha" (6)   8 - 10   10 - 12

Series 1330 "Hiawatha" (6)	10 - 12	12 - 15
SCHULTZ, F.W. (U.S.A.)		
Cowboy Series 1728-1746	8 - 10	10 - 12
1728 "The Outlaw"		
1730 "Alkalai Ike"		
1741 "Roping the Bull"		
"Shooting up the Town"		
Others		

SILHOUETTES

ALLMAHER, JOSEFINE	6 - 8	8 - 9
BECKMAN, JOHANNA	5 - 7	7 - 8
BURKE, PAUL	5 - 7	7 - 8
BORREMEISTER, R.	6 - 8	8 - 10
BRENING, H.	10 - 12	12 - 15
DIEFFENBACH		
Fantasy Children	7 - 10	10 - 15
FORCK, ELISABETH	6 - 7	7 - 10
GRAF, MARTE		
Art Deco Series 1,2,3,4 (743-754)	8 - 10	10 - 14
Others	8 - 10	10 - 12
GROSS, CH.	5 - 7	7 - 8
GROSZE, M.		
P.F.B. in diamond		
Deco Series 2041 "After Bath"	12 - 13	13 - 15
Nude Series 2042	12 - 14	14 - 16
Series 2043	10 - 12	12 - 15
Nude Series 3339	12 - 15	15 - 18

H. Brening, Anonymous

Series 3341, 3342	10 - 12	12 - 15
Others	10 - 12	12 - 14
KASKELINE		
Art Deco Ladies/Children	8 - 10	10 - 12
LAMP, H.		
Series 3, Deco, Dancing	12 - 15	15 - 18
Series 4, Bathing	12 - 15	15 - 18
PEANITSCH, LEO	10 - 12	12 - 14
ROBA		
Deco Fantasy	12 - 15	15 - 18
SACHSE-SCHUBERT, M.	10 - 12	12 - 14
SCHIRMER (Fairy Tales)	10 - 12	12 - 14
SCHONPFLUG, FRITZ	10 - 12	12 - 15
STUBNER, LOTTE	8 - 10	10 - 12
SK		
Meissner & Buch	8 - 10	10 - 12
SUSS, PAUL	10 - 12	12 - 15

OTHER ARTISTS

ALEINMULLER		
Thanksgiving Greetings	3 -4	4 - 5
BAKER, GRANVILLE		
Raphael Tuck		
Military Series (6)	6 - 8	8 - 10
BANKS, E.C. (U.S.A.)		
Halloween Greetings	8 - 10	10 - 12
BAKST, LEON (Russia)		
Ladies in Ballet Costumes (12)	40 - 45	45 - 50
Others	20 - 25	25 - 30
BALL, WILFRED Landscapes	2 - 3	3 - 4
BANESS, MARY Landscapes	2 - 3	3 - 4
BANNISTER, A.		
Salmon		
Aeroplanes of WWII	4 - 5	5 - 6
BATES, MARJORIE		
Shakespeare Characters (12)	8 - 10	10 - 12
BLACK, A.		
Salmon		
Aeroplane Series	5 - 6	6 - 8
Ship Series	4 - 5	5 - 6
BECKER, CARL		
Military	8 - 9	9 - 10
BEERTS, ALBERT		
WWI Patriotics	6 - 8	8 - 10
BENOIS (Russia)		
Ballet Costume Series	30 - 35	35 - 40
Others	15 - 20	20 - 25
BERAUD, N. (France)		
French Military Series	6 - 8	8 - 10

BERTHON, PAUL (France)		
"Music" Series	60 - 70	70 - 80
BERTIGLIA, A.		
Anti-German and Anti-Austrian	12 - 15	15 - 20
BIANCO, T.		
Comics	4 - 5	5 - 7
Political Cartoons	12 - 14	14 - 18
BILLIBINE (Russia)		
Heroes, Costumes, Operas	15 - 20	20 - 25
BOECKER, A. GAMMIUS Fruits	1 - 2	2 - 3
BONORA		
Boy Scout Series 760	16 - 20	20 - 25
BORROW, W.H. English sketches	3 - 4	4 - 5
BUNNELL, C.B.		
4th of July Greetings	8 - 10	10 - 12
BUSI, A.		
Boy Scout Series	16 - 20	20 - 25
CARR, GENE		
4th of July Series	8 - 10	10 - 12
CASSIERS, H. (Belgium)		
Red Star Line Posters	15 - 20	20 - 25
Other Ship Paintings	8 - 10	10 - 12
Costumes	5 - 6	6 - 7
CLARK, ROSE (U.S.A.) See Teddy Bears		

Catherine Klein, Alphabet Series 48
"B"

Mailick, Anonymous
"A Merry Christmas"

CLARKSON
  Raphael Tuck
    Series 3144 (6) Airplanes "In the Air"   8 - 10   10 - 12
CHAPMAN, C. (U.S.A.)
  Patriotics   6 - 8   8 - 10
CRAMER, RIE   8 - 10   10 - 12
CUBLEY, H. English sketches   3 - 4   4 - 5
DeMARIS, WALTER
  Fatherless Children Poster   6 - 7   7 - 8
DENSMORE
  Thanksgiving Greetings   4 - 5   5 - 6
De YONGH
  R&N
    Political "Bill"   12 - 15   15 - 18
DUPUIS, EMILE (France)
  Lady & Men Military Series
    "Nos Allies"   10 - 12   12 - 14
    "Nos Poilus"   8 - 10   10 - 12
    "Leur Caboches"   8 - 10   10 - 12
EMANUEL, F. English sketches   2 - 3   3 - 4
EWIG, ARTHUR
  Series 160 Fraternal   6 - 8   8 - 10
  "B.P.O.E."
  "Woodsmen of the World"
  Others
FIELD, EUGENE
  "Lovers Lane" Series (12)   3 - 4   4 - 5
FLOWER, C.E. London Views, etc.   3 - 4   4 - 5
GALLON, R. Landscapes   2 - 3   3 - 4
HAYES, F.W. Landscapes   2 - 3   3 - 4
GOLAY, MARY
  Fruit, Flowers, Still Life Studies   3 - 4   4 - 6
HALLER, A.
  Flowers   2 - 3   3 - 4
HAMPEL, WALTER (Austria)
  Philipp and Kramer   30 - 35   35 - 40
HOHENSTEIN, A. (Russia)
  Operas, Commemoratives   30 - 35   35 - 40
INNES, JOHN (Canada)
  See Cowboys, Indians
JOTTER Landscapes   2 - 3   3 - 4
KIRK, M.L.
  National Art Co.
    Days of the Week   6 - 7   7 - 8
KLEIN, CATHERINE
  Flowers   2 - 3   3 - 5
  Birds   3 - 5   5 - 7
  Parrots   5 - 7   7 - 9
  Alphabet Series 148 A through T   12 - 15   15 - 18
  U through Z   20 - 22   22 - 25

LEINWEBER		
Old Testament Series	4 - 5	5 - 6
LONGSTAFFE, E. Landscapes	2 - 3	3 - 4
LUDOVICI, ANTHONY		
Tuck Oxford Pageant, 1903	12 - 15	15 - 18
MASTROIANNI, D. Art Sculpture	3 - 4	4 - 5
MORRIS, M. Seascapes	1 - 2	2 - 3
MAILICK (Denmark)		
Hold-to-Light Santas	100 - 110	110 - 135
See Greetings, Children, Animals		
NEWTON, G.E. Seascapes	1 - 2	2 - 3
ORENES, D. (France)	15 - 20	20 - 25
PARRISH, MAXWELL (U.S.A.)		
Scenic Landscapes	20 - 30	30 - 40
Fairy Tales	60 - 70	70 - 80
PAYNE, HARRY (GB)		
Raphael Tuck		
English Military Series (6 ea.)		
Ser. 8625 "The Scots Guards"	10 - 12	12 - 14
Ser. 8738 "Types of British Army"	10 - 12	12 - 14
Ser. 9937 "The Arg. & S. Highlanders"	10 - 12	12 - 14
Ser. 9993 "The Coldstream Guards"	10 - 12	12 - 14
Ser. 9994 "The Blackwatch"	10 - 12	12 - 14
Others	10 - 12	12 - 14
London Life - Policemen, etc. (6)	10 - 12	12 - 14
English Views and Landscapes	5 - 6	6 - 7
See Cowboys and Indians		
QUINTON, A.R. English sketches	4 - 5	5 - 6
REMINGTON, FREDERIC (U.S.A.)		
See Cowboys and Indians		
ROBINSON, FLORENCE (U.S.A.)		
Raphael Tuck		
Views of U.S. Cities	10 - 12	12 - 14
ROBINSON, WALLACE (U.S.A.)		
Heininger Co.		
"Patriotic Kids"	10 - 12	12 - 14
ROCKWELL, NORMAN		
Whitney & Co.		
"Help Him Through the Game..."	30 - 35	35 - 40
"The Fatherless Children of France"		
1 "Help the Fatherless Children..."	30 - 35	35 - 40
2 "Polly Voos Fransay"	30 - 35	35 - 40
3 "Mobilize for Defense" Poster	35 - 40	40 - 45
RUSSELL, CHARLES M. (U.S.A.)		
See Cowboys and Indians		
VAN HIER English Sketches	3 - 4	4 - 5
VEENFLIET, R. (U.S.A.)		
S. Garre		
George Washington's Birthday	6 - 8	8 - 10

THE LINEN ERA ARTISTS

The great depression occurred during the early years of the Linen Postcard Era; times were hard, and postcard production of beautiful artist-signed works of art almost ceased worldwide. Collectors quickly lost their enthusiasm when the beautiful miniature works of art, which for many years were published in Great Britain and the European countries, suddenly became only a memory.

Although thousands of artists turned to other means of earning a living in those difficult times, there were others who continued producing postcards. Many artists continued to sign their works, but others left them unsigned. Therefore, as in earlier days, some of the most beautiful works can only be listed as anonymous.

Unlike other cards of the previous Golden Years, these new linen cards were not collected and saved by hobbyists, so very few early artist-signed cards remain for today's collector. Those that are available usually show the remnants of the Art Deco Era and, because of this, have become very collectible.

Walter Wellman, a carryover artist from earlier years, produced some great comics and blacks from 1930 to 1940. He was probably the most prolific of all the linen era artists. His publishers were Tichnor Bros., Manhattan

Post Card Co., Metropolitan, and others. Distributors such as the Asheville Postcard Co. are also listed as publishers of his works.

Most all of Wellman's cards in the early 30's were of the Deco variety, with great detail and beautiful colors. The advent of WWII gave him, as well as other artists, another great topic. His comic cards of Army, Navy, Air Force, anti-Hitler, anti-Japanese and exaggerated motifs are classics, and are considered among the finest produced. All are eagerly sought by today's collector.

Not to be forgotten during this era are works by British artists such as Donald McGill, Dan Tempest, and A. Taylor. Their fine works, mostly pretty children and comics, had a great impact during the 1930-1940's era. These cards, although not produced on the linen stock used by Americans, contained the same motifs and are probably more in demand by collectors. The Bamforth Co., a British publisher with offices in New York, was the leading distributor.

Later, during the 1940's, the arrival of WWII brought the pin-up back into focus. The serviceman, stationed away from home, yearned for cards to remind them of the American Girl, so artists began producing pin-up beauties to fill the void. Jay Jackson, B. Armstrong, Irby, M.R., and O'Toole were some of the most published. Again, however, many great works were left unsigned.

This was also an era where the artist was very content to produce works that poked fun at blacks, fat ladies, drunks, redneck mountaineers (and their outhouses), and others. Hopefully, there is now no malice against these works by anyone. As every collector knows, the artists of comical works spared no one, and this is probably as it should be.

Values of the early artist-signed linens of the 30's are beginning to escalate as collectors begin to realize that there is a scarcity and demand for them. On the other hand, the common linens of the 40's are rather dormant (except for special motifs) as the supply at this time is above the demand.

The Mutoscope pin-up card was also produced during this

era, and many of the images were produced as postcards. They were beautiful and colorful cards by all the great pin-up artists. K. Munson, Earl Moran, and Zoe Mozert are among those artists most widely collected.

LINEN ERA

	VG	EX
ANDY		
Tichnor Bros.		
Comics	0.50 - .75	0.75 - 1
ARMSTRONG, B.		
Tichnor Bros.		
Pin-ups	2 - 3	3 - 4
BLOODGOOD, DON		
H.S. Crocker Co.		
Outhouse Series	2 - 2.50	2.50 - 3
CHC		
Tichnor Bros.		
Comics	0.50 - .75	0.75 - 1
CARDILL, ANDY		
Manhattan Post Card Co.		
Comics	0.50 - .75	0.75 - 1
Pin-ups	1 - 1.50	1.50 - 2
CHELMON		
Tichnor Bros.		
Comics	0.50 - .75	0.75 - 1
Exaggerated Comics	1 - 1.50	1.50 - 2
Military Comics	1.50 - 2	2 - 2.50
Anti-Hitler, Anti-Japanese	4 - 5	5 - 7
DEAN, H.		
Tichnor Bros.		
Comics	0.50 - .75	0.75 - 1
Fat Ladies & Risque	1 - 1.50	1.50 - 2
Military Comics	1.50 - 2	2 - 2.50
Outhouse Comics	1.50 - 2	2 - 2.50
Animal Comics	0.50 - .75	0.75 - 1
DOOLEY		
Metropolitan Card Co.		
Comics	0.50 - .75	0.75 - 1
Fat Ladies	1 - 1.50	1.50 - 2
DUDLEY, BUD		
Metropolitan P.C. Co.		
Comics	0.50 - .75	0.75 - 1
Risque	1 - 1.50	1.50 - 2
ERICSON, ERIC		
Tichnor Bros.		
Comics	0.50 - .75	0.75 - 1
Military Comics	1.50 - 2	2 - 2.50
Blacks	3 - 4	4 - 6

Walt Munson, Pickaninny Series
"Sure We're Cuckoo..."

Walt Munson, Tichnor Bros.
"Maybe I Am Only..."

FABER
  Tichnor Bros.

Comics	0.50 - .75	0.75 - 1
Fat Ladies	1 - 1.50	1.50 - 2
Exaggerations	1 - 1.50	1.50 - 2

FOX, CRAIG
  Tichnor Bros.

Comics	0.50 - .75	0.75 - 1
Risque	1.50 - 2	2 - 2.50
Animals	0.50 - .75	0.75 - 1
Outhouses	1.50 - 2	2 - 2.50
Fat Ladies	1.50 - 2	2 - 2.50

HAVENSTEIN, BILL
  MWM Color Co.

Military Comics	1.50 - 2	2 - 2.50

HUTSON, H.H.
  MWM Color Litho

Military Comics	1.50 - 2	2 - 2.50

IRBY
  MWM Color Litho

Comics	0.50 - .75	0.75 - 1
Pin-ups	1 - 1.50	1.50 - 2
Animals	0.50 - .75	0.75 - 1
Military Comics	1 - 1.50	1.50 - 2
Blacks	4 - 6	6 - 8

JACKSON, JAY
  Tichnor Bros.
    Glamour Girls Series (10)   3 - 4   4 - 5

JEB
  Tichnor Bros.
    Comics   0.50 - .75   0.75 - 1

LARSEN, DUDE
LARSEN, DOT
    Cowboys, Cowgirls   1 - 1.50   1.50 - 2
    Horses   1.50 - 2   2 - 2.50

LORENZ, P.
  Curt Teich
    Cowboy & Western   1 - 1.50   1.50 - 2

M.R.
  Manhattan P.C. Co.
    Comics   1 - 1.50   1.50 - 2
    Pin-ups   1.50 - 2   2 - 2.50

MANNING, REG
  Curt Teich
    Comic Travel Cards   1 - 1.50   1.50 - 2

McGILL, DONALD
  Bamforth Co.
    Comics   2 - 3   3 - 4
    Blacks   6 - 8   8 - 10

MORAN, EARL
  Mutoscope   4 - 5   5 - 8

Walter Wellman, Manhattan
"Ah's Askin'..."

D. Tempest, Bamforth 2047
"Here's a Quaint Coon..."

Earl Moran, Mutoscope
"Some Chicken"

Samuels, Graphics PC Co.
"Shtop pushin'!"

MOZERT, ZOE
Mutoscope	4 - 5	5 - 8

MUNSON, K.
Mutoscope	4 - 5	5 - 8

MUNSON, WALT
Tichnor Bros. & others
Comics	0.75 - 1	1 - 1.50
Fat Lady Comics	1 - 1.50	1.50 - 2
Animals	0.75 - 1	1 - 1.50
Golf, Tennis	2 - 3	3 - 4
Military Comics	2 - 2.50	2.50 - 3
Anti-Hither, Anti-Japanese	4 - 5	5 - 8
Black Comics	4 - 6	6 - 9
Outhouse Comics	1 - 2	2 - 3

O'TOOLE
Metropolitan P.C. Co.
Military Comics	2 - 2.50	2.50 - 3

PARIS
E.C. Kropp
Comics	0.50 - .75	0.75 - 1
Fat Ladies	1 - 1.50	1.50 - 2
Military Comics	1.50 - 2	2 - 2.50

PAT
Tichnor Bros.
Comics	0.50 - .75	0.75 - 1

Fat Ladies	1 - 1.50	1.50 - 2
SAMUELS		
Graphic P.C. Co.		
Anti-Hitler & Axis Series	7 - 9	9 - 12
SIL, MIKE		
Manhattan P.C. Co,.		
Pin-ups	2 - 2.50	2.50 - 3
SMITH, LARRY		
B.L.& P. Co.		
Comics	0.50 - .75	0.75 - 1
Fat Ladies	1 - 1.50	1.50 - 2
Military Comics	1. 50 - 2	2 - 2.50
Blacks	3 - 5	5 - 8
SULLIVAN		
E.C. Kropp		
Comics	0.50 - .75	0.75 - 1
Military Comics	1.50 - 2	2 - 2.50
TAYLOR, A.		
Bamforth Co.		
Comics	1 - 2	2 - 3
Cats	2 - 3	3 - 4
Dogs	2 - 3	3 - 4
Fat Ladies	2 - 3	3 - 4
Children	2 - 3	3 - 4

E.L. White, Metropolitan
"Well, I ain't the only..."

Dude Larsen
"Just a Pal"

TEMPEST, DAN
Bamforth Co.

Comics	2 - 3	3 - 4
Children	4 - 5	5 - 7
Blacks	6 - 8	8 - 10

TIMMONS, JR.
Tichnor Bros.

Comics	0.50 - .75	0.75 - 1
Blacks	3 - 5	5 - 7

UNK
Asheville Postcard Co.

Comics	0.50 - .75	.75 - 1
Exaggerated Comics	1 - 1.25	1.25 - 1.50

WALTERS, L.
Curt Teich

Comics	0.50 - .75	0.75 - 1
Exaggerated Comics	1 - 1.50	1.50 - 2
Outhouse Comics	1.50 - 2	2 - 2.50
Fat Lady Comics	1 - 1.50	1.50 - 2
Risque	1.50 - 2	2 - 2.50

WARNER, CHET
Asheville P.C. Co.

Risque Comics	1 - 1.50	1.50 - 2
Golf/Tennis	3 - 3.50	3.50 - 5

WELLMAN, WALTER
Tichnor Bros. & others
1930's

Comics	0.75 - 1	1 - 1.50
Animals	1 - 1.50	1.50 - 2
Golf, Tennis	5 - 7	7 - 10
Black Comics	6 - 9	9 - 12
Exaggerated Comics	2 - 3	3 - 4
Fat Lady Comics	2 - 3	3 - 4
Risque	2 - 2.50	2.50 - 3

1940's

Comics	0.75 - 1	1 - 1.50
Animals	0.75 - 1	1 - 1.50
Golf, Tennis	3 - 4	4 - 6
Fat Ladies	1 - 1.50	1.50 - 2
Military Comics	2 - 2.50	2.50 - 3
Anti-Hitler, Anti-Japanese	5 - 6	6 - 10
Black Comics	5 - 6	6 - 10
Outhouse Comics	2 - 3	3 - 3.50
Damn Family	3 - 3.50	3.50 - 4
Exaggerated Comics	1 - 2	2 - 3

WHITE, E.L.
Metropolitan P.C. Co.
1930's

Comics	1 - 2	2 - 3
Fat Ladies	2 - 3	3 - 4
Risque	2 - 3	3 - 4

Appendix

Reference Sources

POSTCARD PUBLISHERS & DISTRIBUTORS

Following are some of the major publishers of postcards world-wide. Minor publishers can be found under each particular listing throughout this book.

A.S.B. -- Greetings
Ackerman -- Pioneer Views of New York City
Albertype Co. -- Pioneer & Expo Views; Local Views
Am. Colortype Co. -- Expositions
American News Co. -- Local Views
American Postcard Co. -- Comics
American Souvenir Co. -- Pioneers
Anglo-Am. P.C. Co. (AA) -- Greetings, Comics
Art Lithograph Co. -- Local Views
Asheville Post Card Co. -- Local Views, Comics
Auburn P.C. Mfg. Co. -- Greetings, Comics
Austin, J. -- Comics
Ballerini & Fratini, Italy -- Chiostri, Others, Deco
B.K.W.I., Austria -- Artist-Signed, Comics
Bamforth Co. -- Comics, Song Cards
Barton and Spooner -- Comics, Greetings
J. Beagles & Co., London -- Artist-Signed, Views
J. Bergman Co. -- Comics, Artist-Signed Ladies, etc.
Julius Bien -- Comics, Greetings
B.B (Birn Brothers) -- Greetings, Comics
Bosselman, A.C. -- Local Views, Others
Britton & Rey -- Expositions, Battleships

Campbell Art Co. -- Comics, Rose O'Neill, etc.
Chapman Co. -- Greetings, College Girls, etc.
Charlton, E.P. -- Expositions, Local Views
Chisholm Bros. -- Expositions, Local Views
Conwell, L.R. -- Greetings
Crocker, H.S. -- Local Views
Davidson Bros. -- Artist-Signed, Greetings, Views
Dell Anna & Gasparini, Italy -- Art Deco Artists
Delta, Paris -- French Glamour
Detroit Publishing Co. -- Prolific View Pub., Artists
EAS (E.A. Schwerdfeger) -- Artist-Signed, Greetings
Faulkner, C.W., Britian -- Artist-Signed, Greetings
Finkenrath, Paul, Berlin (PFB) -- Greetings, Comics
Gabriel, Sam -- Artist-Signed, Greetings
Gartner & Bender -- Artist-Signed, Comics
German-American Novelty Art (also T.S.N.) -- Artist-Signed
Gibson Art Co. -- Comics, Greetings
Gottschalk, Dreyfus & Davis -- Greetings
Gross, Edward -- Artist-Signed, Comics
Gutmann & Gutmann -- Artist-Signed
H.S. Art Co., Germany -- Artist-Signed
Hammon, V.O. -- Local Views, Comics
Paul Heckscher -- Artist-Signed
Henderson & Sons -- Artist-Signed, Comics
Henderson Litho -- Greetings, Comics, Local Views
Huld, Franz -- Installment Sets, Expositions, etc.
Ill. Postal Card Co. -- Greetings, Artist-Signed, Others
Int. Art Publishing Co. -- Greetings by Clapsaddle, etc.
Knapp Co. -- Artist-Signed
Koeber, Paul C. (P.C.K.) -- Artist-Signed, Comics
Koehler, Joseph -- H-T-L, Expositions, Local Views
Kropp, E.C. -- Local Views, Battleships, etc.
Langsdorf, S. -- Alligator and Shell Border Views, Local Views, Etc.
Lapina, Paris -- Color Nudes, French Fashion, etc.
Leighton, Hugh   -- Local Views
Leubrie & Elkus (L.&E.) - Artist-Signed, Comics
Livingston, Arthur -- Pioneers, Local Views
Lounsbury, Fred -- Greetings, Comics, Local Views
Manhattan Post Card Co. -- Local Views, Comics
Marque L-E, Paris -- French Glamour
Meissner & Buch, Germany -- Artist-Signed, Greetings
Metropolitan News Co. -- Local Views, Comics
Mitchell, Edward H. -- Expositions, Battleships, Local Views
Moffat, Yard & Co., NY -- Artist-Signed
Munk, M., Vienna -- Artist-Signed, Comics
Nash, E. -- Greetings
National Art Co. -- Artist-Signed, Greetings, Comics
E. Nister, Britain -- Artist-Signed, Greetings
Novitas, Berlin -- Artist-Signed
Noyer, A., Paris -- Nudes, French Glamour
Owen, F.A. -- Artist-Signed, Greetings

Philipp & Kramer, Vienna -- Artist-Signed, Secessionists
Platinachrome -- Artist-Signed, Earl Christy, etc.
Reichner Bros. -- Local Views
Reinthal & Newman -- Artist-Signed
Reider, M. -- Local Views
Arthur Rehn (A.R.&C.i.B), Berlin, Artist-Signed
Rose, Charles -- Comics, Artist-Signed, Greetings, Song Cards
Rost, H.A. -- Pioneer Views, Battleships
Roth & Langley -- Greetings, Comics
Rotograph Co. -- Artist-Signed, Battleships, Expos, Local Views
Salmon & Co., Britain -- Artist-Signed, Views, Comics
Sander, P. -- Artist-Signed, Comics, Greetings
Sanford, W.H. -- Artist-Signed, Greetings
Santway -- Greetings, Santas, etc.
Sborgi, E., Italy -- Famous Art Reproductions
Selige, A. -- Expositions, Western Views, People, etc.
Sheehan, M.T. -- Artist-Signed, Local Views, Historical
Souvenir Post Card Co. -- Local Views, Greetings, etc.
Stecher Litho Co. -- Artist-Signed, Greetings
Stengel & Co., Germany -- Famous Art Reproductions, Others
Stewart & Woolf, Britain -- Artist-Signed, Comics
Stokes, F.A. -- Artist-Signed, Comics
Strauss, Arthur -- Local Views, Historical, Expositions
Stroefer, Theo, Nurenburg (T.S.N.) -- Artist-Signed, Animals, etc.
Taggert Co. -- Greetings
Tammen, H.H. -- Expositions, Historical, Local Views
Tiech, Curt -- Local Views, Artist-Signed, Comics
Tichnor Bros. -- Later Local Views, Comics
Raphael Tuck & Sons, Britain -- Artist-Signed, Views, Comics, etc.
Ullman Mfg. Co. -- Artist-Signed, Greetings, Comics
Valentine & Sons, Britain -- Artist-Signed, Comics, Views, etc.
Volland Co. -- Artist-Signed, Greetings
Whitney & Co. -- Artist-Signed, Greetings
Winsch, John -- Artist-Signed, Greetings
Wirths, Walter -- Pioneer Views

BIBLIOGRAPHY

The following publications, all related to the collection and study of postcards are recommended for further reading.

American Advertising Postcards, Sets and Series, 1890-1920, Fred and Mary Megson, Martinsville, NJ, 1987.

American Postcard Collectors Guide, 1981, Valerie Monahan.

The American Postcard Guide to Tuck, 1980, Sally Carver, Brookline, MA.

The American Postcard Journal, 1980's, Roy and Marilyn Nuhn, New Haven, CT.

Art Nouveau Postcards, 1977, Alan Weill, Image Graphics, New York.

The Artist Signed Postcard, 1975, Forrest D. Lyons.

Bessie Pease Gutmann, Published Works Catalog, 1986, Victor J.W. Christie, Park Avenue Publishers, NJ.

The Collector's Guide to Postcards, Jane Wood, Gas City, IN.

A Directory of Postcard Artists, Publishers and Trademarks, 1975, Barbara Andrews.

Erotic Postcards, 1977, Barbara Jones and William Ouelette, Britain.

Fantasy Postcards, 1975, William Ouelette, NY.

Harrison Fisher, 1984, David Bowers, Ellen H. Budd, George M. Budd.

How To Price & Sell Old Picture Postcards, 1992, Roy Cox, Baltimore.

I.P.M. Catalogue of Picture Postcards, J.H.D. Smith, IPM Ltd., Britain

Official Postcard Price Guide, 1990, Dianne Allman, NY.

Philip Boileau, Painter of Fair Women, 1981, Dorothy Ryan, Gotham Book Mart, NY.

The Picture Postcard and its Origin, 1966, Frank Staff, Britain.

Pictures in the Post, 1971, Richard Carline, Gordon Fraser, Britain.

Picture Postcards in the United States 1893-1918, Dorothy Ryan.

Picture Postcards, 1974, Marian Klamkin, David & Charales, Britain.

Picture Postcards of the Golden Age, Tonie & Valmai Holt, Britain.

Pioneer Postcards, 1956, J.R. Burdick.

Postcard Collectors Magazine, ca 1954-1955, Bob Hendricks, Pamona, CA.

The Postcard Price Guide, J.L. Mashburn, WorldComm, 1992.

Prairie Fires & Paper Moons: The American Photographic Postcard, 1902-1920, 1981, Andreas Brown, Hal Morgan, Boston, MA.

The Postcards of Alphonse Mucha, Q. David Bowers, Mary Martin.

Reklame Postkarten, Peter Weiss, Karl Stehle, Munich, Birkhauser Verlag, Basel.

Standard Postcard Catalog, James L. Lowe, PA.

The Super Rare Postcards of Harrison Fisher, 1992, J.L. Mashburn, Enka, NC, by WorldComm.

Soumalaista Postikortti Taidetta, 1984, Teuvo Tekomonen, Oy KAJ Hellman Ltd., Espoo.

Till The Boys Come Home, 1977, Tonie & Valmai Holt, Britain.

What Cheer News, 1970-80's, Mrs. E.K. Austin, Editor, Rhode Island Postcard Club.

PERIODICALS

The Antique Trader Weekly, P.O. Box 1050, Dubuque, IA 52004

Antiques & Auction News, P.O. Box 500, Mt. Joy, PA 17552

Collector News, P.O. Box 156, Grundy Center, IA 50638-0156

Barr's Post Card News, 70 S. 6th St., Lansing, IA 52151

Postcard Collectors Marketplace, P.O. Box 127, Scandinavia, WI 54977

Paper Pile Quarterly, P.O. Box 337, San Anselmo, CA 94979

Picture Postcard Monthly, 15 Debdale Ln, Keyworth, Nottingham NG12 5HT, U.K.

Postcard Collector, P.O. Box 37, Iola, WI 54945

Index